Critical
Psychology

The International Journal of Critical Psychology

Issue 8

Spirituality

Guest Editor
Lisa Blackman

ISSN 1471 4167
ISBN 0 85315 978 5

Cover design Art Services
Cover image © Tim Davison
Typeset by E-Type, Liverpool, UK,
Printed and bound in Great Britain by Biddles Ltd,
Guildford and King's Lynn

Critical Psychology is published three times per year by
Lawrence & Wishart
99a Wallis Road
London E9 5LN
United Kingdom

Editor
Valerie Walkerdine (University of Western Sydney)
Email: v.walkerdine@uws.edu.au

Editorial Assistant
Peter Bansel
Email: ijcp@uws.edu.au

Individual subscriptions £40
Institutional subscriptions £120

For advertising information contact contact
editorial@lwbooks.co.uk

Contents

▼

Editorial
Spirituality and psychology; a problem of semantics?

Lisa Blackman

As Thomas Csordas (2002:[1]) notes in his examination of ritual healing within different traditions and communities, religion provides doctrines and moral codes for conducting ourselves as human subjects, as well as a range of practices and techniques of self-transformation which invoke 'powers or entities that (are) by definition wholly other than human'. It is this realm of the sacred and psychology's place as both a key knowledge in the delimitation of what counts as 'spiritual', and how this is and has been articulated, which generated the idea for the special focus of this issue on Spirituality.

In relation to some of the key concepts taken to define normal psychological functioning, there are a range of 'other-worldly' experiences which have been viewed as evidence of psychopathology, a movement towards irrationality, often subsumed within psychiatric categories. William Sargeant (1967), a famous British psychiatrist, was motivated by a fascination with religion and phenomena which, in the cultures he studied, were experienced as signs of a divine, sacred world.[2] One of the key phenomenological criteria for evidence of the sacred, felt by people in and through their bodies, was a spontaneous experience of being possessed.

These modes of being were enacted, often in ritualised settings, through a range of sensory modalities, such as motor dissociation, contortions and tics, trembling, tingling in the hands and other body parts, catatonia, fainting, trances, stupor, collapse and feelings of heat, lightness, heaviness and so on and so forth. Sargeant drew parallels with political techniques of conversion in his preoccupations with Communist, Fascist and Nazi revolutions across Europe, and argued that conversion, both religious and political, could be explained by a physiological mechanism, an abreactive reaction of the brain brought about by rhythmic and repetitive behaviour (ibid:171).[3]

This ethnocentric view typifies the guiding principle underpinning orthodox histories of both psychology and psychiatry. The emergence of the 'psy' knowledges is characterised by a reverence for the heroes of science, seen to offer both disciplines the methods and tools for liberating humanity from prejudice and ignorance. The focus and subject matter of psychology, we are told, has been the rational cogito and its deviations, to be explained through recourse to the biological and life sciences. When the mystery and enchantment of human life is focused upon, it is with the aim of recuperating and containing it as an object that can be known, understood and analysed through the lens of scientific rationality. Some of the papers in this issue, to some extent, bear testament to psychology's cultural purchase and power in providing some of the key concepts through which the realm of the spiritual is increasingly translated and mapped onto the psychological.

Helen Lee and Harriette Marshall's paper on 'Divine Individualism: Transcending Psychology' cogently illustrates the extent to which the terrain of the spiritual is enacted through practices of self-production which invite individuals and groups of individuals to understand the limits of selfhood as subject to their own ability to effect change and transformation in their lives. Focusing upon transpersonal psychology and popular 'mind-body-spirit' literature,[4] they examine the ways in which the discourses of humanistic psychology, associated with Maslow, Rogers and others, have provided the concepts and techniques through which personal development becomes the key site and condition of spiritual self-transformation. The finitude of life is disavowed, one might argue, through cultural narratives which place individuals as participants in their own spiritual health and psychological well-being. Lee and Marshall discuss the moral, ethical and political implications of such spiritual practices, which privilege the individual as a site of change and transformation,[5] rather than forms of spirituality which might help to create more interrelational and compassionate modes of sociality. They are also keen to highlight the dilemma of making critical interventions in relation to psychology at a time when spirituality is marginalised within the discipline, and studied predominantly as part of a broader set of concerns framed by humanistic psychology.

Ian Hodges's paper, 'Assembling the Soul: Self and Media Consumption in Alternative Spirituality' presents a novel and innovative analysis of two conversational encounters on a radio phone-in, where callers are invited to present emotional dilemmas to an expert, who through the use of figurative language, recasts the callers as the target and responsible agent in their own cure. Exploring the enactment and embodiment of the key concepts which Lee and Marshall delineate, Hodges develops an analysis of metaphor and simile to explore the discursive production of therapeutic truth. His argument rests upon the interconnection between popular therapeutic practice and alternative forms of spirituality which are evidenced through their shared concern with an 'ethics of authenticity'. Referring to much more than the linguistic construction of reality (with its implication of the voluntaristic discourse user[6]), Hodges's illuminating analysis shows how callers are invited to take up new ways of understanding themselves, with concomitant rights and obligations (particularly to oneself) within a particular conversational encounter. Rather than liberating the self from the encumbrances of religion and other 'external' forces, he clearly shows how a particular relation of self to self, based upon an ethics of personal autonomy, self-realisation and self-expression, helps to produce a self experienced as 'authentic', but produced upon a particular register of truth framed by the concepts and concerns of humanistic psychology.

Cheals, Morgan and Coombes further explore the centrality of humanistic psychology and its contribution to self-production and narration in their article, 'An analysis of women's spirituality narratives'. Through an analysis of women's accounts informed by Foucault, Lyotard and narrative theory, they explore the ways in which particular metaphors order how women attempt to articulate the meaning of spirituality within their lives. Through an analysis of figurative language, specifically metaphors such as 'journeying', 'self-knowing' and 'turning points', they explore how these contribute to both an 'ethics of authenticity', but also to forms of self-understanding which reproduce what they term a-cultural and a-historical forms of subjectivity unmarked by sexual difference. Although reproducing and translating the concepts central to humanistic psychology, they also reveal how the forms of re-invention made possible are often integral to the survival of experiences of oppression, abuse and inequality. This would seem then to point to questions of the cultural purchase of humanistic psychology and the basis of women's possible subjective commitment to such forms of self-understanding.

Jeremy Carrette, contributing to critical psychology from the discipline of theology and religious studies, argues that critical psychology needs to begin a dialogue with the history of religious ideas in order to further delineate the cultural purchase of humanism and its centrality to the production of new forms of spirituality. His paper, 'Psychology, Spirituality and Capitalism: The Case of Abraham Maslow', expands the theme already governing the papers discussed so far. That is that if we examine the history of religious ideas, we can see the gradual psychologisation of religion, moving away from an 'out-worldly view' (a self created in relation to and dependent upon a non-empirical reality, for example, the 'divine' or 'sacred'), to one which focuses upon an 'in-worldliness' oriented towards a fixed, self-referential essence. He argues that Abraham Maslow was a cultural actor and key psychologist who helped to perform the 'ideological reconfiguration of religious introspection, which prepares the ground for reading spirituality as a production of consumption'. He equates this move as one which was made possible by capitalism, and what he terms psychology's parasitic relationship upon these broader social and cultural processes within American society in the 1960s. Maslow successfully re-modelled religious experience within a humanistic framework through the concepts of 'self-actualisation', the 'peak experience' and 'B-Cognition'. Carrette also considers what is silenced or made absent from this reconfiguration of spiritual semantics. He alerts us to the disavowal more generally within humanistic psychology with what marks our finitude – unbearable loss, pain, terror and uncertainty. Where humanism frames spirituality through a concern with private, intense moments of happiness, he argues that the very fabric of religious experience, its meditation on the suffering body, is eliminated. As he recounts, 'the most rapturous experience may also be the most painful and frightening, as in some near-death experiences or the witnessing of a dying relative'.

This focus upon what is left out or silenced within humanistic psychology is an exclusion which, Paul Stenner argues in his paper 'In the Name of the Father: Dostoevsky and the Spirit of Critical

Psychology', characterises a more general strategy central to the emergence of the discipline of psychology itself. In his call for a revisionist history of the discipline, and its subject matter, he argues that scientific psychology is a form of knowledge that 'keeps half of itself a secret'. He suggests through a critical reading of Darwin, Freud and Dosteovsky, that scientific psychology is defensively structured in relation to concepts which are systematically denied, hidden and occluded, and yet provide the silent preconditions of this particular knowledge formation. These 'masked aspects of half-science' are those concepts which are relegated to alterity and yet constantly threaten to return. These are concepts which have framed questions concerning the 'problem of the individual' in relation to ethics, Christian metaphysics and aesthetics. These are masked, he suggests, through psychology's commitment to neutrality and objectivity, which disavows and refashions such questions within a new semantics of positive scientific knowledge. These then become manifest and hidden but constantly return, for example in the motivations underpinning Darwin's theorisations and musings in his private notebooks.

Stenner's contribution adds further evidence to the role psychology has played in re-working spiritual semantics and supplying new semantic categories authorised through particular appeals to science, truth and objectivity. What is more important, I think, are the implications of this work for how psychology conceives of its subject matter, the rational cogito. It would seem that its focus and interest, from its inception, has been on matters spiritual, religious and unseen, locating them increasingly within a private sphere of choice and psychological autonomy. The articulation of a critical psychological intervention involves more than the opening up of a new and relatively unexplored subject matter for psychology. It must also involve re-writings of the histories of this discipline.

Nick Mansfield presents a paper in this issue which argues that critical psychology itself needs to reflect upon the history of its own development and commitment to 'criticality'. In 'The Subjectivity of Money: Critical Psychology and the Economies of Post-Structuralism', Mansfield responds to an argument made by Margaret Wetherell (1999) about the value of post-Foucauldian and post-structuralist thinking for the project of critical psychology. This itself was a commentary on the value of Marxism as an underpinning for criticality. Mansfield makes a call for critical psychologists to reflect on some of the metaphors implicit and often explicit within the theoretical perspectives which have been mobilised to explore the production of subjectivity. As an example, he suggests that the use of Foucault's work on 'modes of subjectification', as a means of exploring the production of the psychological subject through specific techniques of the self (tied to specific disciplinary practices), fails to capture the network of flows of bodies, pleasures, signs, knowledges, money and so forth which produce an incommensurable and antagonistic realm of possibilities for the experience of subjectivity.

He argues that the metaphor of economy, central to much poststructuralist thought, from Lyotard to Irigaray, makes visible such flows. Indeed, he argues that Foucault was self-consciously aware in his own writings of the metaphorical usage of some of the key concepts he uses to 'think' subjectivity, including the 'panopticon' and the 'aesthetic avant-gardism of the soul'. Rather than develop these as methodologies, he suggests that critical psychologists need to be more aware of the metaphors which inform their own thinking and practice. Mansfield presents a metaphorical usage of 'economy' as a way of framing the network of flows which characterise as much what is possible even if not experienced, a subjectivity that 'will always be defined by what we will not experience'. One role he suggests for Critical Psychology is to plunder the incommensurabilities of these flows.

As a critical psychologist located within the discipline of media and cultural studies, I am delighted to include a paper from a cultural theorist exploring dance, and particularly techno music, as an interface for the production of particular embodied experiences of spirituality on the dance-floor. Hillegonda Rietveld's contribution, 'Entranced: embodied spirituality on the post-industrial dance floor', shows the intersection between critical psychology and other disciplines which seek to understand human subjectivity from broadly discursive or constructionist perspectives. Rietveld's analysis of 'raving' suggests that the autonomous self and its 'undoing' on the dance-floor is produced through a particular assemblage of machine-music-dance-drugs. Although the phenomenological experience is often described and experienced as 'transcendence' or 'freedom from', suggesting a dissolution of the self, she cogently shows how these embodied experiences, often described as 'spiritual', are produced through particular material and social conditions. She argues that this re-making of the self illustrates the contingency of those self/other boundaries so central to the production of rational, autonomous subjectivity. This paper also shows the ways in which the fiction of autonomous selfhood is maintained, re-worked and embodied in social settings seen to be most free from self-governing processes.

The final contribution to this special issue is from the discipline of sociology. Andrew Metcalfe and Ann Game explore and advocate an ethics which moves beyond the persistence of individual selves to a relational logic based on Buber's I-Thou. The paper is an auto-critique of their earlier work, *Passionate Sociology*, which developed an understanding of knowledge production based upon desire. Post-structuralist thought, particularly the work of Hegel, Foucault, Cixous and others informed this work. Writing about their recent book, *The Mystery of Everyday Life*,[7] they explore the implications of moving beyond positional laws of identity, the 'I-It' relation, to an ethics which recognises the 'interbeing' of selves through concepts such as wonder, participation, dialogue, inspiration, presence and so forth. These concepts mark out an ethics of mutuality and relationality which do not perform the kinds of disavowal which they suggest keep self/other boundaries in place (often through a desire to master, appropriate or merge with the Other). Exploring the implications of this ethics for teaching and academic practice, they bring to the fore the sacred and spiritual associations of thinking, when knowledge production is not based upon an accounting of the world, but rather a celebratory unfolding of the world's possibilities.

The issue ends with reviews of three books: Andrew Metcalfe and Ann Game's *Mystery of Everyday Life*, by Louise Chambers, Thomas Csordas's *Body/Meaning/Healing*, by Nigel Danby, and Jeremy Carrette's *Foucault and Religion*, by Linda MacKay.

I hope this diverse collection of papers will help begin a dialogue as to the kinds of intervention we might make as critical psychologists and cultural theorists interested in the realm of the spiritual. I think that the interventions we might wish to make (and indeed are making) would benefit from further collaboration with scholars in other disciplinary locations, framing questions in ways which might transform critical psychology itself. Some of the contributions in this issue from outside the discipline make suggestions for alternative conceptualisations. Although there has been a key focus in this issue on humanistic psychology, we might wish to consider other forms of healing which do invoke powers or entities 'other' than human. What is specifically spiritual about other practices and techniques of self-transformation? What counts and is taken as evidence of the 'spiritual' or 'sacred' in different healing practices? Rather than trying to contain the spiritual as an object that can be known, approaching the 'spiritual' as a contingent realm, existing within wider connected terms and meanings, and shaping our understandings of ourselves as subjects in particular ways, might be apposite. This will take us beyond the linguistic monism which has tended to characterise the discipline, to exploring the embodied practices through which people attempt to transform 'suffering' bodies through particular discourses of hope, survival, health and spiritual and psychological well-being.

Notes

1. His predominant focus is upon the Christian Charismatic Renewal Movement originating within the USA and ritual healing associated with the Navajo Indians in North America.
2. These included the healing methods of 'witch doctors' in Ethiopia, Kenya, Zambia, Nigeria and Dahomey. Firewalking in Fiji, temple drumming and dancing in India, transitional religious practices in Brazil, Voodoo in Haiti, and Revival meetings across North America.
3. See Blackman (2001) *Hearing Voices: Embodiment and Experience,*. Free Association Books: London and New York, for a further discussion of this in relation to the phenomenon of voice hearing.
4. Both taking as their subject Eastern psycho-spiritual traditions.
5. What they term 'self-contained individualism' following a great tradition of critical psychologists.
6. See Blackman and Walkerdine (2001) *Mass Hysteria: Critical Psychology and Media Studies*. Palgrave: Basingstoke and New York.
7. Also reviewed in this special issue.

References

Blackman, L. (2001) *Hearing Voices: Embodiment and Experience*. Free Association Books: London and New York.

Blackman, L., and Walkerdine, V. (2001) *Mass Hysteria: Critical Psychology and Media Studies*. Palgrave: Basingstoke and New York.

Csordas, T. (2002) *Body/Meaning/Healing*. Palgrave: Basingstoke and New York.

Sargeant, W. (1967) *The Unquiet Mind*. Pan Books: London.

Wetherell, M. (1999) 'Beyond Binaries' Comment. *Theory and Psychology*. Vol. 9(3): 399-406.

Divine individualism
Transcending psychology

Helen Lee and Harriette Marshall

Abstract

This paper explores some of the ways in which psychological forms of knowledge produce new forms of spirituality. It is argued that critical work in psychology that has examined the power, role and politics of psychology are as important in explicating new forms of spirituality as they have been for more mainstream psychological concepts. We draw on critical readings of literature produced in two inter-related knowledge sites – transpersonal psychology (academic knowledge site) and popular 'mind, body, spirit' literature (non-academic knowledge site). In that transpersonal psychology has been instrumental in producing knowledge on spirituality within and outside of psychology, it is a critical analysis of this arena that forms a large part of this paper. We refer to historical narratives cited as influential in shaping transpersonal psychology and present a close reading of assumptions within the field which we delineate in terms of divine individualism, consciousness evolution and consciousness or catastrophe. The latter part of the paper explores the inter-relationship between these two knowledge sites by means of reference to a textual analysis of mind, body, spirit literature. Our point of contention centres on transpersonal psychology's individualistic person-orientated forms of knowledge which are problematic because they claims to speak for all human beings and further, they are presented as providing a means of resolving social and global problems.

Introduction

In this paper we argue that theoretical and conceptual knowledge regarding spirituality (a topic marginalised within the discipline) is a matter of concern for critical psychologists. Although spirituality can offer ways of being that might be taken as alternative to and challenge rational scientific modes of thought, we contend it is a problematic area of enquiry that merits critical attention. We begin by outlining briefly what we mean when we refer to spirituality. Then discuss the inter-relationship between transpersonal psychology (a section of the British Psychological Society that has focused specifically on researching eastern psycho-spiritual traditions) and non-academic knowledge sites, before presenting a close critical reading of assumptions within transpersonal academic psychology. Subsequently we draw from a textual analysis to provide a specific illustration of the inter-relationship between transpersonal academic psychology and mind, body, spirit literature. This literature is located often in mainstream bookshops under a section entitled mind, body and spirit (Bruce, 1995). These are texts that draw eclectically from spiritual traditions and practices while offering to heal the mind, relax the body and soothe the spirit as well as promising happiness, success and personal fulfilment. While these texts make mention of spirituality albeit in various ways, they are of interest in this paper because they provide a somewhat popular genre in which new forms of spirituality are constructed.

We work from a perspective informed by a social constructionist concern with somewhat broad-based discourses and the relationship between knowledge and power (Gergen, 1999). To cite Marshall and Woollett: 'we take discourse as being systems of statements, grouped around clusters of terms and figures of speech to articulate particular kinds of knowledge' (2000: 354). We argue that psychological knowledge concerning spirituality provides a powerful form of knowledge which in certain forums can work to legitimate particular ways of doing/being spiritual. We adopt a criticality that is concerned with delineating the underlying assumptions extant within transpersonal psychology and exploring some implications of such a form of knowledge. We argue that this is important precisely because transpersonal psychology has informed constructions of spirituality in a non-academic arena.

Spirituality?

Our intention is not to define spirituality by pinning it down in a narrow sense but to provide some indication of the context informing our approach to spirituality. Our reference to new forms of spirituality in this paper refers to a non-institutional notion of spirituality that is often constructed as separate from religion (Coyle, 2002). Bruce (1995) and Heelas (1996) have been useful in their outline of New Age spirituality as an eclectic engagement with a plethora of spiritual traditions and practices – for example, various forms of meditation, yoga and Native American practices, along with diverse forms of healing including Reiki and crystal healing. Such practices, argues Heelas, are characterised as a means of working on oneself and attaining a sense of self-transcendence, inner transformation or mind, body, spirit holism. This is an elusive and diverse arena and while we cannot address New Age spirituality in its entirety, this depiction of New Age is useful in characterising the new forms of spirituality addressed in this paper – transpersonal psychology and mind, body, spirit. In terms of mind, body, spirit literature Bruce (1995) argues that the 'circulatory system of the New Age body is made up of books, magazines, audio cassettes and public lectures' (103); and, further, 'The New Age's reliance on the printed word gives us a surer way of illustrating the popularity of New Age ideas' (104).

In this paper we acknowledge our partial, critical take on new forms of spirituality. Our reading is informed by our critical analyses of texts from transpersonal psychology and mind, body, spirit literature, and we bring to these texts the first author's engagement with various spiritual practices in the UK.[1] Consequently, we do not claim to speak impartially for all those who engage with spirituality within or outside the UK nor do we offer our reading herein as the only ways of doing/being spiritual.

Knowledge sites
In engaging in the production of psychological knowledge, psychologists have sought to solve social problems for the benefit of human welfare. This mission has inevitably involved offering certain solutions which benefit particular humans and not others under the guise of 'expert'. Some critical psychologists have intervened in such a way as to challenge the legitimacy and power of psychologists claiming 'expert' status (Stainton Rogers, Stenner, Gleeson and Stainton Rogers, 1995). As Rose (1996, 1990a, 1990b) argues, psychology is powerful as it differentiates and defines various groups of people and governs the boundaries around what they might do. In terms of spirituality, it is transpersonal psychology that has been influential in legitimating particular conceptions of spirituality in a non-academic, mind, body, spirit knowledge site.

Institutionally transpersonal psychology was established as a section of the British Psychological Society (BPS) in 1996 (Fontana and Slack, 1996), one explicit aim being to study eastern psycho-spiritual traditions. In North America transpersonal psychology emerged in the 1960s. Though not formally part of the American Psychological Association, the influence of N. American transpersonal psychology since the 1960s is notable as demonstrated by the frequent citations in British transpersonal academic psychology literature. While transpersonal psychological knowledge can be argued as promoting a particular version of spirituality, this knowledge, akin to much of mainstream psychology knowledge, does not remain in the academy but filters through the boundaries of academia to inform common-sense understandings of spirituality such as for example, mind, body, spirit literature (Henderson, 1989; Vitz and Modesti, 1993). Some transpersonal psychologists, for instance Fontana, Wilber[2] and Walsh, publish texts through publishing houses such as Element, Gill and Macmillan that are aimed specifically at a non-academic audience. In addition, forms of knowledge produced by transpersonal psychology appear less directly in a non-academic arena in a manner that resembles Crawford's (1998) reference to the popular text *Men are from Mars, Women are from Venus*. Crawford talks about psychological knowledge being taken up and used although not directly cited in popular literature. In consequence, whether intentional or not, transpersonal psychology plays a key role in producing knowledge that pervades a non-academic arena and in so doing, works to make thinkable and validate certain ways of being spiritual whilst subjugating others.

Transpersonal psychology's constitution of spirituality

It is important to acknowledge certain strengths in addition to our contentions with transpersonal psychology, in line with Gergen's suggestion that a 'balanced appreciation replaces mere assault' (2000, p25). In an attempt to encourage debate rather than alienation and insult a notable strength is a move away from a psychological tradition of scientific obsession with objectivity. Transpersonal psychologists frequently report their own experiences and past experiential accounts have been common place at transpersonal psychology conferences. However, these accounts are rarely accompanied by an acknowledgement of partiality in which particular values, viewpoints and beliefs are taken as part of the knowledge production process. Instead, personal experience tends to be presented as reflective of some underlying reality of the transpersonal that captures what it is to be truly human.

Also while there is a dearth of research on spirituality within mainstream psychology, transpersonal psychology has sought to research what has frequently been rendered beyond the realms of scientific Psychology. Previously, it has been the more formally structured and institutionalised theology/religion that has appeared on a Psychology agenda rather than spirituality per se.[3] Even so any such attention has tended to be on the margins of the discipline and by and large has been written from an ethnocentric stance of Judeo-Christianity (Lee, 2000a). Transpersonal psychology has shifted this balance and taken as central and worthwhile the study of eastern psycho-spiritual traditions. As Tart (1992) argues, a prime concern for transpersonal psychology has been to transgress the matter-spirit dichotomy that has prevailed in scientific study for many years.

However, despite these notable shifts away from traditions in Psychology, of concern from a critical perspective is that despite attempts to break down a spirit-matter dichotomy, transpersonal psychologists often maintain other dualistic divisions, in particular an individual-societal dualism. While transpersonal practices *can be* understood as leading to experiences which likewise *can be* understood in terms of a transcendence of certain dichotomies, this does not necessarily imply a breakdown of all dualisms.

Besanta (2000) discusses the ways in which transpersonal practices can lead to dissolution of a subjective-objective dualism that breaks down a distinction between self and non-self, between internal and external. This dissolution is illustrated in his paper with specific reference to psychic phenomena including clairvoyancy, telepathy and faith healing in which he argues the subjective expands to include parts of the objective. As he contends, 'at very advanced levels attained by spiritual masters who include deep concentration in their training, the "subjective" becomes practically synonymous with the "objective"' (Besanta, 2000: 24). While these specific examples of psychic phenomena *can be* understood in this way, this is just one way of understanding what it is to transgress a subjective-objective, self-non-self or internal-external boundary that is confined to a specific context. An assumption that transpersonal practices work to transcend all dualisms irrespective of context cannot be claimed. Relative to a somewhat broader socially-embodied context[4] transpersonal psychology can be taken as maintaining a modernist individualist ideology. It is this individualism and its implications to which we now turn.

Roots of transpersonal psychology

The prevalence of individualism within transpersonal psychology can be taken as emanating from various sources which include its place within mainstream psychology's individualist ideology. But also individualism shows itself in the work of William James, Carl Gustav Jung and Abraham Maslow. These key figures shared an approach of moving away from conventional forms of religion, and focus on a more personal, inner sense of spirituality/religiosity referenced often as important in the establishment of transpersonal psychology (Edwards, 1999; Fontana and Slack, 1996). We turn briefly at this point to highlight aspects of their work that have been cited as influential for transpersonal psychology.

In James's influential text *The Varieties of Religious Experience* ([1902] 1985) religion is construed in a highly individualistic way. May (1993) argues this line in stating that for James, religion refers to 'the experiences of individual men in their solitude, so far as they apprehend themselves to stand in relation to whatever they may consider divine' (1993: 78). James's experimentation with nitrous oxide as a means of instilling altered or mystical states of consciousness provides an illustration of the importance he placed on inner experience. May argues that James's centralisation of inner experience consequently rendered religious experience asocial and ahistorical. Likewise, Jung moved away from conventional forms of religion, from religious creeds towards a more personal form of a god within oneself which he conceived in terms of the Self (sic) (Jung, 1938). He regarded spirituality as an innate part of being human and necessary for full human functioning. In particular, Jung conceived the process of individuation as a spiritual journey involving the attainment of inner transformation. He posited that this entailed an integration of the unconscious with the conscious mind through close attention to dreams and intuitions (sometimes conceived as an inner voice). These somewhat brief and crude synopses of James's and Jung's work offer glimpses of a select part of their life's work, but our concern at this point is to convey some of the historical narratives which are cited as shaping transpersonal psychology. The focus on 'intra-personal experiences', 'inner-self' and 'recognition of the divine within', along with Jung's spiritualisation of therapy. are evident in transpersonal psychology (Lajoie and Shapiro, 1999).

A third influential figure in transpersonal psychology is Maslow (1968), the humanistic psychologist whose theory assumes an innate need for self-actualisation (Box 1, below) and a fundamentalist conception of human nature as good. His work promoted the notion that a person needs to embark on a journey of self-growth or self-development, in search of self-actualisation.

Box 1. Characteristics of self-actualisation

1. Clearer more efficient perception of reality.
2. More openness to experience.
3. Increased integration, wholeness and unity of the person.
4. Increased spontaneity, expressiveness, full functioning, aliveness.
5. A real self, a firm identity, autonomy, uniqueness.
6. Increased objectivity, detachment, transcendence of self.
7. Recovery of creativeness.
8. Ability to fuse concreteness and abstractness.
9. Democratic character structure.
10. Ability to love.

As in our inclusion of James and Jung above, our aim is to merely point to elements of these characteristics of self-actualisation that are evident in transpersonal psychology. For example, Characteristic 1, the allusion to a 'clearer more efficient perception of reality' is echoed in Tart's (1991) notion of a consensus trance, whereby ordinary waking consciousness is deemed an illusion. Characteristic 3, the notion of integration, wholeness and unity is located in contemporary transpersonal psychology's emphasis on mind, body and spirit holism and intra-personal integration (Lajoie and Shapiro, 1999). Characteristic 6, detachment and transcendence of self, resembles some of the eastern philosophies advanced within transpersonal psychology (Tart, 1992). Like James and Jung, Maslow and humanistic psychology more generally have been of key importance in shaping transpersonal psychology.

These partial representations of James's, Jung's and Maslow's work in transpersonal psychology can be read in different ways. On the one hand they can be taken as influential foundations for transpersonal psychology, providing an important base that has shaped subsequent theory and research in a progressivist search for truth. Conversely we argue that these particular representations of their work serve to delimit the theorisation and conceptualising of spirituality in transpersonal psychology.

Transpersonal psychology knowledge site

We identify three inter-related patterns of knowledge that illustrate assumptions extant in transpersonal psychology. *Divine individualism* informed by humanistic psychology, *consciousness evolution* that embodies a developmental narrative and *consciousness or catastrophe* whereby consciousness evolution attained through contemplative traditions is constituted as means of resolving social and global problems.

Divine individualism

The *Transpersonal Psychology Review* (*TPR*) – the quarterly publication from the section of the BPS – outlines the aims of the section using a terminology of 'self-exploration'; 'self-development'; 'psychological well-being'; 'human potential' and 'personal growth', indicative of humanistic psychology. Also the *TPR* makes reference to 'eastern psycho-spiritual traditions' and in so doing couples a humanistic psychology agenda with an interest in eastern spiritual traditions. As the aims of the *Transpersonal Psychology Review* attest, this coupling makes way for research which converges on 'mystical, transcendental, meditative and peak experiences' as a means of self-improving and maximising 'human potential'. Indeed typically research has centred on exploring certain mystical practices including forms of meditation as well as the use of psychoactive substances such as LSD towards the attainment of transpersonal experiences, in particular transcendent or altered states of consciousness.

> In its strict sense, transpersonal psychology (trans from the Latin for 'beyond' or 'through', and personal from the Latin for 'mask') studies those experiences which allegedly enable the individual to see beyond the conditioned ego, and to identify some deeper and more enduring sense of self (Fontana and Slack, 1996: 267).

The typical humanistic psychology definition of an underlying, enduring, authentic sense of self that exists outside of social constraints can be seen in the above extract. In conveying a notion of a 'deeper and more enduring sense of self' hidden by social conditioning, Fontana and Slack's definition typifies the humanist psychological sense of individualism so central to transpersonal psychology. Of importance in the context of transpersonal psychology is the mission to 'go beyond the conditioned ego' which becomes not just a humanistic psychology endeavour, but becomes something spiritual, a divine form of humanism and in consequence a divine notion of individualism.

Although divine individualism may not be the aim of eastern spiritual traditions, where indeed the goal is to attain a sense of union or connection, one question is the extent to which spiritual practices formulated in a specific socio-cultural and historical context will lead to an attainment of similar goals in a different context. This is important when we consider that transpersonal psychology brings together eastern spiritual traditions with a somewhat western humanistic psychology agenda. While the aim within a western context and indeed within transpersonal psychology still may be to attain a sense of union with whatever is considered divine, the question concerning context should not be ignored. Sampson (1993) contends that an instituting of eastern religion and philosophy as established in collectivist cultures – where a concern for others is deemed foremost – will not achieve the same aim within a culture predominated by a western concept of self-contained individualism, but rather embellishes the self-celebratory program already extant in humanism. Likewise, for Pickering (1994[5]) Buddhism in a western context in contrast to its traditional context – for example Chinese or Tibetan – often takes on a more individualistic stance emphasising transcendence and altered states of consciousness to a greater extent than an embodied sense of interdependence. Likewise, in transpersonal psychology eastern spiritual traditions do not stand alone in a socio-cultural vacuum but rather become orientated with a western humanistic psychology laden with modernist conceptions of the individual; it is this that gives rise to a divine notion of individualism.

Consciousness evolution

Consciousness evolution is most notable in the work of Wilber (1993, 1996), who is cited often in transpersonal psychology literature and referred to as the long sought Einstein of consciousness research (Thomas et al, 1993). Wilber proffers a developmental model of consciousness evolution that comprises a structural analysis of contemplative traditions and practices – he refers to yoga, Buddhist meditation and shamanic journeying. His model posits various levels that constitute a matter-body-soul-spirit hierarchy/holarchy[6] with contemplative practices as central for development to spirit. In building on the work of Maslow as well as Kohlberg's theory of morality, this is a model that postulates levels of self-transcendence that extend beyond stages of self-actualisation and post-conventional morality. Self-transcendence is depicted as bringing a transformation of self, a sense of peace, happiness and tranquillity as the mind is 'freed' from social constraints, and an awareness of union – self with all others – evoking a spontaneous ethics in the sense of care and compassion.

Of note is that Wilber's focus on consciousness evolution forms one part of a wider theory that also includes mention of the importance of cultural understandings and social systems, what he terms the flatland (Wilber, 1995). However Wilber specifically chooses to focus on an interior-individual part of his theory, on an inner, subjective realm that privileges the mind. In consequence, despite acknowledging the inseparability of inner-individual with social and cultural realms, paradoxically he reproduces an individual-society dichotomy by focusing on inner subjectivity as if it exists in a socio-cultural vacuum. His assertion 'what good does it do to adjust and integrate the self in a culture that is itself sick?' (Wilber, 1996: 137) illustrates this dichotomy, implying that it is individual intra-psychic change that is valued foremost.

Although Wilber does not dismiss the importance of lower levels – matter and body – as he claims they are not surpassed but rather encompassed within the higher levels of the holarchy, nonetheless such a notion of development is problematic in its rendering of higher levels of consciousness as 'more valuable' than lower levels (Wilber, 1993:57). Hence spirit is again rendered more important than matter or the body alone. Concomitantly a framework is constructed in which embodiment in the social world is frequently understood as secondary to individual-interior notions of consciousness. In like manner to Wilber's question above concerning a culture that is sick, we argue this hier/holarchy is problematic because action in the social world is preceded by a foremost concern with inner-individual change.

Moreover, in like manner to Gilligan's (1982) critique of Kohlberg's theory of moral development, Wilber can be charged with producing a model of development that promotes independent/individualistic ways of being above and beyond other, alternative ways. For Wilber, while self-transcendence proceeds self-actualisation and both are conceived as higher stages of development, social ways of being are considered less adequate and less valuable (Wilber, 1993). Consequently, it is individualistic, intra-psychic experience that is advanced over social ways of being – this is perhaps somewhat paradoxical to the characterisation of self-transcendence as union – self with all others (Fontana, 1999; Walley, 2002). However, it is important to note that it is a transcendent rather than a socially embodied notion of union that is promoted. Daniels (1998) and Rothberg (1986) writing within transpersonal psychology assert a similar line of argument in contending a hierarchical and somewhat limited sense in which spirituality is construed within the field. Daniels is particularly critical of Wilber who he argues is fundamentalist in acknowledging only certain sorts of experiences as genuinely spiritual.

Consciousness or catastrophe

The final pattern we wish to outline in this paper is intertexually linked with the previous two in its encompassing of self-development and consciousness evolution. It differs in terms of heralding references to social and global problems and asserting contemplative practices as a means of resolution.

> Clearly we are in a race between consciousness and catastrophe. The critical questions of our time, therefore are 1) Can we develop a critical mass of aware, involved people? 2) Can the transpersonal vision be communicated widely enough and effectively enough by each of us to help avert catastrophe and to transform the forces of destruction into forces for awakening and wellbeing? (Walsh, 1993: 132)

Walsh stresses the importance of Wilber's developmental theory of consciousness evolution as a means of resolving certain social and environmental issues including 'population explosion ... pollution increasing ... the insanity of weapons and wars' (1993: 132-33). These are particularly pertinent concerns in the contemporary world. However we take issue with Walsh's offer of contemplative experiences and use of

Wilber's research in particular, as a way of resolving these problems, or in his terms, a way of averting catastrophe. He asserts that transpersonal psychology offers the practices and disciplines through which the 'unity of humanity is realized' and therefore 'ecological concern and compassion spring spontaneously' (Walsh, 1993: 134). These assumptions highlight, in part, typical transpersonal psychological suppositions about the nature of humanity. Walsh suggests that contemplative practices as a means of instilling self-transcendence are the ways and means of addressing concerns of the twenty-first century and of bringing about social and global transformation. It is assumed that changes in one's own lifestyle will occur spontaneously subsequent to a shift in consciousness through contemplation. The question arises as to whether or not this is sufficient. As Prilleltensky and Fox argue, although care and compassion is a fundamental value, its application on an individual basis is not enough to change a society that constantly undermines compassion by promoting competition (1997: 9). As such, even if an ethics of care and compassion does spontaneously arise, is this enough?

If there is a 'race', as Walsh puts it, surely the somewhat slow, often lifelong path of contemplation, is not the only or the most expeditious way of bringing about change. The assumption extant in *consciousness or catastrophe*, that transpersonal consciousness evolution is the only way forward to resolve social and environmental problems, is extremely contentious. It is not simply a case that transpersonal theories and practices are offered as a means of self-development or self-transcendence but, moreover, they are constituted as a means of bringing about social and global transformation. The extent that largely individualistic and intra-personal practices alone can replace and/or be as effective as social action is at the very least disputable. As Prilleltensky (1994) asserts, the humanist assumption that a better world will inevitably occur without any actual intervention or action in the real world is deeply problematic. This assumption is too self-orientated and encouraging of self rather than political expression and as such likely to be ineffective in terms of social change.

Mind, Body, Spirit knowledge site

At this point we wish to draw from a larger textual analysis (Lee, 2000a) to make links between the assumptions delineated above and mind, body, spirit literature. Our aim is to demonstrate the pervasiveness of transpersonal psychology knowledge within a non-academic knowledge site, and in particular to illustrate its role in constituting new forms of spirituality in the form of mind, body, spirit literature.

> ... it is important to realise that our desire to 'serve the planet' might best be approached by working on our own spiritual development and consciousness ... Without specifically setting out to change things, we can ready ourselves by devoting time to practices that assist our opening up to energy, such as meditation, the martial arts, yoga, therapeutic dance and movement. (Original emphasis, Redfield and Adrienne, 1995:123)

> When people ask me what they can do about the problems of the world, I usually suggest that they start recognising and affirming that as they sincerely do their own inner work, the world is being transformed. (Gawain, 1991:173)

The extracts above taken from texts by key authors writing in the mind, body, spirit genre – *The Celestine Prophecy* by Redfield and Adrienne, and *Living in the Light* by Gawain – each exemplify a conceptualisation of personal development as a central and legitimate response to social/global problems. This relationship between personal and social/global change, where it is assumed that self-transformation will inevitably work to alleviate social problems, is reminiscent of the assumptions underlying *consciousness or catastrophe* extant in transpersonal psychology. Simultaneously, in like manner to a transpersonal psychology knowledge site, *divine individualism*, *consciousness evolution* and *consciousness or catastrophe* are extant in this mind, body, spirit knowledge site. As exemplified in these extracts it is inner work; spiritual and consciousness development through specific practices including meditation, yoga, martial arts; and self-transformation as a means of resolving social problems that are valued and deemed first and foremost of importance.

Our concern with the taken-for-granted linkage between personal and social change is echoed by Puttick (1997) who questions the extent to which eastern spiritualities can be brought to a western context as a means of promoting social and political change. She draws on the role of Hindu Goddesses to argue that while a woman in traditional eastern culture might conceive of herself as transcendentally empowered this does not necessarily translate into empowerment in the social world. Similar concerns can be brought to transpersonal psychology's uptake of eastern spiritual traditions and likewise to the uptake of these ideas and practices within 'mind, body and spirit'.

Points of critiques

What we are arguing is that despite maintaining a concern with self-transformation the individualistic intra-psychic stance within transpersonal psychology and mind, body, spirit knowledge sites promotes and encourages a self-contained individualism. We argue this focus relates precisely to the integration of eastern practices with humanistic notions of self-development and psychological well-being that is characteristic of transpersonal psychology. This is problematic not least because of the assumed linkage between personal – social – global, but also, because this individualism is constituted as divine. In line with familiar arguments in critical psychology on individualism, individualistic assumptions concerning person-orientated modes of change are re-created in this forum and, moreover, they are being attributed with notions of divinity. While new forms of spirituality, specifically mind, body, spirit is a relatively new knowledge site, it has potential for critical inquiry because spirituality is being narrowly delineated and quickly colonised by individualistic traditional psychology assumptions. For us, such inquiry underlines the importance of revisiting past critiques even though debates concerning individualism in psychology are well rehearsed. Prilleltensky and Rose amongst others have become notable for their revealing analysis of the role of individualism in psychology in constituting forms of knowledge that speak from and on behalf of a privileged elite and by and large work to maintain the status quo (Caplan and Nelson, 1973; Prilleltensky, 1989, 1994; Rose, 1990b).

Humanistic psychology has been critiqued for its centralisation of the individual:

> Humanistic psychologists took upon themselves that task of creating a self-generated image of the person, an organism that would rise above environmental conditioning and be able to conduct her or himself through life as a self-guided, self-governed individual. (Prilleltensky, 1994: 81)

As Prilleltensky asserts above, humanistic psychology construes a person as having the unlimited potential to surpass social and economic constraints and instil change. Absent is any attention to the structural, economic, or political means that work to oppress, denigrate or otherwise create an impoverished way of life. We argue that in like manner to humanistic psychology, transpersonal psychology has a produced a similar form of subjectivity through the promotion of transcendence and intra-psychic change.

Some critical psychologists have informed us that the promotion of the individual as the site for change is a discourse most thoroughly bound up with systems of knowledge/power (Parker, 1992; Rose, 1990b; Sampson, 1993). Rather than liberation or emancipation from societal constraints, humanistic psychology – and we argue transpersonal psychology – incites invisible forms of regulation which constitute persons as self-governing subjects. Hepburn adopts this line of argument in regard to humanism and quotes Foucault in stating 'The man [sic] described for us, who we are inviting to be free, is already in himself the effect of a subjection more profound than himself' (Foucault, 1997: 30, cited in Hepburn, 1997: 31). Furthermore, she adds, 'resistance merely reinforces our oppression, if it simply involves reaffirming that identity which has been constructed for us within the humanist-modernist narrative' (Hepburn, 1997: 45). So, although transpersonal psychology invites us to be free, to resist social constraints or in the terms used by Fontana and Slack (1996) in the quote cited earlier 'to see beyond the conditioned ego', conversely, any sense of freedom herein is psychical. In that transpersonal psychology and a mind, body, spirit knowledge site promote certain practices as key in attaining self-transformation, their embeddedness in a humanist narrative works to constitute these practices as a form of self-governance as, foremost, they require us to work on and manage ourselves. We become responsible for our own happiness and that of others, because as we engage in transpersonal practices it is assumed we will attain a happier, fulfilled sense of being and spontaneously an ethics of care and compassion. In failing to stress the importance of social action imperative to social change, we are invited to transform ourselves with the promise that things will get better, in our personal lives but also, within the social world.

An inter-related critical point concerns the need to revisit critiques directed towards the notion of self-actualisation. In particular, Wilber's theory of consciousness evolution is of contention as he builds on the concept of self-actualisation to produce a model which he maintains is universal.

> ... the central claim of the perennial philosophy is that *men and women can grow and develop (or evolve) all the way up the hierarchy to spirit itself,* therein to realise a 'supreme identity' with Godhead – the *ens perfectissium* toward which all growth and evolution yearns. (original emphasis, Wilber, 1993: 54)

In aligning his model with perennial philosophy it is produced as a timeless, ultimate and immutable form of knowledge. This immutability is further substantiated as Wilber alludes to 'all growth and evolution', imparting naturalistic assumptions and conceiving his model of consciousness as something applicable to each and every person. Arguments that have highlighted self-actualisation as a class concern – as something that is more available to members of a white, Western, affluent world – are relevant here (Sampson, 1993).

> To self-actualise meant to realise one's own potential as a human being: to explore, develop and grow; to be creative and enlarge one's currently restricted range of opportunities ... The Humanistic movement offered a way of living for people who had the luxury of time and money to explore their own personal world and to find their way through the complex and constraining mazes of modern life. (Sampson, 1993: 58)

We align our position with Sampson's in arguing that in like manner to humanism, transpersonal psychology represents the interests of an elite, though it paradoxically offers discourses that we are all invited to take up – despite classed, gendered and other identities. This is important because in equating spirituality with a limited sense of transpersonal psychology and promoting narrow means through which such transcendence is deemed attainable, in a similar vein to self-actualisation, self-transcendence is argued as something that is more available to the affluent middle and upper classes. It is far from representative or equally applicable to all. Taken together with our concern about transpersonal psychology as inciting forms of self-transformation in place of social action, the issue of class is pertinent. If it is intra-psychic transformation that is granted primacy first and foremost, then it will be those most disadvantaged within society that stand to lose as they are most in need of material change.

Dilemmas and possibilities

This paper has sought to explicate some of the ways in which transpersonal psychology constitutes knowledge concerning spirituality. Links between an academic and a non-academic knowledge site, specifically that of mind, body spirit literature have been outlined as a means of highlighting the power of psychological knowledge in enabling and constraining new forms of spirituality. In the early part of this research Helen (first author) became concerned with the usefulness of questioning conceptions of spirituality and challenging an area that is marginal in both psychology and western culture. While a spiritual position is often constituted as a form of resistance to a more rational, scientific worldview it can be viewed as counter-productive for critical psychologists concerned with challenging scientific psychology to explicate spirituality. Dilemmas arose for her concerning the usefulness of discrediting voices just as they are beginning to be heard and critiquing psychological research on spirituality just as it is beginning to be taken seriously – at least by some sections of psychology.

While this may be so, in like manner to mainstream psychological forms of knowledge, transpersonal psychology has in the past been, and continues to be, a powerful, influential knowledge site. Transpersonal psychological forms of knowledge play an important role in constituting spiritual subjectivities through, for instance, a mind, body, spirit knowledge site. When taken as an exemplar of what constitutes 'real' or 'genuine' spirituality, assumptions extant within transpersonal psychology work to legitimate only certain ways of being spiritual at the same time as constraining possible spiritual subjectivities that stand outside of transpersonal forms of knowledge (Lee and Marshall, 2002). By means of example, alternative possibilities to those created within transpersonal psychology are located in some (but by no means all) feminist conceptions of spirituality.[7] Most specifically, we refer to feminist spiritualities informed by earth-based spiritualities that conceive spirituality as inextricable from political forms of action (Finlay, 1991; Spretnak, 1994; Starhawk, 1989, 2002[8]). Miriam Simos, alias Starhawk, self-defined feminist witch and political activist, provides one such example in arguing for the importance of what she terms outer work, that is, action in the world.

Similarly, Sylvia Boyes from Ploughshares Trident Action[9] (a group engaging in direct action against Trident nuclear missiles) provides another example whereby spirituality is inseparable from direct action.

In this context, spirituality influences, instigates and initiates the action. It is also embodied in the ways in which the action is carried out as informed by issues of responsibility, accountability and non-violence. Although underdeveloped in our research we have referred to these somewhat socially and politically-embodied ways of doing spirituality as they stand outside of transpersonal psychology's conceptualisation of spirituality.

In regard to the dilemmas mentioned above, while transpersonal psychology fails to provide a space for these somewhat divergent conceptions of spirituality, whether marginal or not, we consider critical inquiry of transpersonal psychology and spirituality justifiable and important. However, we hope the critiques raised in this paper are not heard as destructive in the sense of discrediting recently heard voices. Rather, our aim has been to question the contributions, limitations and implications of transpersonal psychological knowledge, and subsequently provide an opening in which other ways of delineating spirituality can be acknowledged and given serious consideration.

Notes

1. Her involvement with various practices predates her research herein and includes for example, meditation (London School of Buddhism and The Dhyana Centre, London); shamanic dance; yoga; seminars at the Theosophical Society and Alternatives at St. James, Piccadilly, London; Dharma Classes in Tibetan Buddhism, Dharamsala, India; as well as attendance of seminars at Mind, Body, Spirit exhibitions.
2. Though not specifically a transpersonal psychologist, Wilber is often cited within humanist and transpersonal psychology publications – see Lajoie and Shapiro (1999), also Thomas et al (1993).
3. Zinnbauer et al (1997) discuss the relationship between religion and spirituality. They note that while no such distinction was made until the rise of secularism in the 1900s, frequently religiousness is taken to signify church attendance, religious rituals, and is associated with a formally-structured theology, while spirituality is often assumed representative of personal transcendence, supra-consciousness, meaningfulness in life as well as 'mind, body and spirit' and 'new age'. They add that while religion and spirituality are not synonymous, that they neither are separate and distinct.
4. Gregory Jones (1997) talks of a socially-embodied spirituality whereby spirituality is inextricably embodied within social and political action. Building on from his work Lee and Marshall (2002) point to spirituality as extant within a direct-action collective in which spirituality is bound up with actively changing their local environment. They add that while religion and spirituality are not synonymous, neither are they separate and distinct.

5. Go to www.warwick.ac.uk/~psrev/psybnd.html for an online copy.
6. Wilber (1993) argues that the stages/levels of his model are non-linear, that they are ordered but that one stage does not supplement another. Consequently, he uses hierarchy and holarchy interchangeably, the latter implying that preceding stages/levels are encompassed and expanded in succeeding stages – in similar manner to a nest of boxes.
7. Although united in challenging the power of male-centred forms of spirituality, feminist spirituality is an umbrella term representing diversity which includes post-Christian spiritualities, women's spirituality with a focus on Jungian psychology, as well as earth-based spiritualities such as Wicca (see Lee, 2002; Puttick, 1997 and Woodhead, 1993).
8. See also www.starhawk.org
9. Ploughshares website www.gn.apc.org/tp2000/html/ploughs.html

References

Besanta, C. (2000) Spirituality and western psychology. *Transpersonal Psychology Review* 4 (3): 23-28.

Bruce, S. (1995) *Religion in Modern Britain*. Oxford: Oxford University Press.

Caplan, N., and Nelson, S. D. (1973) 'On being useful: The nature and consequences of psychological research on social problems'. *American Psychologist* March.

Coyle, J. (2002) 'Spirituality and health: towards a framework for exploring the relationship between spirituality and health'. *Journal of Advanced Nursing* 37: 589-597.

Crawford, M. (1998) 'Mars and Venus': Gender Representations and their Subversion. Keynote presentation at International Conference in Discourse and the Social Order, Aston Business School, Birmingham, UK. 16-17 July 1998.

Daniels, M. (1998) 'Transpersonal psychology and the paranormal'. *Transpersonal Psychology Review* 2 (3): 17-31.

Edwards, A. (1999) 'A brief history of transpersonal psychology'. *Transpersonal Psychology Review* 3 (2): 4-9.

Finlay, N. (1997) 'Political activism and feminist spirituality'. *Sociological Analysis* 52: 349-362.

Fontana, D., and Slack, I. (1996). 'The need for transpersonal psychology'. *The Psychologist* 9: 267-269.

Fontana, D. (1999) 'Inner transformation and outer behaviour'. *Transpersonal Psychology Review* 3 (1): 5-13.

Foucault, M. (1977) *Discipline and Punish: The Birth of the Prison*. London: Penguin.

Gawain, S. (1991) *Living in the Light: A Guide to Personal and Planetary Transformation*. London: Bantam.

Gergen, K. J. (1999) *An Invitation to Social Constructionism*. London: Sage.

Gergen, K. J. (2000) 'Emerging challenges relux'. *Theory and Psychology* 10 (1): 23-30.

Gilligan, C. (1982) *In a Different Voice*. Cambridge: Harvard University Press.

Gregory Jones, L. (1997) A thirst for God of consumer spirituality? Cultivating disciplined practices or being engaged by God. In L. Gregory Jones and J. Buckley (Ed), *Spirituality and Social Embodiment*. Oxford: Blackwell.

Heelas, P. (1996) *The New Age Movement: The Celebration of Self and the Sacralization of Modernity*. Oxford: Blackwell.

Henderson, B. (1989) 'Self-help books emphasising transpersonal psychology: are they ethical?' *The Journal of Transpersonal Psychology* 15: 169-171.

Hepburn, A. (1997) 'Teachers and secondary school bullying: a postmodern discourse analysis'. *Discourse and Society* 8: 31.

James, W. ([1902]1985) *The Varieties of Religious Experience*. London: Penguin.

Jung, C. J. (1927) *Collected Works 8 – The Structure of the Psyche*, London: Routledge and Kegan Paul Ltd.

Jung, C. J. (1938) *Psychology and Religion*. London: John Wiley and Son.

King, A. (1996) 'Spirituality: Transformation and metamorphosis'. *Religion* 26:343 351.

Lajoie, D. H. & Shapiro, S. I. (1999) 'Definitions of transpersonal psychology: The first 23 years'. *Transpersonal Psychology Review* 3(1): 12-25.

Lee, H. (2000a) Explicating Spirituality through Different Knowledge Sites, Unpublished PhD thesis. Staffordshire University.

Lee, H. (2000b) 'Towards ungendered relationality: Psychology and feminist spirituality'. *Feminism and Psychology* 10: 470-474.

Lee, H. and Marshall, H. (2002) Embodying the spirit in psychology: Questioning the politics of psychology and spirituality. In V. Walkerdine (Ed), *Challenging Subjects*. Basingstoke: Palgrave.

Marshall, H. and Woollett, A. (2000) 'Fit to reproduce? The regulative role of pregnancy texts'. *Feminism and Psychology* 10: 351-366.

Maslow, A. (1968) *Towards a Psychology of Being*. Princeton N.J: Van Nostrand.

May, R. M. (1993) *Cosmic Consciousness Revisited*. Shaftesbury: Element Books Ltd.

Parker, I. (1992) *Discourse Dynamics*. London: Routledge.

Pickering, J. (1994) Selves are Bodies Too: The Limits to the Explicit. Paper presented at the BPS conference, Institute of Education, London 19 – 24 Dec 1994.

Prilleltensky, I. (1989) 'Psychology and the status quo'. *American Psychologist* 44: 795-802.

Prilleltensky, I. (1994) *The Morals and Politics of Psychology: Psychological Discourse and the Status Quo*. Albany: State University of New York Press.

Prilleltensky, I., and Fox, D. (1997) Introducing critical psychology: values, assumptions and the status quo. In D. Fox and I. Prilleltensky (Eds) *Critical Psychology: An Introduction* 3-20. London: Sage

Puttick, E. (1997) *Women in New Religions*. London: Macmillan Press Ltd.

Redfield, J. & Adrienne, C. (1995) *The Celestine Prophecy: An Experiential Guide*. London: Bantam.

Rogers, C. (1961) On *Becoming a Person*. Boston: Houghton Mifflin.

Rose, N. (1990a) *Governing the Soul: The Shaping of the Private Self.* London: Routledge.

Rose, N. (1990b) Psychology as a 'social' science. In I. Parker and J. Shotter (Eds), *Deconstructing Social Psychology* 103-116. London: Routledge.

Rose, N. (1996) *Inventing Our Selves: Psychology, Power and Personhood.* Cambridge: Cambridge University Press.

Rothberg, D. (1986) 'Philosophical foundations of transpersonal psychology: An introduction to some basic issues'. *The Journal of Transpersonal Psychology* 18: 1-34.

Sampson, E. E. (1993) *Celebrating the Other.* Hemel Hempstead: Harvester Wheatsheaf.

Spretnak, C. (1994) *The Politics of Spirituality.* New York: Doubleday Publishing Group Inc.

Stainton Rogers, R., Stenner, P., Gleeson, K., and Stainton Rogers, W. (1995) *Social Psychology: A Critical Agenda.* Cambridge: Polity Press.

Starhawk (1989) *The Spiral Dance.* New York: HarperCollins.

Starhawk (2002) *Webs of Power: Notes from the Global Uprising.* Gabriola Island: New Society Publishers.

Tart, C. T. (1991) ' Influences of previous psychedelic experiences on students of Tibetan Buddhism: A preliminary exploration'. *The Journal of Transpersonal Psychology* 23: 139-173.

Tart, C. T. (1992) *Transpersonal Psychologies: Perspectives on the Mind from Seven Great Spiritual Traditions.* San Francisco: Harper Row.

Thomas, E., Brewer, S. J., Kraus, P. A., and Rosen, B. L. (1993) 'Two patterns of transcendence: An empirical examination of Wilber's and Washburn's theories'. *Journal of Humanistic Psychology* 33: 66-81.

Vitz, P. C., and Modesti, D. (1993) 'Social and psychological origins of new age Spirituality'. *Journal of Psychology and Christianity* 12: 45-57.

Walley, M. (2002) 'Towards a psychology of inter-being: Putting the heart back into psychology'. *Transpersonal Psychology Review* 6 (1): 3-11.

Walsh, R. (1993) 'The transpersonal movement: A history and state of the art'. *The Journal of Transpersonal Psychology* 25: 123-139.

Wilber, K. (1993) 'The great chain of being'. *Journal of Humanistic Psychology* 33: 52-65.

Wilber, K. (1995) 'An informal overview of transpersonal studies'. *The Journal of Transpersonal Psychology* 27: 107-129.

Wilber, K. (1996) *A Brief History of Everything.* Dublin: Gill and Macmillan.

Woodhead, L. (1993) 'Post-Christian spiritualities'. *Religion* 23: 167-181.

Zinnbauer, B. J., Pargament, K. I., Cole, B., Rye, M. S., Butter, E. M., Belavich, T.C., Hipp, K. M., Scott, A. B., and Kadar, J. L. (1997) 'Religion and spirituality: Unfuzzying the fuzzy'. *Journal for the Scientific Study of Religion* 36: 549-564.

Assembling the soul
Self and media consumption in alternative spirituality

Ian Hodges

Abstract

The interconnectedness of alternative spiritualities and therapeutic ethics and practices is explored in this paper, in particular through a focus on what has been termed an 'ethic of authenticity' (c.f. Taylor, 1991). The practical, discursive techniques involved in the constitution of the self or 'soul' are examined through an empirical analysis of therapeutic discourse operating within a media setting. Foucault's analytics of subjectification and ethical self-formation (c.f. Foucault, 1988, 1992) are used to inform a discursive analysis – with a particular focus on the deployment of figurative language – of two calls to a radio-phone-in broadcast. It was found that the use of metaphor and simile on the part of the therapist opened up new possibilities for accounting for self and for altering individual conduct (c.f. Hacking, 1995) such that in this setting callers were invited to account for themselves as both the target of and the responsible agent in their own cure. It is suggested that the search for real, authentic, 'natural' selves (and/or 'experience') – which is often regarded as a liberatory element of many forms of alternative spiritual practices – is both tied to the operation of power and a reflection of a ubiquitous 'therapeutic' moral order.

Introduction

The diverse practices, beliefs, 'experiences' and moralities – both religious and secular – subsumed under the term 'spirituality' have recently attracted scrutiny within critical psychology (for example, Game, 2001;

Blackman, 2002; Lee & Marshall, 2002; McPhillips, 2002). In this paper I am concerned with 'alternative' spiritualities, often described using the term 'New Age'.[1] In particular I consider the interconnectedness of alternative forms of spirituality with 'popular' therapeutic practice and ethics. This interconnectedness is most powerfully evidenced in a shared concern with what has been termed an 'ethics of authenticity' (Taylor, 1991), that is an ethics based upon personal autonomy, self-realisation and self-expression. Thus, in much alternative spirituality the search for a 'true' self devoid of the encumbrances of traditional religion and other institutional authority is a key element along the path to enlightenment.[2]

It has been argued that alternative spiritualities should, in part, be understood as 'audience cults' (Stark & Bainbridge, 1985; Hamilton, 2000) where membership is primarily based upon consumption of cultural, especially media, products. These arguments suggest that spiritual life in this context is focused upon leisure and consumption such that individuals – through consumer choice – put together their own version of spirituality through a process of 'bricolage' (c.f. Van Hove, 1999) to suit their current needs and aspirations. This process of assemblage may incorporate a range of sources, especially media such as books (including self-help publications), magazines, the internet and television and radio broadcasts, including those with 'therapeutic' content. In this paper I follow the arguments of Heelas (2000) who proposes that it is 'expressive authenticity' – that is, a humanist doctrine based upon the authenticity (and subsequent authority) of inner experience – that influences the most significant number of individuals in contemporary culture and which has had the most profound role in the decline of traditional religious practices and allegiances:

> Expressivist discourse generally takes a 'humanistic' rather than an explicitly religious form: the language of the 'true' or 'natural' self, not of the 'soul' or 'spirit'. But this should not blind us to the implied religious ontology and capacities … Themes to do with 'being ourselves', 'finding ourselves', 'expressing ourselves', 'developing ourselves', and 'fulfilling ourselves', all premised on there being an inner *source* … run through countless lives … (Heelas, 2000: 247 original emphasis).

Much of our current understanding of self within contemporary Western culture draws upon what might be termed a 'therapeutic' moral order (c.f. Rieff, 1987; Rose, 1989, 1996; Hodges, 2002) which focuses on the notion of a true, authentic self discoverable through particular kinds of therapeutic work. I contend here that this therapeutic moral order provides one of the key constituents of contemporary practices of 'spirituality' as they have moved away from traditional religious doctrines. In this paper I draw upon the work of Michel Foucault to examine the therapeutic/ethical construction of selves in a popular media setting and argue that the forms of self produced through 'expressive authenticity' are far from 'liberated' or 'natural' and 'authentic' but rather operate (via therapeutic discourse and its articulation with power) to enhance the individual's capacity for self-discipline and self-regulation such that individuals may better align themselves to prevailing social and moral norms.

Following a brief exposition of a Foucauldian approach to the analysis of talk I examine two calls to a radio counselling phone-in broadcast[3] focusing on the ways in which callers' presentations of self are shaped-up by therapeutic discourse, in particular through the deployment of simile and metaphor which form key elements of 'popular' therapeutic discursive practice. I show that therapeutic intervention within this media setting opens up alternative ethical understandings of self (including its rights and obligations) and its relationship both to itself and others. Finally, I conclude by discussing the ubiquitous operation of a therapeutic moral order in which responsibility to and for oneself is paramount and return to a consideration of the effects of reconceptualising the nature of 'authentic/humanistic expressivity' in terms of the power of therapeutic discourse and its centrality to much alternative spiritual practice.

For Foucault a major way in which power has its effects is through the production of truth, here I focus on the production of truth about oneself. Thus, I present an analysis of therapeutic discourse where the notion of 'power' is operationalised in terms of practices concerning the constitution and regulation of the self (c.f. Miller, 1987:17). Although Foucault never extended his methods to the level of conversational interaction, his methodological framework suggests that an analysis of therapeutic discourse should commence through recognising the therapeutic exchange as the operation of a micro-power, with respect to which Foucault (in Gordon, 1980: 99) has said:

One must conduct an ascending analysis of power ... starting ... from its infinitesimal mechanisms ... their own techniques and tactics ... and then see how these mechanisms of power have been ... invested, colonised, utilised, involuted, transformed, displaced, extended etc. by ever more general mechanisms and forms of global domination.

Thus, before any broader, cultural questions can be considered we need to begin by mapping the (technical) micro-operation of therapeutic discourse conceptualised as a form of 'subjectification' – which refers to the processes through which persons are 'made subject' to discourse. Thus, in this paper I report an empirical analysis of the deployment of therapeutic discourse and its relation to self-formation to illustrate both the concrete, technical aspects of the constitution of self or 'soul' and a method for analysing these.

The ethical operation of power

Foucault's distinction between morality and ethics (c.f. Foucault, 1992) provides a key methodological element of an analysis of therapeutic discourse. For Foucault, morality is understood in terms of codes, but codes which themselves do not determine in any specific way how persons conduct them, while the space of the ways one might conduct oneself always remains a space of indetermination. Foucault calls those ways in which individuals might relate themselves to the moral code a space of 'ethics'.

Prior to his death, Foucault began to write more specifically about this domain of ethics, outlining (1988: 18) four major forms of (cultural) 'technology': 1) technologies of production, 2) technologies of sign systems, 3) technologies of power, and finally 4), technologies of the self – which:

> ... permit individuals to effect by their own means or with the help of others a certain number of operations on their own bodies and souls, thoughts, conduct and way of being so as to transform themselves in order to attain a certain state of happiness, purity, wisdom, perfection or immortality.

It is argued here then, that Foucault's distinction between morality and ethics provides a formula for analysing the conversational interaction itself. Foucault's conceptualisation of ethics is quite different to that of the moral philosophers, aiming his analysis at a lower level (Couzens Hoy, 1991); examining the ways the self regulates itself. For Foucault

(1992: 26) the most interesting questions are concerned not so much with the codes themselves but rather with the ways in which individuals practice them:

> Given a code of action and with regard to a specific type of actions (which can be defined by their degree of conformity with or divergence from the code), there are different ways to 'conduct oneself' morally, different ways for the acting individual to operate, not as an agent but as an ethical subject of his [sic] own actions.

Here then, Foucault introduces a third domain (in addition to the code and the individual's behaviour in relation to it), the ways in which individuals form themselves as the ethical subject of their own actions. Foucault (1992: 26-28) devised a four-way conceptualisation of the self's relation to itself as follows:

1) The determination of the ethical substance:
   ... that is the way in which the individual has to constitute this or that part of himself [sic] as the prime material of his moral conduct.

2) Mode of subjection:
   ... the way in which the individual establishes his relation to the rule and recognises himself as obliged to put it into practice.

3) Forms of elaboration of ethical work:
   ... the forms of ... ethical work that one performs on oneself, not only in order to bring one's conduct into compliance with the given rule, but to attempt to transform oneself into the ethical subject of one's behaviour.

4) Telos of the ethical subject:
   ... an action is not only moral in itself, in its singularity; it is also moral in its circumstantial integration and by virtue of the place it occupies in a pattern of conduct.

Thus, therapeutic discourse can be examined as not only providing codes of conduct in relation to a moral order but also as *utilising* the self's relation to itself to achieve its ends (that is, as a strategic means), most importantly aiming to make the self accountable to itself. In relation to the four axes above then, four key questions inform the empirical analysis:

1. How is the caller made subject to therapeutic discourse, that is, how are the callers brought to recognise themselves as therapeutic subjects? (This links to the 'mode of subjection'.) For example, are there identifiable modes of discourse that, in some sense, align the caller to novel forms of self-understanding?
2. What kinds of techniques are offered for the turning of oneself into a therapeutic subject? (This relates to 'ethical work'.) What techniques for work upon the self can be identified within the data?
3. What kinds of substances are constituted as the 'prime material' for therapeutic practice? (This relates to the 'ethical substance'). What are the objects with which callers must concern themselves?
4. Towards what 'mode of being' (Foucault, 1992: 28) does the discourse move its subjects? (This relates to the ethical 'telos'.) Are there identifiable goals to which callers are enjoined to strive? What values are present within these goals?

It is important to remember however, that Foucault's four-way 'map' of ethical self-formation does not necessarily refer to distinct objects or processes but rather offers a means of understanding subjectification, in other words they do not refer to planes of reality, that is to ontologically distinct zones, but offer a practicable method of cutting into the data under examination.

A Foucauldian framework then, offers a means of reflecting upon the constitution of selves through a developed theory of the operation of power in relation to language and through which we might understand the regulatory nature of therapeutic discourse. Furthermore, Foucault's later work – with its emphasis upon self-regulation and self-discipline – enables a consideration of the therapeutic construction of selves as a form of subjectification (involving truth-telling[4]) in which the ethical operation of therapeutic discourse – its mode of subjection, ethical substance, ideal outcome (telos) and the work involved in achieving this – provides a way of understanding how the discourse gets 'inside' the subject. In other words by undertaking a detailed analysis of therapeutic subjection we might begin to understand the ways – within this popular media setting – that subjects fold discourse into themselves (c.f. Rose, 1996: 142). Thus, the therapeutic conversation is understood as a site of the production of truth through the subjectification of persons within discursive practices/techniques, including ethical self-formation on the part of the client/analysand or within this setting, the caller.

The ethical operation of therapeutic discourse

One key effect of therapeutic discourse is that it offers clients/callers new ways of understanding themselves; new ways of describing their histories, their present experiences and their future goals. These descriptions – offered within therapeutic discourse as objective and factual and hence authoritative – provide clients with the possibility of changing their idea of the person they take themselves to be. Hacking (1995: 21) proposes that descriptions of certain kinds of person generate expectations from those in authority – those experts in a position to offer the description. Such descriptions operate within a feedback loop consisting of the constitutive elements of expert descriptions and the need for these descriptions to respond to changes in patterns of behaviour which they subsequently are unable to capture. Hacking terms this process 'the looping effect of human kinds' (21). This 'looping effect' refers to more than the linguistic construction of reality but suggests that sense of self is intricately bound up with the production of knowledges and practices concerning it.

Using this model then, therapeutic discourse can be seen to operate on clients' existing sense of self, which will be bound up with their existing everyday practices, in part through altering expectations of conduct; thus I will show in this paper that what makes therapeutic discourse 'effective' is its operation upon callers' self-expectations. Fundamentally, descriptions of kinds of person open up new avenues for conduct. In relation to the data analysis which follows we are thus concerned with the shaping effects of therapeutic techniques on the caller's self-understanding.

Analysing figurative language

Here I use the term 'metaphor' to refer to a form of figurative language which (re-)places its object within an entirely new arrangement of paradigmatic and syntagmatic associations. Lakoff & Johnson (1980: 3) usefully argue that metaphor is not merely a literary device but profoundly structures our everyday understandings. They claim that language takes second place to concepts, using the familiar model of language as representation – where a word has a direct relationship to the concept it represents, and in turn, the concept has a direct relationship to the 'reality' it indexes. Put another way, they make their claims from a psychologistic rather than semiotic position and consider metaphor as bound up with 'psychological' processes which ultimately have their origin in our experience of the materiality of our bodies and the world with which they interact. I take selectively from semiotics the importance of metaphor as an aspect of semiosis and concur with Jackobson's (1956) suggestion that metaphor is fundamental to the referential function of communication (quoted in Fiske, 1990: 92).

My analysis of figurative language then, recognises the therapeutic process as semiotic in nature, in other words as a process of signification rather than meaning; structural rather than interpretive. I use semiotics to refer to the analysis of sign systems, derived originally from Saussure's (1916/1995) work but modified to give the signifier priority over the signified (for useful summaries see for example, Walkerdine, 1988: 2-5; Silverman, 1994: 71-72, 78). Lakoff and Johnson focus attention on the systematicity of metaphor, that is they suggest that we can trace a system of 'entailment relationships' for a particular metaphor by which they mean the conceptual relationships it makes possible or 'entails', thus if we accept their claims from a semiotic rather than 'psychological' viewpoint, identifying the deployment of metaphor during the therapeutic interaction may index some important features of the process of signification as it operates as an element of discursive (and therapeutic) practice.

Analysis of transcript data

In the data analysis which follows I focus on the shaping effects of therapeutic techniques on the caller's presentation of self. This occurs, I suggest, through the production of truth concerning it, or put another way, from a Foucauldian perspective the forms of self found in the therapeutic conversations analysed here are *produced* rather than reflected through this technical operation of discourse. Given this, I completed a systematic examination of the transcript data, identifying the accomplishments of each statement (utterance) and focused upon those utterances which appeared to play an important role in the problematisation of the caller's past, present and future conduct and concomitantly the subjection of the caller through therapeutic discourse. In this paper I focus on the counsellor's deployment of figurative language (though I have explored other aspects of the therapeutic process elsewhere (Hodges, 1995, 1998, 2001, 2003), and examine two calls which were selected from a larger data archive (given the substantive role played by figurative language within the counsellor's interventions). However, I am not suggesting that the exchanges analysed here are representative of therapeutic practices and/or the discursive construction of selves in general, rather the aim of the analysis is to provide an in-depth examination of the discursive operation of popular media counselling and thus to *exemplify* some of the processes involved in both therapeutic and possibly other practices of self-formation.

The therapeutic deployment of figurative language
In the following analysis (and excerpts from transcript data) the counsellor is referred to as A (for advisor[5]) and the caller as C. Transcript line numbers are given in brackets.

BELINDA'S CALL

EXCERPT 1 (T3: 181-222)

181 C: =the thought of her alone with him for three and a half hours on the motorway fills me with
182 absolute horror I mean his attention span (.5) I think there's something wrong with him but I mean
183 I'm not a doctor but his attention span is about half an hour
184   [
185   [
186 A: Belinda you (1) you sound like somebody who (.) likes to please people
187 and who doesn't want to let them down and I think what we've got in here hidden away in this
188   [
189
190 C: [sighs]
191
192 very complex story is what I call guilt and what we all know
193   [
194 C: Mm
195
196 as guilt.hh you feel (.75) guilty about the grandmother (y-)
197   [[
198 C: I don't (want to)   terribly
199
200 yes you feel you're letting her down.hh you fee-
201   [
202 C: I've I've said I'll take her down there
203

```
204   A: yes=
205
206   C: =why can't he bring her down
207
208   A: yes yes=
209
210   C: =and I say you're joking (wha- ) supposing he wants to take her to the loo or or
211                                                       [
212                                                       [
213   A:                              well well th- th- this this is a the is an issue of not going.hh
214   on being Mrs. Nice for the rest of your life.hh and that sometimes
215                      [
216   C:                              see the grandmother threatens to have a nervous breakdown on me
217                                                                                   [
218                                                                                   [
219   A:                                                  no no no but this is upsetting you
220   isn't it when I say to you don't be nice to somebody you get a bit cross with me and you say well I
221   want to go on being nice.hh sometimes in life.hh truth has to take precedence over niceness now
222   that is a very important guiding principle.hh
```

At (181-182) C deploys a metaphor as follows:

181-182 C: =the thought of her alone with him for three and a half hours on the motorway *fills me with absolute horror* ... (my emphasis)

which firmly situates the problem with the caller's husband and entails an understanding of the consequences of unsupervised contact with his child as 'horrific' – implying that such contact would constitute an extremely high risk. A then interrupts with a fundamentally different understanding of the problem, one which bears little relation to the previous turn (187-189):

```
186   A:                      Belinda you (1) you sound like somebody who. likes to please people and
187   who doesn't like to let them down and I think what we've got in here hidden away in this
```

A suggests C sounds '... like somebody who likes to please people ...' (186-187) – where the deployment of simile offers a resemblance rather than an equivalence (which would be produced with metaphor). A then suggests that something is 'hidden away' (187) in the 'very complex story' (192) and that what is hidden away is guilt (196), recognisable not only to A but also to 'we all' (192-196).

During this turn A's metaphor 'hidden away' (187) produces the following effects, implying that: 1) It is C who is culpable (perhaps consciously or unconsciously) for the hiding, for it is C who has produced the story – moreover, it is easier to conceal something in a 'very complex story' (192); 2) C has hidden away her 'true' feelings – 'you feel guilty' (196) – where this emotion is recognisable to all, 'what we all know as guilt' (192-196). Here the collective pronoun could be heard as including the overhearing audience, the advisor and possibly the caller too – A invites C (and the overhearing audience) to recognise her authentic emotion.

These two elements of A's interpretation – concealment and authentic emotion – I suggest combine to produce a compelling subjection. C is the responsible/culpable agent here – she is concealing something, moreover what she is concealing – not only from A and the overhearing audience but also from herself – is not only her 'authentic' emotion – guilt – but also its cause; her 'true' self, 'someone who likes to please people' (186-187). I will show later that this figurative mode of subjection can, in addition, provide evidence for its claims within the interaction itself. It is interesting to note at this point that these forceful effects have been constituted through a combination of colloquial, informal ideas and statements – guilt hidden away in a story – the technical language characteristic of some schools of psychotherapy and counselling is entirely absent.

Immediately following A's interpretation, C appears to offer some agreement at (198) with 'terribly' but then continues to present the grandmother's perspective – as she understands it – until at (213) A interrupts with another metaphor which includes an extreme case formulation (c.f. Pomerantz, 1986) and which is again deployed as an interpretation (213-214):

213   A: well well th- th- this this is a the is an issue of not going hh on
214   being Mrs Nice for the rest of your life hh and that sometimes

Here, A once more links the problem to the caller through the deployment of a metaphor which operates as a proper noun – 'Mrs Nice' (214) while at the same time presenting the extreme case 'for the rest of your life' (214). This metaphor serves (at least) three purposes: 1) It emphasises C's position as woman and wife through the form of address 'Mrs'

(214); 2) It constructs a sense both of inescapability and exigency concerning the disposition (and problem) 'Mrs Nice', unless properly dealt with it will be life-long, and most importantly, 3) it makes the caller the responsible agent in resolving the problem, that is, I suggest, a specifically 'therapeutic' responsibility – it is her disposition as well as her conduct that is the problem – as someone who likes to please people.

A goes on to frame the caller's previous responses to his interpretation as providing immediate evidence for it (219-222):

```
219   A:                                              no no no but this is
220   upsetting you isn't it when I say to you don't be nice to somebody you get a bit cross with me
221   and you say well I want to go on being nice.hh sometimes in life.hh truth has to take precedence
222   over niceness now that is a very important guiding principle.hh
```

The suggestion that hidden guilt is operating not only within the situation recounted by the caller but in the telephone interaction itself, once again forcefully situates the problem within the caller. Thus, a process that psychoanalytically oriented practitioners might term 'transference' or 'resistance' operates here to augment the mode of subjection in that the caller herself is constituted as both the immediate cause, and means of rectifying, her 'presenting' problem.

SALLY'S CALL
EXCERPT 2 (T10: 144-170)

```
144                         I'm obviously being punished for something that I've done
145   (.) you know
146
147   A: Well not necessarily you may have just (.) I mean this may be like slipping on an ice mountain
148   you might be walking down this ice mountain you take the wrong foot and you start slipping
149   and one of the problems about eating disorders is that once (.) you see the body is like a very
150   delicately balanced spring in a way and it knows exactly when it's had enough and it knows
151   exactly when it's full up and it knows when to stop eating and when to start eating now that
152   mechanism's incredibly delicate and what has happened and what happens to so many people
153   most bulimics and most eating disorders start with some kind of dieting
154          [
155   C:          yeh mine did
156
157   A: and that seems to upset the body's regulation mechanism (.) it like you know you fiddle around
158   with the thermostat on the central heating system and once you've got it out of order it finds it
159   incredibly difficult to get itself back in in order again (.) and so it doesn't help you and I don't
```

160 think it's even true to say that your compulsive eating or your endless eating is (.) is really the
161 result of your own failure it's because the mechanism of your body sensing when you're full up
162 has got overridden (.) now the answer for you is can you get control of your weight again and if
163 you can believe in yourself and trust yourself and care for yourself then you might be able to (.)
164 and I mean the way forward as I see it is to really try and commit yourself to a diet and to get into
165 a relationship with somebody who will stand by you and rather than at this stage being admitted
166 somewhere and spending all your parents' money if you could afford to go to a counsellor even
167 two or three times a week (.) but it's got to be someone who's experienced in this field it's no good
168 going to somebody (.) you know who's got a counselling diploma from here or there or
169 somewhere (.) eating disorders are their own special (.) very difficult er problem and you've got to
170 be experienced in them if you're going to help somebody

At (144-145) the caller offers an account of her bulimia '... I'm obviously being punished for something that I've done'. A replies with an alternative in the form of a simile, the problem is 'like slipping on an ice mountain' (148) and develops this in what might be termed narrative style, that is, he presents the events in their order of imagined occurrence:

147 A: well not necessarily you may have just (.) I mean this may be like slipping on an ice mountain
148 you might be walking down this ice mountain you take the wrong foot and you start slipping ...

At (149-150), A introduces a second simile concerning the body, 'the body is like a very delicately balanced spring' and then develops this simile by switching the word 'body' with a pronoun 'it'. The deployment of a pronoun at this point invites reference not only to the body (in general) but also to the previous reference (simile) which likened the body to a machine, so that what began as a resemblance 'the body is like a machine' we are now asked to accept as fact. A then places this 'factual' description within a further metaphor:

151 exactly when it's full up and it knows when to stop eating and when to start eating now that
152 mechanism's incredibly delicate and what has happened and what happens to so many people ...

where the determiner 'that' appears to refer back to the simile 'body is like a very delicately balanced spring' (149-150). Here again, this is offered as fact rather than resemblance and is then related to an aetiology (158-160) where dieting 'upsets the body's regulation mechanism' (157), which is again offered as fact and which, in turn, becomes the object of a further simile – this mechanism is like 'the thermostat on the central heating system' (158):

157 A: and that seems to upset the body's regulation mechanism (.) it like you know you fiddle around
158 with the thermostat on the central heating system and once you've got it out of order it finds it
159 incredibly difficult to get itself back in in order again (.) and so it doesn't help you and I don't

How can we make sense of this complex chain of metaphor and simile? At (159-161), A refers directly to the caller's problem as not the result of her own failure and goes on to provide another metaphor which draws together the events of all of the previous ones, (161-162):

159 incredibly difficult to get itself back in in order again (.) and so it doesn't help you and I don't
160 think it's even true to say that your compulsive eating or your endless eating is (.) is really the
161 result of your own failure it's because the mechanism of your body sensing when you're full up
162 has got overridden (.) now the answer for you is can you get control of your weight again and if

Thus, by following the entailment relationships (c.f. Lakoff & Johnson, op cit) we can observe that what begins as a simile (at 147) becomes a *description* of the body's mechanism (150-152) and finally a *factual* statement (161-162) regarding the aetiology of the condition itself (bulimia). The metaphor of damaged thermostat shifts seamlessly into a description of a physiological cause; offered as fact.

The key effects of this final metaphor (161-162) are that: 1) The body is given a certain autonomy in its physiological processes, seemingly exonerating the caller from any culpability regarding her condition, 2) This factuality is conveyed in a pseudo-scientific language (an 'overridden' mechanism), and was developed through a series of metaphorical references that began as similes. In other words, what we are offered as fact relies upon the previous use of simile and metaphor for its intelligibility in that A's reformulated account initially utilised resemblance but culminated in a factual description. Put another way, here we see the discursive production of truth.

We can identify then, a discursive technique which involves moving from simile (and resemblance) to metaphor (and factuality). What, however, are the ethical effects of the mobilisation of these similes and metaphors? A's interpretation initially appears to avert culpability from the caller after her self-blaming interpretation at (144-145); however, if we once again consider A's deployment of metaphor at (157-159):

157　A: and that seems to upset the body's regulation mechanism (.) it like you know you fiddle around
158　with the thermostat on the central heating system and once you've got it out of order it finds it
159　incredibly difficult to get itself back in in order again (.) and so it doesn't help you and I don't ...

there is a sense in which these utterances are anomalous in that A
appears to produce culpability through an ambiguous use of the
pronoun 'you' in relation to dieting. That is, the pronoun could equally
apply to the caller or dieters in general. However, at 159-161 A
dismisses a general notion of the caller's failure in favour of an overridden body mechanism but this seeming exoneration shifts once more
as A urges C to get control of her weight (162); so that culpability
appears to have returned through an implication that control has – at
some time – been lost by the caller:

162　has got overridden (.) now the answer for you is can you get control of your weight again and if ...

Thus, through these complicated moves A's deployment of metaphor
and simile carefully balances the issue of culpability. A's discourse
relieves C from the responsibility for her condition but at the same
time opens a space of accountability through her dieting and finally
goes on to constitute C as responsible for her cure through attending to
her relation to herself (162-166).

162　has got overridden (.) now the answer for you is can you get control of your weight again and if
163　you can believe in yourself and trust yourself and care for yourself then you might be able to (.)
164　and I mean the way forward as I see it is to really try and commit yourself to a diet and to get into
165　a relationship with somebody who will stand by you and rather than at this stage being admitted
166　somewhere and spending all your parents money if you could afford to go to a counsellor even

Thus, as with the previous call, the deployment of metaphor within A's
discourse conveys sophisticated ethical constructions – averting blame
for the condition but encouraging a therapeutic responsibility by
making the self accountable to itself. Within A's turn (162-163) the
caller's relation with herself is constituted as the prime material upon
which she must work, where self-belief, self-trust and self-care is the
work to be performed.

　　In this relatively short section of the turn (157-170), A has produced
a therapeutic responsibility on behalf of the caller which above all

entails care of the self. What is most interesting is that these broad and sweeping imperatives 'trust in yourself' are offered without instructions for their exact implementation, implying that they are already understood and accepted by both C and the overhearing audience and thus perhaps constitute an element of a therapeutic moral order.

Conclusion

The discursive processes examined in this analysis were identified as techniques which operated in relation to the production of truth, thus the shaping-up of C's account through the (therapeutic) deployment of figurative language was shown to be a forceful mode of subjection. Here the advisor did much more than tell persuasive stories, that is the interventions were more than rhetorical, rather the techniques deployed within the broadcast produced the strategic effect of shaping-up the caller's account and realigning accountability via the callers' relationship to themselves. Moreover, the deployment of figurative language operated as a discursive technique which was all the more forceful because it functioned not only to construct the truth about the caller's problem but also to enable the caller to tell the truth about *themselves* – and this is the sense in which the processes identified here can properly be termed 'subjectification'. I also identified other ethical features of therapeutic discourse including the constitution of ethical substance (for example, guilt) and telos (for example, taking responsibility for oneself and one's problems). Although there were no detailed instructions given to callers with regard to 'therapeutic work', broad imperatives were provided (for example, 'trust in yourself', 'care for yourself'[6]). Furthermore, given A's interventions appeared to alter the ethical relations (for example with respect to accountability) already present in the problem C brought to the broadcast, therapeutic discourse (as one example of a practice involved in the construction and transformation of selves) must be considered far from disinterested or value-free.

In both of the exchanges considered here the caller is made the responsible agent in resolving their problem. In particular, I observed a link between the deployment of figurative language involving the constitution of 'psychological substances' (for example 'guilt' and 'niceness') and the production of selves which are urged to account for themselves as both the target of and the responsible agent in their own cure. Thus, we might understand the *strategic* operation of the therapeutic exchange as in some way involving a reformation (and self-reformation) of selves that engenders a particular relation to a 'therapeutic' moral order – where authority is conveyed through expressive authenticity. Put another way, we must remember that self-formation here is much more than the construction of biographical knowledge but concerns ethical practices and techniques which may be deployed to transform oneself in some way and where such transformation will reflect some or other (cultural) system of morals, values and ideals.

Therapeutic means of understanding oneself and others can be found in an astonishing array of locations, not only the established arenas of psychotherapeutic and counselling provision (which themselves have colonised an increasing range of sites) but also in self-help texts, media broadcasts (including the rise of 'confessional' TV) and other cultural products such as popular music and advertising. A key element of what I have termed the 'therapeutic' moral order is that issues of morality must ultimately be played out upon the terrain of self. Thus, it is the 'interior' which must be made to yield its secrets rather than some external, 'natural' or even divine force. While therapeutic discourse presents the path to enlightenment as obtainable through authenticity of self, it can be argued that the so called 'triumph of the therapeutic' (c.f. Rieff, 1987) has in fact inaugurated a shift in the ways individuals are made subject to power and regulation where self-identity, self-realisation and self-formation are indispensable to current forms of governmentality (c.f. Rose, 1999).

In relation to alternative spiritualities, although therapeutic practices are presented (and consumed) as a means to personal enlightenment through uncovering real or authentic selves, it can be argued that rather than escaping the effects of powerful and authoritative institutions, therapeutic discourse forcefully draws the individual into a therapeutic moral order in which 'authenticity' is offered in the shape of 'sanctioned' forms of personhood and conduct which in turn are related to particular forms of moral order and modes of authority. Thus, rather than focusing on the 'deeper' experiences of self as somehow ephemeral, sacred, mysterious, linked to the 'natural' and so on, we might recognise the 'soul' as a product of the practical, concrete construction of self-identity. Thus, by adopting a Foucauldian approach I have shown that it is possible to map the technical constitution of experience of the 'interior' where this 'interior' is conceived as a folding of discourse. What is important here is that power not only operates through more tangible 'external' structures such as our governing institutions and practices but also – and arguably more effectively – at the 'deepest' levels of our sense of self.

Therapeutic discourse then, provides an array of cultural resources that individuals can draw upon when assembling their spiritual lives, including concrete practices for the construction of the self or 'soul' as 'natural', 'authentic' and unencumbered by external influences. While there are numerous other practices, techniques, products and so on which individuals may incorporate into their spiritual lives, the search for authentic selfhood will be powerfully reinforced through the saturation of our contemporary culture with the 'ethic of authenticity'. As Bruce (2000: 234) argues:

> Insofar as it [new age spirituality] is popular, it is so because its individualistic epistemology, consumerist ethos and therapeutic focus resonate with the rest of our culture. The New Age is important not for the changes it will bring but for the changes it epitomises.

It is important however, to remember that a relatively short phone-call to a counselling broadcast may or may not constitute a therapeutic/transformative event in the everyday life of the caller. Rather, the practices illustrated here exemplify one way in which a discursive mode of subjection (the deployment of figurative language) opened up new possibilities for conduct via the provision of new understandings of oneself and its relation both to itself and to others (c.f. Hacking, 1995). The analysis presented here illustrates the sense in which our desire for knowledge of who and what we are does not necessarily culminate in 'natural', 'authentic' modes of being but rather the process of subjectification, of folding discourse into oneself, involves incorporating *cultural* systems of values, beliefs, moralities and so on which are aligned with the operation of power and which potentially impact upon one's relationships with oneself and others. It is these 'therapeutic' aspects of self-identity, I argue, which offer the greatest purchase on diagnosing contemporary forms of spirituality and the 'soul'.

Notes

1. Most commentators agree that the term 'new age' is problematic given that a) it often (and confusingly) subsumes a vast range of practices, beliefs, products, ideologies and so on and b) the term is often seen as unhelpfully

pejorative and judgmental, that is, as a description of shallow, vague and faddish beliefs and practices. Heelas (2000) for example suggests that the term should be avoided in scholarly work and for these reasons I use the (somewhat) more neutral term 'alternative spirituality'.

2. I am not arguing that an ethics of authenticity is necessarily central to alternative spiritualities but that it may form one of the major elements. Possamaï (2002) argues that alternative spiritualities, especially those designated as 'new age' encompass: a) a monistic interpretation of the cosmos, b) a striving toward personal growth, c) a search for spiritual knowledge, either knowledge of the universe or of the self (or both if understood as interrelated). Note that both b and c encompass aspects of therapeutic ethics.

3. The two calls analysed here are taken from a larger archive originally used for my PhD thesis (Hodges, 1998) and were chosen because figurative language forms a key element of the counsellor's interventions. Originally three complete broadcasts of the LBC (London Broadcasting Corporation) 'counselling hour' were recorded off-air between August 1991 and May 1992 (exact dates: 12.8.91; 16.3.92; 11.5.92). From these broadcasts ten complete telephone exchanges were selected in order to provide: a) as broad as possible a range of problems/topics, b) a balance of gender (five women and five men), c) a range of three different advisors, d) inclusion of the two different days/times of the broadcast (the counselling hour went out weekly on Mondays from 9-10 p.m. and Wednesdays from 12.00-1.00 a.m.). The exchanges were transcribed using accepted transcription notation conventions (c.f. Atkinson & Heritage, 1984) as required by conversation analytic research.

4. Although it is important to remember that callers are only able to 'tell the truth' because what they say is in some way placed upon a 'register' of truth.

5. The term advisor was used to incorporate interventions from counsellors, 'agony aunts' and psychiatrists, all of which were represented in the larger data archive. The advisor for Sally and Belinda's calls was a male consultant psychiatrist.

6. I discuss more detailed examples of therapeutic 'ethical work' elsewhere (Hodges, 1998). Later in Belinda's call (428-429) A suggests that '... a little more assertion and truth would help your case a lot ...'

References

Atkinson, J. M., & Heritage, J. (Eds), (1984) *Structures of Social Action: Studies in Conversation Analysis*. Cambridge: Cambridge University Press.

Blackman, L. (2002) 'A Psychophysics of the Imagination'. In V. Walkerdine (Ed), *Challenging Subjects: Critical Psychology for a New Millennium*. Basingstoke: Palgrave.

Bruce, S. (2000) 'The New Age and Secularism'. In S. Sutcliffe & M. Bowman. (Eds.), *Beyond New Age: Exploring Alternative Spirituality*. Edinburgh: Edinburgh University Press, 220-236.

Couzens Hoy, D. (1991) Introduction. In D. Couzens Hoy (Ed), *Foucault: A Critical Reader*. Oxford: Basil Blackwell, 1-25

De Saussure, F. (1995) *Course in General Linguistics*. La Salle, Illinois: Open Court Classics.

Fiske, J. (1990) *Introduction to Communication Studies* (2nd ed.). London: Routledge.

Foucault, M. (1980) 'Two Lectures'. In C. Gordon (Ed), *Power/Knowledge: Selected Interviews and Other Writings, 1972-1977 By Michel Foucault* 78-108. Hemel Hemstead: Harvester Wheatsheaf.

Foucault, M. (1988) 'Technologies of the Self'. In L. Martin, H. Gutman, & P. Hutton (Eds), *Technologies of the Self: A Seminar with Michel Foucault* 16-49. London: Tavistock.

Foucault, M. (1992) *The Use of Pleasure: The History of Sexuality Volume Two*. London: Penguin.

Game, A. (2001) 'Creative Ways of Being'. In J. R. Morss, N. Stephenson, N. & H. Van Rappard (Eds), *Theoretical Issues in Psychology*. MA: Kluwer

Hacking, I. (1995) *Rewriting the Soul: Multiple Personality and the Sciences of Memory*. New Jersey: Princeton University Press.

Hamilton, M. (2000) 'An Analysis of the Festival for Mind-Body-Spirit, London'. In S. Sutcliffe & M. Bowman. (Eds.), *Beyond New Age: Exploring Alternative Spirituality*. Edinburgh: Edinburgh University Press, 188-200.

Heelas, P. (2002) 'Expressive Spirituality and Humanistic Expressivism: Sources of Significance Beyond Church and Chapel'. In S. Sutcliffe & M. Bowman. (Eds.), *Beyond New Age: Exploring Alternative Spirituality*. Edinburgh: Edinburgh University Press, 237-254.

Hodges, I. (1995) 'Changing Your Mind: Therapeutic Discourse and Foucault's Ethics'. In I. Lubek, R. van-Hezewijk, G. Pheterson, & C. Tolman. (Eds), 'Trends and Issues in Theoretical Psychology'. New York: Springer, 301-305.

Hodges, I. (1998) 'A Problem Aired: Exploring Radio Therapeutic Discourse and Ethical Self-Formation'. Unpublished PhD Thesis: University of London.

Hodges, I. (2001) 'A Problem Aired: Radio Therapeutic Discourse and Modes of Subjection'. In J. Morss, N. Stephenson, H. Van Rappard (Eds), *Theoretical Issues in Psychology*. MA: Kluwer

Hodges, I. (2002) 'Moving Beyond Words: Therapeutic Discourse and Ethical Problematisation'. *Discourse Studies* 4: 455-479.

Hodges, I. (2003) 'Broadcasting the Audience: Radio Therapeutic Discourse and its Implied Listeners'. *International Journal of Critical Psychology* 7, 74-101.

Jackobson, R. & Halle, M. (1956) *The Fundamentals of Language*. Quoted in: J. Fiske (1990) *Introduction to Communication Studies* (2nd ed.). London: Routledge.

Lakoff, G. & Johnson, M. (1980). *Metaphors We Live By*. Chicago: Chicago University Press.

Lee, H. & Marshall, H. (2002) 'Embodying the Spirit in Psychology'. In V.

Walkerdine (Ed), *Challenging Subjects: Critical Psychology for a New Millennium*. Basingstoke: Palgrave.

McPhillips, K. (2002) 'Refiguring the Sacred'. In V. Walkerdine (Ed), *Challenging Subjects: Critical Psychology for a New Millennium*. Basingstoke: Palgrave.

Miller, P. (1987) Domination and Power. London: Routledge & Kegan Paul.

Pomerantz, A. (1986) 'Extreme Case Formulations: a way of legitimising claims'. *Human Studies* 9: 219-230.

Possamaï, A. (2002) 'Cultural Consumption of History and Popular Culture in Alternative Spiritualities'. *Journal of Consumer Culture*. Vol. 2(2) 197-218.

Rieff, P. (1987) *The Triumph of the Therapeutic: Uses of Faith After Freud*. Chicago: University of Chicago Press.

Rose, N. (1989) *Governing the Soul: The Shaping of the Private Self*. London: Routledge.

Rose, N. (1996) 'Identity, Genealogy, History'. In S. Hall & P. du Gay (Eds), *Questions of Cultural Identity* 128-150. London: Sage.

Rose, N. (1999) *Powers of Freedom: Reframing Political Thought*. Cambridge: Cambridge University Press.

Silverman, D. (1994). *Interpreting Qualitative Data: Methods for Analysing Talk, Text and Interaction*. London: Sage.

Stark, R. & Bainbridge, W. (1985) *The Future of Religion*. Berkeley: University of California Press.

Taylor, C. (1991) *The Ethics of Authenticity*. London: Harvard University Press.

Van Hove, H. (1999). L'Emergence d'un 'Marché Spirituel'. *Social Compass*. Vol. 46 (2): 161-172.

Walkerdine, V. (1988). *The Mastery of Reason: Cognitive Development and the Production of Rationality*. London: Routledge.

Speaking from the margins
An analysis of women's spirituality narratives

Kirsti Cheals, Mandy Morgan and
Leigh Coombes

Abstract

Feminist theory and research in psychology has identified women's exclusion and marginalisation within the discipline for some decades. This paper addresses spirituality through feminist and critical psychology. The research values women's accounts of their experience and was undertaken as a specific political intervention into epistemological social power relations. While the paper refuses to foreclose the meaning of spirituality, it analyses the narratives of spirituality told by women and discusses the subject positions opened through their narratives.

> Stories go in circles. They don't go in straight lines. So it helps if you listen in stories because there are stories inside stories and stories between stories and finding your way through them is as easy and hard as finding your way home. And part of the finding is in the getting lost. [For] if you're lost, you really start to look around and listen. (Metzger, 1986: 104)

The past three decades of feminist writing and research in psychology have produced powerful feminist voices speaking to the long term absence and marginalisation of women's accounts of their own experiences within the discipline (Morawski, 1997; Nicolson, 1992; Parlee, 1979; Russo & Denmark, 1987; Squire, 1989). Feminist discourse has articulated critiques of methodological practices complicit with marginalising and silencing women's voices (Riger, 1992; Wilkinson, 2001), and constituted research strategies enabling women's voices to be heard in a space of choral support (Code, 1995). Choral support is read here as a location within a community where women's understandings of their experiences are supported and valued (Morgan, 1999). Wherever such a community is formed the history of gendered social power relations is implicated in political struggles over the meaning and value of women's ways of knowing for themselves.

This project was undertaken as a political intervention into the social power relations of the academy, an intervention into epistemological power relations. We regard the opening of inclusive spaces for speaking spirituality as a specific political intervention into the historical marginalisation and exclusion of women's experiences in psychology (Coombes & Morgan, 2001; Lee, 2001). We take this special issue as a rare opportunity, in psychology, to speak to issues of spirituality. Because we cannot make sense of ourselves without including our spirituality, we have engaged in research as a strategy of legitimating women's knowledges of spiritual experiences and legitimating spirituality as a sensible and legitimate process of producing subjectivities. This paper reports a study of the narratives told by nine women speaking of spirituality in a social relationship of choral support.

There are diverse accounts of spirituality within many disciplines, including feminist and psychological accounts.[1] In writing feminist spirituality, Starhawk (1979) and Daly (1978) trace the historical movements that alienated women who legitimately held positions of social power and knowledge, herbalists, midwives and priestesses. Lee (2001: 153) reads this feminist writing as an 'alternative to patriarchal conceptions of God', as well as to traditions that dislocate spirituality from community, interconnectedness, everyday life and politics. By these accounts spirituality is a site of the oppression of women within patriarchal power relations. Within psychology, spirituality has been largely excluded from legitimated accounts of human subjectivity. Coombes and Morgan (2001) identified humanistic psychological accounts as dominating psychology's writing of spirituality. These accounts constituted spirituality as belief system, personal growth, and search for the meaning and purpose of life. By these accounts spirituality is constituted as an internal dimension of the individual without regard for social power relations.

Rather than contest the multiplicity of accounts of spirituality by privileging a specific definition this project refuses to foreclose the meaning of spirituality. We do not attempt to elaborate the form of spiritual experience as if it were some *thing* conducive to an empirical gaze. We assume spirituality is intangible, multiple, fluid and shifting across time and space. We understand that definitions and accounts of spirituality are engaged in political struggles over meaning and legitimacy. Each account engages political concerns in specific ways. For example, while Lee (2001) also refuses to foreclose the meaning of spirituality, she asks what form a critical politics of spirituality might take. Here, we ask how accounts of spirituality may inform critical politics, and in particular the politics of epistemological power relations in which women's accounts of their own experience have been traditionally excluded, marginalised or devalued. This question depends on readings of some poststructuralist writing that theorises the field of epistemology and social power relations.

THEORETICAL ASSUMPTIONS OF THE PROJECT

Knowledge, discourse, narrative

From Foucault (1972, 1980, 1983) we take the notion that knowledge is always already discursively constituted and legitimated within fields of social power relations. Discourse is implicated in all forms of knowledge. In this reading the term discourse is inclusive of the implicit rules, material practices and technologies that govern the formation of meaningful statements as knowledge. These processes of governing knowledges and ways of speaking are political processes in as much as they reproduce social power relations by exclusion, marginalisation and domination. This theory of knowledge disrupts notions of objectivity in scientific practices of psychological research by proposing that all scientific knowledge is a body of discourse. Foucault insists that knowledge and discourse be analysed in relation to social power relations of domination and least domination. While Foucault's projects are concerned with the development of forms of subjectivity that resist state control (Dormer & Davies, 2001), our feminist use of Foucauldian theory is more concerned with forms of gendered subjectivity that resist patriarchal power relations, specifically the domination and subordination of women. Within the field of legitimated knowledges implicating epistemological power relations feminist challenges to the marginalisation and exclusion of women's ways of knowing are refigured as discursive strategies of intervention into social power relations of domination.

Foucault's emphasis on knowledge and social power relations resonates with Lyotard's (1984) notion of narratives as a form through which social relations are organised, and complicit in organising hierarchies of power. Lyotard argues that narratives specify the criteria by which knowledge is legitimated. As narrative form, stories of science have traditionally authorised knowledge according to criteria of factuality, derived from values of singularity and objectivity and producing truth statements. This authorisation constitutes psychological knowledges as metanarratives of human subjectivity. Lyotard argues against the totalising effects of metanarratives and suggests attending to specific narrative forms that challenge social power relations of domination by authorising specific knowledges. So as to pay attention to specific narrative forms, we draw on particular theories of narrative.

Narrative theory

Narrative theories have become increasingly important to making intelligible the ways in which we make sense of our lives (Freeman, 1993; Murray, 1999; Polkinghorne, 1995; Reissman, 1993; Sarbin, 1986). Narratives or stories are understood as a form of ordering the often chaotic and seemingly unconnected events into meaningful trajectories. As ordering devices narratives represent lived experience, however the processes of representation are neither linear nor transparent. Reissman (1993) complicates any simple notion of representing experience in stories by suggesting that five 'levels' of representation are involved in any academic re-telling of research participants' life experiences. She argues that coherent sense is made of experiences through social processes of selection and negotiation in dialogue between storytellers and their audience. We cannot assume that stories transparently represent experience in itself. Experience is constituted through discourse (Gavey, 1989; Hollway, 1984) and dependent on the specific temporal and social locations in which sense making is performed. As such, narrative theory suggests that the study of experiences represented through stories is always already the study of discourse, the forms through which experience is articulated, and the social power relations implicated in the dialogue between storytellers and audiences. Through this reading, narratives are understood as the culturally available resources used to make sense of the events in our lives.

The specificity of narrative as a discursive form is often theorised in terms of the sequencing of events in time. Narratives organise a temporal sequence of events so that they tend towards an explicit or implicit ending (Sarbin, 1986). White (1987) suggests that this trajectory towards an ending implicates a moral endpoint rather than an ending to events in real time. In this way the endings of narratives are ascribed to a moral order. Because, through narrative, events are represented in relation to a moral order they are also constituted as socio-political events. The representation of experience through narrative positions the storyteller within a moral order at the same time that events are organised in a temporal sequence authorised by that moral order. As storytellers are positioned in the moral order they are also constituted as particular kinds of subjects with specific social obligations, rights and duties (Davies and Harré, 1990). Narrative form produces subject positions.

From these readings of narrative theory we draw on three key terms: structure, configuration and function. Structure evokes the notion that events, objects and persons are represented in the organisation of talk. Attending to structure enables us to identify stories told in talk about spirituality. Configuration evokes the notion that the structure of a story is not simply the creation of a temporal succession of events, but the organisation of a sequence so that it serves a particular moral function. Attending to configuration enables us to identify culturally available linguistic devices used to organise story content so as to enable shared intelligibility. Function evokes the notion that stories that are told through culturally available narrative forms are active in positioning subjects within moral orders. Stories are neither simple representations nor passive reflections of lived experience.

From these readings of poststructuralist and narrative theories our concern with the way in which spirituality may inform critical politics is transformed into specific research questions: how are women's accounts of their spiritual experiences storied? How do these stories draw on culturally available resources so as to configure events, objects and persons? How do the subject positions constituted through these configurations enable resistance to patriarchal social power relations?

RESEARCH CONDUCT

Generating stories for analysis

To gather the women's stories of their spiritual experiences the first author invited nine women to participate with her in a one-to-one interview. The women were recruited to participate through snow-balling, a technique that involves using personal contacts to extend invitations to people with an interest in the research topic. Invitations were not extended on the basis of any criteria other than the women's interest in spirituality. No one was invited or excluded on the grounds of religious affiliation or spiritual convictions. Nine women accepted the invitation to participate. Each woman chose a pseudonym for herself and provided information on her age. The participants were Artemis, 59; Agnes, 44; Belinda, 23; Caesal, 29; Drizzle, 25; Fathom, 24; Jonesy, 73; Maria, 23 and Sianan, 17.

Interviews were unstructured, conversational and lasted for around an hour. Unstructured interviews were chosen to enable participants to actively construct their own account (Mishler, 1986). Each woman was encouraged to say what spirituality meant for her and how spirituality enabled her to make sense of herself. Interviews included many moments in which the women commented on the difficulty they experienced in finding the right words to say what they wanted to say. For most of the participants, spirituality is deeply personal and rarely discussed with anyone else. Some participants commented that they had not put words to spirituality until they were invited to take part in the research.

Each interview was audiotaped and transcribed. Transcription included both interviewer and participant turns, sufficient punctuation to make sense of the text, and pauses measured in seconds. Transcripts were returned to the participants for comment. Few participants added or changed anything, and additions or changes were incorporated into the transcript used for analysis.

Conceptualising stories as knowledge

Lyotard's (1984) reformulation of the relationship between metanarrative, legitimate knowledge and social power relations informs the conduct of our research project.

We honour women's stories of spiritual experience as legitimate forms of knowledge in themselves. This strategy disrupts the metanarrative of scientific psychological knowledge by treating the 'raw data' of women's talk in interviews as already legitimate without needing to pass through a process of 'objective analysis' to be reformulated as fact. Our analysis is not focused on the content of the stories, but on the cultur-ally available narrative devices through which the women are able to constitute themselves as specific spiritual persons. By refusing to attend to commonality in the content of the stories we attempt to resist creating an alternative metanarrative of women's spiritual experience. Instead, we focus on identifying specific stories, identifying shared cultural resources used for organising story content and discussing the subject positions enabled for women through their stories.

Analytic strategies

i. Identifying specific stories

The first phase of our analysis involved identifying specific stories within the interview transcripts. We made use of Labov's (1972) structural analysis of oral storytelling. Labov identifies six elements that form a story in conversation: an abstract, orientation, complicating action, evaluation, result or resolution, and coda. The *abstract* takes the form of a summary or evaluation of the narrative that follows, perhaps a clue to the reader/listener of how to respond. The *orientation* component generally indicates time, place, persons and their activity, and situation. Clues of the when, where, who, what do not necessarily depend on the temporal sequence (Tuffin, Morgan & Stephens, 2001). The *complicating action* indicates the temporal sequence of events that followed. And the order matters to the meaning of the narrative. The *evaluation* element provides the means through which the narrator is able to convey the significance of the events, how it should be understood, 'why it is told, and what the narrator is getting at' (Labov, 1972: 366). The element *result* or *resolution* tells of the culminating event or outcome of the complicating action. The final element, the *coda*, suggests an ending to the narrative at the same time as signalling a return from the past of the story to the present of the storytelling (Tuffin et al, 2001).

This first phase resulted in a collection of stories that were used to identify shared cultural resources for organising events, objects and persons into a narrative.

ii. Identifying organising devices

Adams (1996) suggests that all narrative theories 'presuppose[s] the concept of configuration' (157). Configuration is understood as the shape, or form, that emerges from the process of organisation in storytelling. To identify culturally shared organising devices, it is necessary to specify the meaning of 'configuration'. Adams (1996) talks of the image of causality as one possible meaning of configuration. In our analysis we relied on an image of configuration drawn from Sarbin's (1986) argument for narrative as a root metaphor for psychology. When Sarbin makes his argument he tells a story of psychology that presupposes the configuration of the discipline in and through root metaphors. This presupposition implies that configuration may be conceptualised as metaphor. To identify culturally shared resources within the women's stories we read for commonly used metaphors that served to shape the trajectory of events told in the interview texts.

This second phase of analysis resulted in identifying three organising metaphors commonly used across the women's stories. Naming these metaphors enables us to speak of specific narrative forms that constitute particular subject positions within social power relations.

iii. Speaking of subject positions

Having grouped specific stories according to their metaphors of configuration, their narrative form, we read within each group to identify specific subject positions enabled by the stories. Our understanding of subject positions draws on Davies and Harré's (1990) explication of them as sets of rights, duties and obligations that may be offered, accepted or refused in the social processes of conversation. Stories told in conversation enable or constrain particular subject positions in as much as the moral order through which their trajectories are organised legitimates certain rights, duties and obligations (Morgan & Coombes, 2001).

Since we were particularly interested in the way in which spirituality might inform a critical politics with regard to patriarchal power relations, we focused our attention on subject positions that were complicit with or resistant to the phallocentric positioning of women.[2]

In the following sections we exemplify each phase of our analysis, though the full analyses are beyond the scope of this paper.

ANALYSES

Structural analysis

Engaging Labov's (1972) structural analysis of oral storytelling, interview transcripts were searched for specific stories of spirituality. Initially phrases that could be identified as abstracts or orientations were located. The text that followed these phrases was then read for the other four components of story structure: complicating action, evaluation, result or resolution, and coda. For example, the following text was identified as a complete story:

> Maria: Like I had one woman telling me about my spirit guides who were women – thus easier to identify with. And it was like a secret magical relationship that I had that no one ever sort of knew about. It was something that I always had access to and it was really good for me like that. I think, um, from that point I developed ... I guess I was getting more self-esteem and stuff and I became more social. And as soon as I got into a more social scene that spiritual stuff was sort of put on a back-bench. It was still there but I wasn't spending so much time meditating or thinking about it or (.) doing much around that ... To me now it's not just meditating, it's going and being by yourself somewhere and thinking. It's just, um, going off into another dimension you know. I found that the more I spent time with other people the less I did that. Then I started to meet other people that um ... introduced me to new things or talked about some of those spiritual things. And they had their own ideas which sort of made me (.) open up new doors (Maria 1.6)

This story does not begin with an abstract, but the reader is oriented through the representation of a particular person and her activity: *I had one woman telling me about my spirit guides who were women.* The complicating action that follows includes a sequence of events in which the speaker firstly recognises and characterises the relationships she has with her spirit guides. She then identifies herself as becoming more social and less involved in *spiritual stuff.* This active movement sets up a conflict between her spiritual life and her social life. She then meets people who are also interested in spirituality and is able to resolve the conflict between her social and spiritual life through *open[ing] up new doors.* Evaluation occurs throughout the story both explicitly through phrases such as *it was really good for me* and implicitly through devices such as negative comparisons, *the more I spent time with other people the less I did that.* Through these evaluations readers are informed of the significance of the movement from the spiritual to the social to a renewed spiritual. As with many examples of oral storytelling, this story also has no coda.

Some of the stories identified in the interview transcripts did include abstracts and codas. For example, Fathom begins a story of her adolescence with the following abstract:

> Fathom: I think when I was younger my friends went to church and I went to church too and my mum was really into going too ... and then I came to the decision that church wasn't for me and so ...

The story of Fathom's rejection of church-going concludes with an account of the way in which academic study enabled her to be cynical of church-going among Christians:

> Fathom: I'm quite cynical about ... a belief system based around the bible because I have academically looked at it in that kind of way.

Immediately following this conclusion, Fathom offers the following coda:

> Fathom: I believe that people probably do get the kind of healing and, um, what they're looking for through the church mainly because of support maybe ...

This statement signals a return from the past of her academic study to the present conversation about spirituality and asserts her contemporary belief that while she may find little of value in Church-going for herself, this does not preclude others finding what they are seeking.

The process of identifying stories within the interview transcripts involves careful decision making in sorting through text that is frequently non-linear. As Metzger (1986) suggests there are stories within stories and between stories. Even with Labov's structural model of stories as an interpretive framework, this phase of the analysis involved close reading and attention to the voices of the women who had spoken with Kirsti.

Analysis of organising metaphors

Once the stories within the interview transcripts had been identified, they were read for common metaphors that operated to organise the storied events within particular moral trajectories. Three metaphors were identified: the journeying metaphor, the metaphor of self-knowing and the metaphor of turning points. In the following illustration of this phase of the analysis we include examples from transcripts to show how the metaphors were engaged in the stories, and we also discuss the trajectories and end points that implicate moral orders.

i. *Journeying*

The metaphor of journeying was engaged in various stories that spoke of spirituality as an experience of movement, of opening up possibilities, of consciousness and surrender. The following extract Fathom uses the metaphor of journeying to characterise spirituality as a form of conscious travelling. Consciousness of the journey is critical to distinguishing between a spiritual journeying and a kind of aimless searching.

> Fathom: I was thinking about it [spirituality] ... Like what is spirituality to me. And it is ... a journey. Going along but being conscious of it being a journey (.) because that way you're open to new ideas. And you're open to things that make you feel good and you're also aware that you don't have to take them on board. [It's] kind of proactive and internal. Not like searching like a lost soul ...

The distinction drawn between travelling and searching implicates a tension in the character of the spiritual traveller. The activities of *going along* and *being open* may be read as relatively passive in comparison to *searching*. However, the conscious traveller is not passive, but *proactive* and *aware*. Even though the journeying may not be directed towards a particular goal the spiritual traveller is engaged in making choices.

In another example of journeying as a configuring metaphor, Artemis distinguishes between submission and surrender:

> Artemis: I realise my journey has been going from submission to the external to surrender to the internal ... Submission to the external is disempowering and surrender to my god within – the divine within – is the most empowering powerful thing you can ever do ... It empowers me in every way ... And my whole journey has been about going ... from external to internal.

Here, the journey itself is represented as a movement from the outside to the inside of the traveller. This distinction carries implications for the characterisation of the spiritual traveller as *empowered*. The empowered traveller *surrenders* to the inside without *submitting* to the outside.

This movement also characterises the journey as a movement towards empowerment.

As narrative form, journeying configures events in a trajectory towards revealing the interior of the traveller. The journey itself is devalued in relation to the value of the experience of travelling for the traveller. To realise the value of the journey, the traveller must be conscious and aware of themselves and the movement of the journey. As a trajectory towards a moral endpoint, the journeying narrative organises events and characters so as to value movement and consciousness *within* the traveller.

ii. Self-knowing

The metaphor of self-knowing was engaged in stories that told of spirituality as self, and as a process of gaining knowledge for and about oneself. In the following extract Drizzle speaks of spirituality as her self, and the notion of selfhood she engages evolves.

> Drizzle: For me spirituality is my self it um (.) oh I change all the time … I find I learn new things every day and I put that into myself which is which becomes my own sort of spirituality.

In accounting for the transformation of her *self* across time Drizzle represents a process of learning that internalises *new things*. This process establishes a relationship between the inside of the self and the external world. Spirituality is spoken across the boundary of self and other, inside and outside, as a self produced through the relationship between self and other, inside and outside.

Reading knowledge as a process of *finding out*, Sianan makes use of a self-knowing metaphor in speaking of the multiple possibilities for being spiritual.

> Sianan: I don't think my way is right. I don't think any way is right. I think you should find out for yourself. What makes your spirit feel good.

According to this account the self and the spirit are intimately related, though not quite isomorphic. For the spirit to *feel good* the self *should find* the form of spirituality best suited to that end. Thus the *self* tends to the *spirit* through knowledge.

Jonesy speaks of spirituality in terms of being *in tune with* ourselves.

To the extent that being *in tune* requires knowledge, this phrase evokes a notion of harmony within the self that requires self-knowing. Harmony implies a multiplicity of selves with the potential to be out of tune among themselves.

Artemis evokes a relationship between knowledge, self and spirituality through speaking of the truth of the spirit.

> Artemis: That's your truth and that's all it ever can be for anybody ... there can't be any more need for it to be anything else ... how splendid if each of us stands in our truth. That for me is about standing in the spirit.

Here truth is specific to particular persons. To be able to stand in the truth (spirit) requires knowing the truth of the self, for the self. This relationship between knowledge, self, spirit and truth implies that truth is multiple and simultaneously specific to *each of us*.

As narrative form, the self-knowing metaphor configures a trajectory towards valuing authenticity of selfhood. Knowing about and for the self values the uniqueness of individuals. Simultaneously, this trajectory also tends towards valuing multiplicity and specificity: multiple paths to authentic spirituality, specific truths for each spiritual being.

iii. Turning points

Stories organised through the metaphor of turning points told of moments where personal loss or abuse in heterosexual or familial relationships was transformed. In the following extract Belinda tells of losing herself in her heterosexual relationship.

> Belinda: yeah I was losing myself and I was really really lonely in my own relationship and I thought um you know I just can't spend the next (.) I cant wake up at forty and look in the mirror at this hag that's been nagging and crying and whinging for forty years you know I've got to um (.) I've got to yeah honour myself ... I need to be free and that's a whole part of the spirituality thing.

Here losing *self* is represented simultaneously with being lonely in relation to another. Self and other are not separate or discrete because what happens in relation to the other affects the self. The damaging effect of loss of self is represented through negative images of femininity, *nagging and crying and whinging*. In contrast to loss of self, honouring the self is represented as necessary to freedom and spirituality.

Agnes uses the metaphor of turning point explicitly in her account of an *emotionally abusive* relationship. She makes use of representing her own experience to create an image of feminine spirituality shared in a community of women living through the effects of abuse and violence.

> Agnes: So that was a really big turning point for me again um (.) I'd gone through this thing with my ex husband ... It was quite an emotionally abusive situation ... I think you create your own *[spirituality]* internally I think you have to, to survive ... I mean you take the battered woman. Somewhere she's got this little spiritual core and I mean I think you would find that if you speak with any battered woman that there's a piece of them that's untouched ... every one of them has got something (.) even if it's just the tiniest spark. And I think for me, that's feminine spirituality (Agnes 16.4-8).

The *tiny spark* that Agnes represents as feminine spirituality is explicitly located within the person and as a creation of the person. The *spark* connotes light, energy and liveliness. Here spirituality is told as a core of a woman's self that remains *untouched* by the effects of violence and abuse and enables survival. This core is specified as the core of a woman's self.

The moral endpoint of the trajectory of these turning point narratives values movement away from lonely, abusive or violent relationships as a process of moving beyond oppressive patriarchal relationships. Femininity as core to women's spiritual being, their self, is specified as necessary to survival and freedom. In narratives configured through this metaphor, the moral trajectory of the organisation of relationships among events and persons tends towards valuing the specificity of women.

Subject positioning

In moving towards the end of our own narrative of this research process we discuss the ways in which subject positions enabled through the narrative configurations we have identified position subjects with regard to patriarchal power relations. Here we return to the question of how spirituality might inform a critical politics of gendered power relations. Our own understanding of spirituality as intangible, fluid and multiple locates women's stories of their spiritual experience as discursively rather than ontologically constituted. As discursive, women's stories of spiritual experience may be legitimated as knowledge and simultaneously read for the subject positions they open up for the women speaking. Subject positioning serves the purpose of locating subjects within specific moral orders. We are particularly interested in those positions that enable resistance to patriarchal social power relations of domination and disturb the phallocentric positioning of women in psychological discourses.

The three narrative configurations we have identified through the women's stories have been read for their trajectories towards moral endpoints. These moral endpoints involve simultaneously valuing movement and consciousness within the speaking subject, uniqueness of self and multiplicity of truth and authenticity, femininity and the core of women's spiritual selves that enables survival.

With regard to the narrative of journeying, valuing qualities *within* the subject risks positioning women within phallocentric relationships that constitute all persons as individuals: unique, bounded and motivated from within. This constitution of the subject resonates with humanist psychology's construction of the subject as a unique individual: 'acultural, ahistorical and unmarked by sexual difference' (Coombes & Morgan, 2001: 12). By this account women are constituted as the same as men and the specificity of women's histories is excluded from legitimate knowledge of psychology. However, valuing the specific qualities of movement and consciousness disrupts psychology's subject within the journey narratives we were told. While consciousness is implicated in psychology's construction of the subject as unified and rational, movement is implicated in instability and change over time. Positioning women within a moral order where both consciousness and movement are valued within the person disturbs the phallocentric positioning of women as the same as men by including a characteristic of subjectivity historically represented as feminine: the instability of women.

Self-knowing narratives value the uniqueness of individuals simultaneously with valuing multiplicity and specificity in relation to truth and authenticity. Uniqueness, truth and authenticity are characteristics of humanistic psychology's subject. The self of humanistic psychology is essential to the uniqueness of each individual regardless of sexual specificity. Positioning women in relation to such a self risks constituting women as the same as men and excluding women's experiences of social power relations of domination from the characteristics of women's selves. However, the multiplicity of truths and authentic ways of being valued in the women's telling of unique selves disturbs the constitution of the humanist subject as universal. Positioning women within a moral order that values uniqueness, multiplicity and specificity opens the possibility of transforming psychology's totalising metanarratives towards multiple, diverse and specific stories.

Turning point narratives value femininity and the spiritual core of the self. Again a moral order valuing spirituality as a core of the self risks reproducing psychology's humanist subject and positioning women as the same as men. However, the specificity of femininity valued through incorporation into the core of the self, or through resistance to negative images of the feminine, insists on the specificity of gendered experiences of social power relations. The turning point narratives read through our analysis specified moving away from, and beyond, gendered power relations of domination as a movement towards women's survival and freedom. These narratives are *inclusive* of women's specific experiences.

These readings valuing movement *and* consciousness within the speaking subject, uniqueness of self *and* multiplicity of truth and authenticity, femininity *and* the core of women's spiritual selves that enables survival, disturb the constitution of the women speaking as simply similar to or different from men. This disturbance resists the return of Man as the figure of the unified rational subject, the representative of psychology's metanarrative of universal personhood. Simultaneously such both/and valuing produces the figure of feminine spirituality as resistant to and disruptive of gendered power relations of domination.

From our analysis it seems that women's talk about their spiritual experiences may offer a critical politics of gendered power relations a way of construing the both/and valuing as a means of redressing the exclusion and marginalisation of women in the production of psychological knowledges. By enacting tensions between positions as subjects of humanistic psychology and positions specifying women's experiences the participants in our research were able to tell stories that functioned to resist patriarchal power relations.

Notes

1. Because of our location within feminist and psychological discourses we do not extend our discussion of accounts of spirituality beyond these two fields. We understand our discussion of these accounts as partial and limited.

2. According to Grosz (1989), phallocentric positioning takes three forms: whenever women are represented as the opposites or negatives of men; whenever they are represented in terms the same as or similar to men; whenever they are represented as men's complements. In all three cases, women are seen as variations or versions of masculinity – either through negation, identity or unification into a greater whole.

References

Adams, J-K. (1996) *Narrative explanation: A pragmatic theory of discourse*. New York: Peter Lang.

Code, L. (1995) *Rhetorical spaces: essays on gendered locations*. New York: Routledge.

Coombes, L., & Morgan, M. (2001) 'Speaking from the margins: A discourse analysis of ten women's accounts of spirituality'. *Australian Psychologist* 36: 10-18.

Daly, M. (1978). *Gyn/Ecology: The metaethics of radical feminism*. Boston, Massachusetts: Beacon Press.

Davies, B., & Harré, R. (1990) 'Positioning: The discursive production of selves'. *Journal for the Theory of Social Behaviour* 20: 42-63.

Dormer, S., & Davies, B. (2001) 'Desiring women and the (im)possibility of being'. *Australian Psychologist* 36: 4-9.

Foucault, M. (1972) *The archaeology of knowledge*. (A. Sheridan, Trans.). New York: Pantheon Books.

Foucault, M. (1980) *Power/knowledge: Selected interviews and other writings, 1972-1977*. (C. Gordon, Ed. & Trans.). New York: Pantheon Books.

Foucault, M. (1983) 'The subject and power'. In H. Dreyfus & P. Rabinow (Eds), *Michel Foucault: Beyond structuralism and hermeneutics*. Chicago: University of Chicago, 208-226.

Freeman, M. (1993) *Rewriting the self: History, memory, narrative*. London: Routledge.

Gavey, N. (1989) 'Feminist poststructuralism and discourse analysis. Contributions to psychology'. *Psychology of Women Quarterly* 13: 459-475.

Grosz, E. (1989) *Sexual subversions*. Sydney: Allen and Unwin.

Hollway, W. (1984) 'Gender differences and the production of subjectivity'. In J. Henriques et al (Eds), *Changing the subject: Psychology, social regulation and subjectivity*. London: Methuen, 227-263.

Labov, W. (1972) *Language in the inner city*. Oxford: Basil Blackwell.

Lee, H. (2001) 'Towards a critical politics of spirituality'. *The International Journal of Critical Psychology* 1: 153-157.

Lyotard, J-F. (1984) *The postmodern condition. A report on knowledge*. (G.

Bennington & B. Massuni, Trans.). Minnesota: University of Minnesota Press.

Mishler, E. G. (1986) *Research interviewing: Context and narrative*. Cambridge, Massachusetts: Harvard University Press.

Metzger, D. (1986). 'Circles of stories'. *Parabola* IV: 104-105.

Morawski, J.G. (1997) *Practising feminisms, reconstructing psychology. Notes on a liminal science*. Ann Arbor: University of Michigan Press.

Morgan, M. (1999) 'Touches of the institution: An informal curriculum of teaching about violence towards women'. *Women's Studies Quarterly* XXVII: 185-196.

Morgan, M., & Coombes, L. (2001) 'Subjectivities and silences, mother and woman: Theorizing an experience of silence as a speaking subject'. *Feminism and Psychology* 11: 361-375.

Murray, M. (1997) *Narrative Health Psychology* (Visiting Scholars Series No. 7, Department of Psychology). Palmerston North: Massey University.

Nicolson, P. (1992) 'Feminism and academic psychology: Towards a psychology of women?' In Kate Campbell (Ed), *Critical Feminism. Argument in the disciplines*. Philadelphia: Open University Press, 53-82.

Parlee, M. B. (1979) 'Psychology and women'. *Signs, Journal of Women in Culture and Society* 5: 121-133.

Polkinghorne, D. E. (1995) 'Narrative configuration in qualitative analysis'. In J. A. Hatch, & R. Wisniewski (Eds), *Life history and narrative*. London: Falmer Press, 5-23.

Riessman, C. K. (1993) *Narrative Analysis*. California: Sage.

Riger, S. (1992) 'Epistemological debates, feminist voices. Science, social values, and the study of woman'. *American Psychologist* 47: 730-740.

Russo, N. F., & Denmark, F. L. (1987) 'Contributions of women to psychology'. *Annual Review of* Psychology 38: 279-298.

Sarbin, T. (1986) 'The narrative as a root metaphor for psychology'. In T. Sarbin (Ed), *Narrative psychology: The storied nature of human conduct* 3-21. New York: Praeger.

Squire, C. (1989) *Significant Differences*. London: Routledge.

Starhawk. (1979) *The spiral dance. A rebirth of the ancient religion of the great goddess*. New York: Harper & Row.

Tuffin, K., Morgan, M., & Stephens, C. (2001) 'Jane's jealousy: A narrative analysis of emotion experience in its social context'. *International Journal of Group Tensions*, 30(1): 55-68.

White, H. (1987) *The Content of the Form: Narrative, discourse and historical representation*. Baltimore: John Hopkins University Press.

Wilkinson, S. (2001) 'Theoretical perspectives on women and gender'. In R. Unger (Ed), *Handbook of the psychology of women and gender*. New York: John Wiley & Sons, 23-27.

Psychology, spirituality and capitalism
The case of Abraham Maslow

Jeremy Carrette

> People know what they do; they frequently know why they do what they do; but what they don't know is what what they do does.
>
> Foucault, in Dreyfus and Rabinow, 1982:187.

The discourse of religion has co-existed, throughout history, with other forms of institutional authority. Such a co-existence has often meant that the boundary between the religious and the so-called 'secular' discourses is difficult to define. It is often assumed that religious knowledge adapts itself to existing political structures in order to survive, but it is more accurate to recognise that new discourses appropriate older regimes and traditions of power in order to displace authority from within. In such a situation, religious institutions, once all-powerful in the Western world, inescapably move within other systems of power-knowledge. In this territorial struggle for an authoritative discourse, knowledge of what it is to be human is a central site of contestation, because to claim authority on the nature of being human is the technology of government.[1] To know what we are is to know what we should be doing or, more precisely, to construct and politically imagine a discourse of what we are is to convince people to voluntarily become 'subject' to such knowledge. General psychology, for instance, provides the anthropological sub-structure for capitalism (the ideology of efficiency for profit motive), because it provides a utility and measurement of human functioning and performance for modes of production and consumption. This is, to develop Dumont's (1986) conceptual distinction, the logic of an 'in-worldly' (a fixed, self-referential, essence), as opposed to an 'out-worldly' (an open-ended, interdependent and non-empirical), individualism. The unity of psychology and capitalism, established through the politics of 'in-worldly individualism', was not simply an economic alliance, but an operation of the nation state to order populations. If populations were to be ordered it was also necessary to pacify potential revolutionary discourses, which may disrupt the status quo. It was therefore necessary, as Nikolas Rose (1996) has shown, to 'psychologise' society through a network of institutions and practices. The rise of the nation state is, therefore, also the assimilation of all aspects of life – the policing of life – through technologies of the psychologised self. This policing of life required a knowledge of self which would undermine the rationality of existing discourses of being human, or at least pacify such categories of knowledge for the service of the state. It is my contention in this paper that the gradual psychologisation of religion in the twentieth-century, the rejection of an 'out-worldly individualism', was part of the disarming of a theological knowledge of the self – that is a 'self' created in relationship to, and dependent on, a non-empirical reality. The psychologised subject of capitalism provided the technology for rethinking the ontology of ourselves through the acts of measurement and analysis, which closed down the liminality of self – a self developed at the limits of knowledge and established in its illusion and disappearance – found in the history of religious ideas and the 'sacrifice of the self', which Foucault identified, in Christian history.[2]

The appropriation of the discourse of 'spirituality' by psychology in the twentieth-century is one instance of the psychologisation of human beings for the services of capitalism and the undermining of religious subjectivity. This is not to presume that psychologists were always aware of what they were doing, but to recognise that the psychologisation of life provided a new currency for thinking about being human. Following the 'naturalisation' of religion in science and philosophy from the Enlightenment, psychology converted the 'out-worldly' individualism of religion into the capitalistic utility of psychological knowledge. The idea of 'spirituality' assumed particular importance in the history of Western capitalism because it allowed American psychology to invade the territory of religion and take over some of its authority. In order to understand how this shift occurred, I want to identify one key figure in the cultural transformation of 'spirituality', one historical vignette of a complex historical transformation. However, before we can do this we need to understand how the discourse of spirituality mutates through history and briefly mark out the relationship between psychology, religion and capitalism.

Spirituality: the politics of a shifting signifier

The signifier 'spirituality' has been reconstructed throughout history according to the socio-political demands placed on religious discourse. Its meaning shifts according to, what Foucault (1989: 98) called, the 'enunciative field' – the discursive networks which make a particular utterance possible. 'Spirituality' is therefore a site of knowledge through which certain discursive regimes – theology, psychology, religion – value acts, events or experiences. Representing the 'spiritual' is therefore a political act, positioning the beliefs and actions of a culture. There is no essence to 'spirituality', but rather a set of competing social demands, which will carry a certain efficacy for a society. Thus, the word 'spiritual' has shifted its meaning under different conditions of knowledge in Western thought.

Following Walter Principe's 1983 article 'Toward Defining Spirituality', it is possible to see a series of historical shifts in the use of the term 'spirituality'. We find a moral register in the letters of St. Paul, where there is a sense of life in the Spirit as opposed to the flesh (Gal.3:3, 5:13, 16-25; I Cor. 3:3:1-3, Rom 7-8). Later, in the medieval church, we find legal and ecclesiastical forms of the idea of the spiritual, related to ecclesiastical jurisdiction and property. A distinction was made between types of persons and property by designating them either spiritual or temporal, a distinction between 'lords spiritual' and 'lords temporal', or between the property of the church and the king. From the seventeenth-century, in Madame du Guyon's writings in France, 'spiritualité' came to refer to an 'interior knowledge', to an inner devotional state. Despite the development of the term by Madame du Guyon, during the eighteenth and nineteenth centuries there was relatively infrequent use of the term 'spiritualité', but in the twentieth-century the term began to emerge more strongly in a popular psychological usage. This psychological framing of spirituality referred to various states of being, ranging from 'universal connectedness' and 'inner meaning' to general ideas of 'well-being' and 'wholeness'. In this complex set of discursive shifts, it is important to identify how 'spiri-tuality' became a psychological discourse in the twentieth-century and what political values sustained such a move. This discursive shift did not happen by chance, but through an ideological necessity of a culture driven by psychological ideologies of meaning.

In the ideological shifts of the twentieth century, religion had to find a discourse which blended with, but did not threaten, the values of the religious tradition.[3] Psychology was, therefore, an ambiguous friend to religion. The religious institutions, particularly in their pastoral forma-tions, did not recognise that such an alliance had wider political ramifications for the construction of a 'religious subject'. The psychol-ogisation of 'spirituality' was one of the central tactics of modern regimes of knowledge to break the ideology of the self found in pre-capitalistic societies. In the twentieth century, the trajectory of the psychologisation of religious discourse can be traced through the work of William James, Gordon Allport and Abraham Maslow in the USA. Even though they would not necessarily sanction the political ideolo-gies that supported their work, they were nonetheless, due to their popularity, key players in the shift of 'spirituality' towards a private, individual construction.

Abraham Maslow

I want to demonstrate the psychological shift in the representation of 'spirituality' in the ideological space of individualism, by focusing on the work of Abraham Maslow (1908-1970) – often regarded as the most significant psychologist in the mid-twentieth century. I want to concentrate on his work, not because he initiated the move towards the psychologisation of spirituality (he was clearly part of a wider histori-cal process), but because his work in the USA reflects a very poignant ideological transformation of spirituality inside American capitalism. Indeed, I would want to go further and suggest that Maslow's psychol-ogy was caught in a post-war market demand for a 'spirituality' that was compatible with capitalistic ideology. However, I would also like to suggest that Maslow started to recognise the dangers of his own psychologisation of religion later in his career.

I will begin this paper by giving a brief context to the history of psychological accounts of the 'spiritual' and then show how Maslow categorised the 'religious' as 'psychological' in a discursive-political battle for authority over experience. What I am suggesting is that psychology, and Maslow's psychology in particular, is an ideological reconfiguration of religious introspection, which prepares the ground for reading 'spirituality' as a product of consumption. What this means is that Maslow is taking the open-ended reflections of 'self-in-relation' to sacred mystery (God, Being, non-empirical reality) as self-referential statements of fixed, measurable, essences. This re-orders the introspection of religion as private, separate and distinct modes of operation, which can be identified, measured and sold as attitudes or moods (products), rather than seeing religious introspection as a dynamic of a paradoxical self in relation to mystery (that which is not fully known or understood). Such re-ordering extrapolates concepts from religious traditions, without the history, context and processes of formation, and (falsely) assumes that they describe the same experience. This shift would eventually provide the platform for the so-called 'New Age' market of spirituality and the post-Thatcherite management use of 'spirituality' for marketing and personal/commercial growth. By focusing on Maslow we can unravel some of the intricate relationship between psychology, capitalism and spirituality.

Hidden relations: capitalism, psychology and religion

In his 1987 work *Religious Thought and Modern Psychologies*, Don Browning attempts to examine the ethical dimensions of modern psychology through an analysis of the metaphors embedded in the conceptual system of psychologies. He believes traditional religion and modern psychology have a special relationship because 'both of them provide concepts and technologies for the ordering of the interior life' (Browning, 1987:2). He goes on to state that psychologies are 'instances of religio-ethical thinking', 'mixed disciplines' containing religious, ethical and scientific discourses (1987: 8). While recognising the value of the dialogue between theology and psychology, Browning believes it is necessary to develop a critical perspective. While Browning identifies the correlation between the 'values of individualism' and capitalism in psychology, he seriously underestimates the critical project required to interrogate such a relationship.

Interestingly, Browning's work appears at the beginnings of the emergence of 'critical psychology' and he cannot therefore appreciate the technicalities of later writings in critical psychology, not least on the question of religion.[4] He does, nonetheless, acknowledge that critical psychology sees the models of previous psychologies as 'unreflective, naïve, and philosophically and ethically immature if not downright dangerous' (1987: 244). Nonetheless, his conclusion that critical psychology and descriptive and normative value-free psychology need to work together only waters down the ethical commitment, allowing psychologies to flourish even in their abuses. He is, however, rightly sensitive to the fact that writers in the arena of critical psychology 'seem to find no place for the role of religion' (1987: 245). Such a concern emphasises the importance of undertaking a closer examination of the relationship between religion, capitalism and psychology in terms of 'spirituality'. Maslow's so-called 'third-force', or humanistic psychology, of the 1950s and 1960s serves this purpose. It not only seeks a kind of translation of religious discourse into psychological discourse, but is also firmly grounded in the context of American capitalism, having impacts on business and other organisational structures. It is possible to suggest that Maslow provides a new 'currency' for reading spirituality in the psychological market place, a kind of 'motivational' model for market forces and a hierarchy for capitalistic need. If critical psychology is to be effective in its analysis it can no longer hide the religious dimensions of Western culture. Religion is cultural ideology and psychology borrows and mutates such ideologies for its own purposes, even in its very rejection of such discourses.

Maslow's psychology

According to Ruth Cox, Maslow 'captured the spirit of his age' and his psychology was 'woven into the very fabric of American life' (Cox, 1987:264). While Cox offered this as a positive afterword to the third edition of Maslow's 1954 *Motivation and Psychology*, the very fusion of Maslow's psychology with American life is also its critical downfall. Maslow's psychology, for instance, is not born in the Two-Thirds world or even in the land of his parents in Eastern Europe. Maslow's psychology is reflective of the optimistic post-war American political and economic climate and cannot be separated from such a context. It captures a period of economic optimism, increased production and individual consumer power. Maslow rejects the angst of European culture in Freud and the mechanistic models of Watson as negative evaluations of the human being and sets about a political reconfiguration of 'motivation' as human potential. This focus on 'motivation' is, therefore, not simply a reflection of the biological foundations of his work and a development of Kurt Goldstein's organismic theory, which recognised a drive towards wholeness in brain injured soldiers from World War 1, it is a social statement of capitalistic desire hidden in the fabric of the so-called 'science' of his psychology. Maslow's theory of motivation shifts, in a post-war consumer society, from biology to social manifesto, particularly in its mirroring of the models of economic production. While Maslow's work clearly reflected positive re-evaluations of the human person in humanism and existentialism, his ideas of 'deficiency' and 'growth' motivation and the distinction between 'becoming' and 'being' also played into wider social trends of market 'efficiency'. The subsequent establishment of a hierarchy of needs, which has 'self-actualisation' as its highest achievement, was not simply a naturalistic understanding of human experience, but rather an adoption of the values of individualism and the American dream. The capitalistic substructure of Maslow's psychology reflects the ideological weight of knowledge behind the self in Western culture, but what is more significant for our concerns is how such notions of 'self-actualisation', 'peak-experience' and 'B-cognition' have all played a key part in the creation of late capitalistic spiritualities – that is a 'spirituality' coterminous with consumerism.[5] Maslow is not alone in his contribution to the commodification of spirituality, but his concepts and re-framing of religious tradition and experience into the instrumental operations of psychological knowledge captures the wider representational shift of 'spirituality' into the psychological machine of capitalism.

Remodelling religious experience

According to Maslow's biographer Edward Hoffman, after the 1954 publication of *Motivation and Personality* – the work which established Maslow's hierarchy of needs – Maslow started to gather material on so-called ecstatic and mystical experience, reading works from Eastern traditions, Krishnamurti, Watts, and Jung, or, as Maslow phrased it, 'the immense literatures of mysticism, religion, art, creativeness, love, etc' (Hoffman, 1962: 69). Such reading was also accompanied by personal interviews with 80 people, fifty 'unsolicited letters' and written responses by 190 college students to a set of instructions – a reflection of the distorted sample analysis involved in Maslow's work.[6] Hoffman believed no one had gathered more material on this area of religious experience since William James.[7] He listed 'transcendent' experience under the heading of '(Inner) timelessness' and identified

20 features in his 1956 paper 'Cognition of Being in the Peak-Experiences', later appearing as chapter 6 in his 1962 *Toward a Psychology of Being*.

Maslow's overall aim was to extract from religious history aspects of experience for a different historical ideology and reposition them in the discursive structures of psychology. Rejecting the move by nineteenth-century atheism to eradicate everything of religion, he states in his short work *Religions, Values and Peak-Experiences* in 1964: 'One could say that the nineteenth-century atheist had burnt down the house instead of remodelling it' (1964: 18). The specificity of Maslow's 'remodelling' of religious experience is a careful adaptation of religious ideas for the purposes of a psychological ideology. He was trying to reconfigure experience once held under the categories of religious discourse into a (pseudo) scientific analysis of the facts. However, the attempt to 'naturalise' religion needs to be questioned from the perspective of the history of ideas. In this sense we need to interrogate the 'religious myths' of psychology, which requires us to see 'religion' not as superstition or oppressive false beliefs but as cultural practices, for cultural practices persist in society irrespective of their truth-claims. Critical psychology requires critical religion to understand the history of ideas.[8]

Before taking a closer look at his excursion into religious language in his *Religions, Values and Peak-Experiences*, it is interesting to note *how* he framed his written instructions for data gathering in his earlier exploration of peak experiences. The instruction stated:

I would like you to think of the most *wonderful* experience or experiences of your life; *happiest* moments, *ecstatic* moments, moments of *rapture*, perhaps from being in love, or from listening to music or suddenly 'being-hit' by a book or a painting, or from some great creative moment. First list these. And then try to tell me how you feel in such *acute* moments, how you feel differently from the way you feel at other times, how you are at the moment a *different* person in some ways (emphasis added, Maslow, 1962: 67).

From this instruction we can easily see how experience is remodelled in terms of private, intense experience. Maslow has already re-written his concepts in terms of the psychological self. The experience is wonderful, happy, ecstatic, rapturous, acute and leaves you different.

The extraordinary element of this analysis is that, in reaction to Freud and behaviourism, Maslow has turned and fetishised the positive dimensions of experience – 'high level of maturation, health and self-fulfilment' as opposed to Freud's 'deficiency' model of neurosis, anxiety, pathology – but in the very process he has eliminated the fabric of religious experience. To highlight the 'feel good' dimensions of experience reflects an economic possibility that the conditions of expression and experience carry the value of the positive experience. It also reduces religion to its euphoric dimensions, rather than the character formation of many religious traditions, which develop from the integration of, and meditation on, suffering. The agonies of Job, the emptiness of the desert, the dark night of the soul and a theology of crucifixion, to recall the Judaic-Christian tradition, have all been eliminated. Maslow fails to see how experiences co-exist with more painful and testing events. The most rapturous experience may also be the most painful and frightening, as in some near-death experiences or the witnessing of a dying relative. Maslow's remodelling is therefore distorting an experience for the purposes of a particular politic of optimism and euphoria – the hopeful dynamics of consumption, without responsibility for suffering.

It is also significant that Maslow notes that no one responding to his survey reported his full 'syndrome'. This is problematic not only because of the issues of correspondence to his 'impressionistic, ideal, "composite photograph"', but because experience has been re-written in terms of 'syndrome' (Maslow, 1962: 67). The remodelling of religious experience in terms of 'syndrome' is an example of Rose's (1996) 'psychologisation' of experience, the reading of all human experiences in terms of psychological discourse. The extent to which 'syndrome' can be grafted into religious discourse shows the powerful dimensions of Maslow's reconfiguration of the spiritual. As Frager notes, Maslow saw the revolution he and others led in psychology as 'solidly established' in 1968. 'Furthermore', as Maslow argues, 'it is beginning to be *used*, especially in education, industry, religion, organisation and management therapy and self-improvement' (Frager, 1987). Here we see the application of psychological knowledge becoming parasitic on existing discourses and 'remodelling' them to the concerns of a different knowledge sustainable for a new society, a society determined by instrumental rationality, efficiency regimes and market forces. Maslow's work is one striking example of how humanistic psychology remodelled religion for a materialistic politic, blending psychology with American capitalistic values in a distinctive and accessible manner. To appreciate this in more detail we must look more closely at his commentary on religious experience from 1964.

Remodelling the transcendent

The key strategy of Maslow's appropriation of religious language for psychology can be seen in his reconfiguring of the signifier and signified in religion and spirituality. This is a process of retaining the religious signifier but removing the signified of religious language, so that it operates according to psychological regimes of knowledge. It is the creation of an epistemological rupture. The authority of the religious institution (through its own willingness to engage the power of psychological language) is undermined by coupling religious ideas with scientific and 'naturalistic' contexts. The move towards a new representation of spirituality in Maslow's work was initiated by his concern that those who wished to establish a legal ban on prayers in schools were some how seen as not interested in 'spiritual values'. Maslow, in the attempt to claim institutional power over the religious organisations, sought to take 'spiritual values' away from the church by rejecting what he saw as 'the erroneous definition and concept of spiritual values' (1976: 3). Maslow thus starts a battle to take over religious discourse from organised Religion (with a capital R to distinguish it from it practices) for the victory of psychology – that is to take over the power of religious institutional discourse and bring a new authority to the psychological institutions and practices. He rejects, in propagandist terms, the domination by organised Religion of '*the* path' to a life of righteousness, justice and the good. As he states, in a revealing footnote:

> As a matter of fact, this identity is so profoundly built into the English language that it is almost impossible to speak of the 'spiritual life' (a distasteful phrase to a scientist, and especially to a psychologist) without using the vocabulary of traditional religion. There just isn't any other satisfactory language yet (Maslow, 1976: 4).

One interesting feature of Maslow's particular take-over of religious language for psychology was that it gave the impression it was in the service of the church, but paradoxically it undermined the authority of the church from the inside. Once the churches started to use psychological registers, within and alongside its own (institutional) discourse, it gave away its authority to speak the 'truth' about human experience and became a host for the parasite of psychological discourse. Maslow's battle, of course, was part of a wider war going on between the church and the ideology of science. While modern physics challenged Christian cosmology, psychology undermined Christian anthropology and ontology. Unlike William James – whose work *The Will to Believe* Maslow regarded as 'the last despairing rationalisation of a previous believer in God' – Maslow eradicated the mystery of experience and read it back into human potentiality (Maslow, 1976: 38-39). As he remarked:

> I want to demonstrate that spiritual values have a naturalistic meaning, that they are not the exclusive possession of organised churches, that they do not need supernatural concepts to validate them (1976: 4).

A less critical reading of Maslow might suggest his work was an important post-war effort to rescue 'spiritual values' for a society rejecting them as out-dated, something the so-called 'New Age' movement claims as its own moral authority. Such movements, however, are hiding an ideology of psychologised 'truth' and an allegiance to the market values of capitalism (even in the outward rejection of such values). Many new patterns of religion which adopt psychology are supporting the consumer mentality that Maslow initiates in his work, a consumer mentality that positions the spiritual inside the psychological for redistribution.

'Motivational' factors are re-written in terms of commerce and competition and there is a subtle elision of ideas, especially when an increase in human potential is indistinguishable from an increase in capital. It is always the utilisation of motivation and potential towards capital not any other social task. I will return to this later, but what we see in Maslow is an efficient relocation of religion according to a set of discursive moves in the process of psychologisation. We can organise these moves of psychologisation into four areas: the rejection of tradition and religious institutions, the extrapolation of ideas from religion useful for psychological individualism, the territorial claim to the 'transcendent' – one of the most powerful conceptual terms of Western metaphysics – and, finally, the repositioning of religious experience inside psychological discourse – the final disempowering of religious authority and the opening of capitalistic determinism. It is worth looking at these moves of psychologisation in more detail.

Tradition, science and religion

Maslow's first move in the psychologisation of religion, and subsequently 'spirituality', is to reject tradition and the religious institutions that preserve these traditions. However, when Maslow says society can 'no longer rely on tradition', 'cultural habit' and the 'unanimity of belief', he is unaware of how traditions operate and how he performs the very dichotomisation of science and religion he tries to overcome. In this sense, Maslow's arguments are constructed on a manipulation of knowledge for advancing the ideology and authority of psychology. Maslow's argument is that the split between science and religion misguides science and religion. In line with Nietzsche and James before him, Maslow rejected institutional religion as dogmatic sheep-following, it was 'arbitrary and authoritarian' (1976: 14).

Once Maslow has marked out the territory, he then carries out his second move of psychologisation by isolating the aspects of religion most amenable to psychological adaptation, what he identifies as the 'core' aspect in terms of 'naturalised' states of the psychological condition. According to Maslow, the 'core' of religion – significantly – is read as private and individual, which enables Maslow to isolate the institutional authority and the traditions of communities to an atomistic unit of the psychological self (1976: 27-28). Such a model, to some extent, echoes William James's analysis of individual religious experience in his *The Varieties of Religious Experience* (1902), but where James respects the limits of his project Maslow is unrelenting in his task.[9] Maslow is emphatic about the 'essential' and 'intrinsic' aspects of religious experience. He argues that the 'nucleus of every known high religion ... has been the private, lonely, personal illumination, revelation, or ecstasy of some acutely sensitive prophet or seer', which it 'subsumes' under revelation, the mystical and the ecstatic or transcendent experience – what Maslow coined 'peak-experience' (1976: 19). As Maslow forcefully argued:

> As a consequence, all the paraphernalia of organised religion – buildings and specialised personnel, rituals, dogmas, ceremonials, and the like – are to the 'peaker' secondary, peripheral, and of doubtful value in rela-

tion to the intrinsic and essential religious or transcendent experience (1976: 28).

The erosion of institutional religion and the assertion of the psychological state above community, tradition and social rituals is a central move in the privatisation of religion. As Maslow goes onto acknowledge, 'each "peaker" discovers, develops, and retains his *own religion*' (1976:28). The creation of a private religion is the key market strategy that brings Maslow's psychological evangelism into direct support of American capitalism – the individual agent forming the basic unit of consumption. What is even more interesting is the way he builds his argument openly to appeal to the American political climate of the 1960s Cold War in his attempt to eradicate religious community.

> I may go so far as to say that characteristically (and I mean not only the religious organisations but also parallel organisations like the Communist Party or like revolutionary groups) these organisations can be seen as a kind of punch card or IBM version of an original revelation or mystical experience or peak-experience to make it suitable for group use and for administrative convenience (Maslow, 1976: 22).

The concept of an original revelation or peak experience detached from the cultural environment raises the question of whether one can have such a 'raw unmediated experience', religious or not.[10] (Following Foucault, I see experience as a discursive and embodied process. History and culture create and shape experience. Experience is, therefore, the conscious register of events in time and space, which by definition cannot be extrapolated from their conditions of emergence.) To argue that experience is inwardly driven according to psychological events and not social ones creates the market conditions for a 'supermarket of spiritualities', the 'pick and mix' mentality of private religious ideas and practices. Such a model means that everyone has their own 'private religion' created from their own 'private experience'. However much Maslow might suggest self-actualisation brings about compassion and social concern, his psychologisation is a serious misunderstanding of social values, shared rituals and symbolic practices. My own counter-discourse in this examination of Maslow uses a different ideological rhetoric to bring psychology under critical examination; it seeks to reveal the politics of experience in Western thought. By showing the complexity of religious introspection, the ideology of psychology can be questioned and ways of undermining capitalistic constructions of the self can be established. The history of religious ideas offers a political resource for rethinking psychology. This is not to assert a doctrinal affirmation but to recognise, with Foucault, how 'the self is nothing else than the historical correlation of the technology built in our history' (Foucault, 1980: 181). In this sense, religious history provides ethical resources for opposing psychology and capitalism.

In order to remove the power from religious authority Maslow has to undermine the value of such traditions. This he does by making a third move in the psychologisation war, the territorial claim to the 'transcendent'. This psychological reductive move occurs when he states that so-called 'supernatural revelation' can be seen as 'perfectly natural, human peak-experiences' (Maslow, 1976: 20). The reality of experience is taken outside religious authority and reduced to human experience. Not only have the Gods become human experiences, but, echoing Huxley's perennial philosophy, he makes the imperialistic move in stating that 'all religions are the same in their essence and always have been the same' (Maslow, 1976: 20). Maslow has now universalised psychological knowledge and taken the imperialistic Western move in assuming that all human experience and all senses of the self are the same, irrespective of culture and history. If such a move was not sufficient, Maslow then sets up a division between 'non-theistic religious people' and 'conventionally religious people' and makes the claim that the former have *more* religious experiences' than the latter (1976: 30). This is an extraordinary move that uses the quantity of religious experiences as a register of value. The logic is deeply flawed, not only in assuming religiousness is a separate and distinct process from everyday life, but also that there is something called 'religion' which can be identified as such and can be separated from culture.[11] It would, in effect, be like the church claiming that you could have more psychological experiences in non-psychological people, which is an absurd statement.

Maslow continues this line of argument by claiming that the individual who struggles to create 'a system of faith' has a more 'serious' relationship to values, ethics and life-philosophy, but that 'system' – and note the irony of this word, in so far as a 'system' implies a worked out tradition of theological/religious reflection – could be anything from personal fascism to hedonism. The individualism of creating a 'faith' can only support a system which promotes the self-creating faiths as valuable to its efficiency, notably a regime that promotes a diversity of products for strengthening the market. Maslow, therefore, uses frequency and depth as ways of rejecting organised religion and then makes the claim that '"orthodox religion" de-sacralises much of life' (1976: 33). Maslow is now in all out attack on institutional religion. He argues that religion separates the 'transcendent and the secular-profane'. He then appeals to Eastern traditions to show that the religious and the secular, the sacred and the profane, are not separate, but Maslow's entire argument is built on the assumption that religions are claiming something different to naturalise psychological events. The contradictions abound, to reveal the polemical nature of Maslow's 'scientific' project.

Maslow's work becomes even more confused when – the exciting – peak experience is contrasted with habitual religious practices, the latter dulled through 'familiarisation and repetition' (176: 34). He argues that the transcendent or religious experience occurs more regularly outside traditional religion because of the repetition in institutional rituals. The splits and dichotomisation he criticises is here brought into full view. He even makes the claim, in a footnote which undermines his entire position, that 'it is easier to be "pure"' outside an organisation, whether religious, political, economic, or for that matter, scientific. And yet 'we cannot do without organisations' (1976: 34). His recognition that we cannot do without 'organisations' undermines this attempt to extrapolate a 'raw' experience from the fabric of institutions. The constant reference to the 'transcendent' is also a reflection of the way Maslow is dependent on religious tradition in the very act of rejecting it. His entire argument is a psychological polemic for privatising the religious for an American market, not least for a generation of college students disillusioned with the past.

The fourth and final move towards psychologisation comes when he repositions the religious experience in the psychological space. He sets up a distinction between the 'naturalistic' and 'supernatural', without giving any sense of what these terms mean in practice, and argues that all the dimensions of religion are reflections of the capacity of human beings. He wants, for example, to find a scientific view of the 'transcendent', but the language is under great strain at this point (Maslow, 1976:44). Even Maslow thinks the 'semantic confusion' is difficult to work out. He believes, appealing to Paul Tillich's theology of Being, that 'all the concepts which have been traditionally "religious" are redefined and then used in a very different way' (Maslow, 1976; 45). Tillich, of course, did provide a different ontology for theology and was sympathetic to psychoanalysis, but the move to the singular psychological referent did not occur in his work.[12]

Maslow's move is to claim religion for psychology and, in turn, to move authority and power to such discourses (1976: 46). He seeks an ultimate separation of religion from the church by arguing 'that spiritual, ethical, and moral values need have nothing to do with any church' (1976: 57). Maslow's argument is overstated, as historically the spiritual, ethical and moral values emerge from religious/cultural traditions, even in their Enlightenment formation. The binary construction of the secular and sacred is therefore a false separation, as religious ideas feed the so-called 'secular' institutions. Maslow's move is, nonetheless, a tactical disassociation, as can be seen in the shifts from 'spiritual values' to 'higher values', from 'peak-experience' to 'transcendent experiences' (1976: 42). There is constant moving back and forth to displace the language of religion and replace it with a monolithic language of psychology.

Psychology, politics and economics

The political nature of Maslow's project becomes even more apparent when he attempts to pacify the role of the churches. He states:

> Even the social act of belonging to a church must be a private act, with no great social or political consequence, once religious pluralism has been accepted, once any religion is seen as a local structure, in local terms, of species-wide, core-religious transcendent experience (1976: 55).

While Maslow was clearly part of a wider social trend in the privatisation of religion, his particular psycho-politics contributed to the pacification of American religion as a challenge to state politics by selectively picking out religious themes for individual experience. Religion was brought into the private sphere, enforced by the discourse of spirituality, and was in consequence reduced to individual choice (private spirituality) as opposed to carrying forward the powerful strands of social justice found in many religious traditions – the revolutionary social perspective of religion.

Maslow never identified the ideological position behind his psychology, but Hoffman's biographical work does provide some insights into the political location of Maslow's thinking. His personal engagements with the business world also provide some immediate evidence of the commercial applicability of his psychology. We can, of course, never rely on these assessments alone, but they do contribute to the wider picture of Maslow's psychology and the positioning of his work. This is not to say Maslow was not concerned with justice and social values, but he fails to realise the political weight of his psychological model.

The most revealing correspondence of Maslow's developing psychology with capitalism can be seen from the fact that in the summer of 1962 he become a visiting fellow at the Non-Linear Systems, Inc. plant in Del Mar, California, invited by its President, Andrew Kay. Impressed by their working models he formulated a response to the structures of the industry. Deborah Stephens, who reissued his work on business management, with the support of the Maslow family, has more recently promoted this alignment between Maslow and business. The original 1965 work, *Eupsychian Management*, was republished under the new title *Maslow on Management* (1998), which included many extracts and interviews from leading captains of the business world. This republication of Maslow's work was also supported by a collection of pieces by Maslow called *The Maslow Business Reader* (2000). In the preface to *The Reader*, Stephens points out that Maslow is even more important to practices of American business today. Referring to Douglas McGregor's *The Professional Manager* and Maslow's own studies, Stephens states 'both men developed theories that are now imperative to the success of business in a global economy' (in Maslow, 2000: vii). The words are telling and support the general contribution Maslow's work makes towards enhancing the substructure of business, particularly in places like Silicon Valley. Maslow's work offered a model for 'motivating' the work force – so they could flourish in their skills – but what is never considered is how this creative flourishing in the work place is always linked to profit margins and capitalistic investment. Building models of human flourishing on the efficiency of production neglects how human flourishing requires social justice and the end of human poverty. Maslow's model is human flourishing for the privileged of capitalism.

Maslow believed that his work on management was a way of reaching the wider public, beyond the restricted institutional base of education and psychology. His management model was based on the idea of a 'eupsychian' culture, that is a culture generated by self-actualising people, which moved towards 'psychological health'. The assumption was that this would create 'synergy', a 'resolution of the dichotomy between selfishness and unselfishness, or between selfishness and altruism' (Maslow, 1998:22). But this 'synergy' disguised visions of global capitalism behind a rhetoric of 'health' and 'human potential'. As Maslow indicated: 'Enlightenment economics must assume as a prerequisite synergetic institutions set up in such a way that what benefits one *benefits all*. What is good for General Motors is then good for the US, what is good for the US is then *good for the world*, what is good for me is then good for everyone else, etc' (emphasis added, Maslow, 1982: 23). Such a claim reveals the imperialism of American capitalism behind Maslow's psychology.

Plateau and peak experience: rescuing the tradition

Maslow eventually saw how his and other such humanistic psychologies were being abused in the prevailing culture. This can be seen in his later critique of the Esalen Institute and his disillusionment with how his own work was being developed.[13] After critiquing the values of religious traditions Maslow is forced to acknowledge that:

> There needs to be a better balance at the Esalen between the Dionysian and the Apollonian. There needs to be more dignity, politeness, courtesy, reserve, privacy, responsibility, and loyalty. There should be much less talk about 'instant intimacy' and 'instant love' and much more about the necessity for Apollonian controls of such a space and style (1996: 130).

He goes on to ask whether the Esalen institute could 'make for a better society' (1996: 131). This revealing question continued to concern Maslow in his later life, as seen in his 1970 presentation at the Transpersonal Psychology conference, held at Council Grove in Iowa, which led to the revised 1970 preface of his *Religions, Values and Peak Experiences*.[14] As Hoffman shows in his biography, Maslow conceded he was 'originally naïve' about 'the dangers of an overzealous interest in mysticism and the purely experiential aspects of religion' (Hoffman, 1999: 310). He was concerned about the 'over-extreme, dangerous, and one-sided' use of his work and believed he had been 'too imbalanced toward the individualistic and too hard on groups, organisations, and communities' (Maslow, 1976: vii & xiii). In response to this situation Maslow revised his 'peak-experience' concept with the idea of 'plateau experiences', which were 'less intense' and required 'long hard work', as found in the formation of many religious traditions (1976: xv-xvi). Maslow is here recognising the dangerous results of extrapolating the 'experience' from the 'tradition' which creates the experience, recognising perhaps that the marketing and psychologisation of the 'spiritual' could only corrupt the object. In the new 1970 preface, he was critical of the American counterculture misuse of 'spiritual disciplines', believing the drug culture and consciousness expanding groups had misconstrued the insights of religious traditions. As Hoffman recalls Maslow, there was an attempt to correct this misunderstanding:

> The great lesson from the true mystics ... [is that] the sacred is *in* the ordinary, that it is to be found in one's daily life, in one's neighbour, friends, and family, in one's backyard, and that travel may be a *flight* from confronting the sacred ... To be looking elsewhere for miracles is a sure sign of ignorance that *everything* is miraculous (Hoffman, 1999: 312).

Maslow may have realised the problems with his psychology too late, for the very marketing of intense, short-lived experiences was a joy for the capitalistic world. Spirituality had become a psychological product and in a world of late-capitalism, following the deregulation of the markets by Reagan and Thatcher, the late 1980s and 1990s saw the spirituality market burgeon even more than before.[15] Maslow's efforts to reposition his psychology also faced calamity when he saw how his work inspired the privileged culture of capitalism. In an attempt to save his psychological creation from its own potential injustice, Maslow had argued: 'Unfortunately, physical and economic wealth do not inevitably get used for higher need gratification. Higher needs can be gratified under poverty, it's harder, but possible if we remember what we're dealing with – respect, love, self-actualisation, *not* autos, money, bathtubs.'[16]

What Maslow had failed to realise is that his hierarchy of needs was a hierarchy of capitalistic values and the idea of 'self-actualisation', however much it appealed to 'synergy', was locked into a fundamental individualism and motivation of capital. Maslow could not see how his psychology was formed and shaped by capitalism, because he could not problematise the ideology of psychology and its re-framing of religious experience.

Conclusion: religion of the self

In Paul Vitz's timely little volume in 1977, *Psychology as Religion: The Cult of Self-Worship*, we see the central problems of Maslow's psychologisation of religious experience. Maslow and humanistic psychology were putting forward a new kind of religion of the self – an 'in-worldly individualism' of utility and measurement. As Vitz argued: 'Psychology has become a religion, in particular, a form of secular humanism based on worship of the self' (Vitz, 1994: 7). However, what Vitz's, somewhat limited, study did not appreciate was how this 'religion of self' was fundamentally tied to a capitalistic sub-structure within psychology, or at least he did not theorise the full implications of his position. This new religion of the self was the psychologised religion of capitalism and its appropriation of the discourse of 'spirituality' was it central hallmark. The attempt now to integrate 'spirituality' into health treatment and education is a complex re-formulation of religious truth, which desperately masks the social and economic vacuum of capitalistic ideology. In an attempt to meet the needs of uncertainty, mystery and liminality in human life, the product of 'spirituality' – with its undifferentiated meaning – silences the non-psychological worlds of the human imagination in order to continue the perpetuation of a regime of knowledge which seeks nothing else but accumulation of wealth. As long as 'spirituality' remains a 'psychological' construction, divorced from its theological and religious history, it will continue to suffocate the traditions that make such a discourse possible – the cultural implications of which are still unclear. Psychology is not a liberation from an oppressive religious paradigm; it is the creation of a different ideological structure with its own oppressions. Under the regime of psychology, 'spirituality' has become the new opium for a capitalistic ideology tortured by its own angst and consumer vacuum. Paradoxically, only in critically re-evaluating and re-imagining religious tradition, with its sacrifice of self and its politics of community, can the ideology of a capitalistic self, found in psychological spirituality, be overcome. As Foucault stated, 'may be the target nowadays is not to discover what we are, but to refuse what we are' (1982: 216).

Notes

1. See Foucault [1979] 'Pastoral Power and Political Reason' in *Religion and Culture by Michel Foucault*, Selected and edited Jeremy Carrette, Manchester University Press/Routledge, London, 1999, pp135-152.

2. Foucault [1980] 'The Hermeneutics of the Self', in *Religion and Culture* p180. For a wider discussion of Foucault's relationship to Christianity, and the underlying use of Foucault in this essay, see Carrette, J. R., *Foucault and Religion: Spiritual Corporality and Political Spirituality*, Routledge, London 2000.

3. See, for example, Graham Richards, 'Psychology and the Churches in Britain 1919-1939: Symptoms of Conversion' in *History of the Human Sciences*, Vol. 13, No.2, 2000, pp57-84.

4. See, for example, Jeremy Carrette, 'Post-Structuralism and the Psychology of Religion', in *Religion and Psychology: Mapping the Terrain*, Diane Jonte-Pace & William Parsons (eds), Routledge, London 2001, pp110-126.

5. See Carrette, J. & King, R. *Capitalistic Spirituality* (Routledge, London, forthcoming).

6. See Maslow, *Toward a Psychology of Being*, p67.

7. See Hoffman, *The Right to be Human*, p206.

8. I would like to thank Paul Stenner for raising this issue. I would also like to thank Paul Stenner and my other (anonymous) reviewer for their comments, particularly in requesting clarification of concepts, ideas and assumptions lost in the translation between the disciplinary regimes of psychology, politics and religion.

9. James develops the ideas of the 'More' and 'over-beliefs' to preserve a mystery and refuse a closure on the religious subject. See William James, *The Varieties of Religious Experience*, Centenary Edition, Routledge, London 2002, pp394ff.

10. See Steven Katz, 'Language, Epistemology and Mysticism', in *Mysticism and Philosophical Analysis*, Ed. Steven Katz, Oxford University Press, Oxford 1978, pp22-74.

11. The idea of 'religion' and its relation to culture has been critically examined in recent years. See Richard King, *Orientalism and Religion*, Routledge, London 1999; and Timothy Fitzgerald, *The Ideology of Religious Studies*, Oxford University Press, Oxford 2000. William James recognised the problem with the idea of religion in 1902, see James *Varieties*, p26.

12. See Paul Tillich, *The Courage To Be*, Collins, Glasgow [1952] 1980.

13. See Hoffman, *The Right to Be Human*, p309; Abraham Maslow, *Future Visions: The Unpublished Papers of Abraham Maslow*, Edited Edward Hoffman, Sage, London 1996, pp129-131.

14. See Hoffman, *The Right to Be Human*, p310.

15. See Wade Clark Roof, *Spiritual Marketplace: Baby Boomers and the Remaking of American Religion*, Princeton University Press, Princeton, New Jersey 1999.

16. See Maslow in Lowry, R.J., *The Journals of A.H. Maslow* (Vols. 1 & 2) 1979, Monterey, CA: Brooks/Cole, pp373-374, quoted in Ruth Cox, 'Afterword', in Maslow, *Motivation and Personality*, p262.

Bibliography

Browning, D. (1987) *Religious Thought and Modern Psychologies*. Philadelphia: Fortress Press.

Carrette, J. R. (2000) *Foucault and Religion: Spiritual Corporality and Political Spiritual*. London: Routledge.

Carrette, J. R. (2001) 'Post-Structuralism and the Psychology of Religion'. In D. Jonte & W.Parsons (Eds), *Religion and Psychology: Mapping the Terrain*. London: Routledge, 110-126.

Cox, R. (1987) 'Afterword: The Rich Harvest of Abraham Maslow'. In A. Maslow (Ed), *Motivation and Personality*, Third Edition. New York: Harper Collins, 245-271.

Danziger, K. (1990) *Constructing the Subject*. Cambridge: Cambridge University Press.

Dreyfus, H.L. & Rabinow, P. (1982) *Michel Foucault: Beyond Structuralism and Hermeneutics*. London: Harvester Wheatsheaf.

Dumont, L. (1986) *Essays in Individualism*. Chicago: University of Chicago.

Foucault, M. [1969] (1989) *The Archaeology of Knowledge*. London: Routledge.

Foucault, M. [1979] (1999) 'Pastoral Power and Political Reason'. In J. Carrette (Ed), *Religion and Culture by Michel Foucault*. London: Manchester University Press/Routledge.

Foucault, M. [1980] (1999) 'About the Beginning of the Hermeneutics of the Self'. In J. Carrette (Ed), *Religion and Culture by Michel Foucault*. London: Manchester University Press/Routledge, 158-181.

Foucault, M. (1982) 'Afterword: The Subject and Power'. In H.L. Dreyfus & P. Rabinow, *Michel Foucault: Beyond Structuralism and Hermeneutics*. London: Harvester Wheatsheaf, 208-226.

Fitzgerald, T. (2000) *The Ideology of Religious Studies*. Oxford: Oxford University Press.

Frager, R. (1987) 'Foreword: The Influence of Abraham Maslow'. In A. Maslow (Ed) *Motivation and Personality*, Third Edition. New York: Harper Collins, xxxiii-xli.

Hoffman, E. [1988] (1999) *The Right to be Human: A Biography of Abraham Maslow*. New York: McGraw-Hill.

James, W. [1902] (2002) *The Varieties of Religious Experience*, Centenary Edition. London: Routledge.

James, W. [1896] (1903) *The Will to Believe*. New York: Longmans Green and Co.

Katz, S. (1978) 'Language, Epistemology and Mysticism'. In S. Katz (Ed), *Mysticism and Philosophical Analysis*. Oxford: Oxford University Press.

King, R. (1999) *Orientalism and Religion*. London: Routledge.

Maslow, A. H. [1954] (1987) *Motivation and Personality*, Third Edition. New York: Harper Collins.

Maslow, A. H. (1962) *Toward a Psychology of Being*. Princeton, New Jersey: D.Van Nostrand Company, Inc.

Maslow, A. H. [1964] (1976) *Religions, Values and Peak Experiences*. New York: Penguin Books.

Maslow, A. H. (1996) *Future Visions: The Unpublished Papers of Abraham Maslow.* Edward Hoffman (Ed). London: Sage.

Maslow, A. H. (1998) *Maslow on Management,* with Deborah Stephen and Gary Heil. New York: John Wiley & Sons. [Previously published as: Eupsychian Management: A Journal, Homewood (1965). Illinois: Richard D. Irwin Inc. & The Dorsey Press.]

Maslow, A. H. (2000) *The Maslow Business Reader.* Deborah C. Stephens (Ed). New York: John Wiley & Sons.

Principe, W. (1983) 'Towards Defining Spirituality'. *Sciences Religieuses/Studies in Religion* 1983 (12) 127-141.

Richards, G. (2000) 'Psychology and the Churches in Britain 1919-1939: Symptoms of Conversion'. *History of the Human Sciences* 13 (2) 2000: 57-84.

Roof, W. C. (1999) *Spiritual Marketplace: Baby Boomers and the Remaking of American Religion.* Princeton, New Jersey: Princeton University Press.

Rose, N. (1996) 'Power and Subjectivity; Critical History and Psychology'. In C. Graumann & K. Gergen, *Historical Dimensions of Psychological Discourse.* Cambridge: Cambridge University Press, 113-114.

Tillich, P. [1952] (1980) *The Courage To Be.* Glasgow: Collins.

Vitz, P. [1977] (1994) *Psychology as Religion: The Cult of Self-Worship,* (Revised Edition). Grand Rapids, Michigan: Eerdmans.

In the name of the Father
Dostoevsky and the spirit of critical psychology

Paul H. D. Stenner

Abstract

Through a discussion of Dostoevsky in relation to Darwin, Nietzsche and Freud, the argument is raised that metaphysical questions of spirituality were central to the emergence of modern psychology. Metaphysical concerns relating to the materialist translation of Christian doctrine and imagery were fundamental to Darwin's interests, for instance, although they remained in his private notebooks. In this context, thinkers such as Dostoevsky and Nietzsche began 'unmasking' the hidden side of this developing positive knowledge of human nature. This unmasking was considered part of the emergence of a new and integrated 'true' psychology, and it took place during the very decades when modern experimental psychology was forming itself from a flux of possibilities. Freud's development of psychoanalysis, itself heavily influenced by Nietzsche and Dostoevsky, as well as Darwin, must also be viewed in this context. A focus on the topic of spirituality thus necessitates a re-telling of the history of psychology, in which the re-working of spiritual semantics is central to the birth of the discipline. A consideration of Dostoevsky's work hence becomes especially salient for critical psychologists articulating a discourse on spirituality.

Section I: Orientation and socio-historical context[1]

I i *Orientation*

Yes indeed! Look more carefully! After all, we don't even know where this life is at the moment, or what it is, what it's called. Leave us alone, without books, and we'd instantly trip up, get lost – we don't know where to place our allegiance, what to hang on to; what to love and what to hate, what to respect and what to despise. We even find it difficult to be human beings – human beings with our *own* real flesh and blood; we're ashamed of it, we consider it a disgrace and strive to be some kind of imaginary general type. We are stillborn, and for a long time we have not been begotten of living fathers and this pleases us more and more. We are acquiring the taste. Before long we'll think up a way of being somehow begotten by an idea. But enough; I don't want to write any more 'from the underground'.

> Dostoevsky, *Notes from the Underground*, 1864: final paragraph

The primary medium within which identities are created and have their currency is not just linguistic, but textual: persons are largely ascribed identities according to the manner of their embedding within a discourse – in their own or in the discourse of others.

> Shotter and Gergen, *Texts of Identity*, 1989: sleeve notes

It is instructive to juxtapose the above two quotations, one from the great nineteenth-century Russian novelist, and the other from a key text of late twentieth-century critical psychology. Dostoevsky can here be read as critically prophesying what Shotter and Gergen discuss positively under the rubric of the textualisation of identity. Dostoevsky points to the role of books in supplying identity texts for moral and spiritual guidance, as satirised so effectively by Cervantes some 350 years previously in *Don Quixote*. Without these mediating texts, he suggests, we would instantly trip up and get lost. He points to the centrality of affect in the mediating process. At stake is the ordering role these texts play in the organisation of our emotional identifications: what to love and respect and what to hate and despise. He points to the negative relationship to human embodiment that is engendered by this process of textualisation. We are, he says, ashamed of our own real flesh and blood. And he suggests that in place of such concrete embodiment we strive towards an imaginary, general and ideal existence – a form of life determined through-and-through by ideas, narratives, texts. As a result of this fleeing from the concrete towards the abstract, he predicts, we will eventually think up a way of being begotten by an idea, thus completing our disconnection from the world of the living. This prophecy of de-realisation, it appears, comes true in the diagnosis of Shotter and Gergen. We are, they declare, textual beings in so far as our very identities are constructed in the talk of self and others.

For Shotter, Gergen and other contemporary critical psychologists, the case for the discursive nature of identity is positive because, in part at least, it represents a critique of essentialist tendencies on the part of mainstream scientific psychology: better to accept a fragmented and multiple identity than to be defined by the practitioners of psychometrics. Dostoevsky's negative assessment of what we might for convenience call the *textualisation thesis* stems, paradoxically, from a not dissimilar critique of the positivistic and scientistic tendencies that the writer saw as acquiring a position of increasing dominance both in the West and in his own native Russia (Frank, 1986). Dostoevsky's critique of these tendencies, unlike those critical psychologists have so far offered, as based on a complex and ambivalent position regarding what can broadly be described as *spiritual* questions. Given that questions of spirituality are now being addressed by critical psychologists themselves, this critique becomes newly relevant. It becomes relevant not simply as subject matter for the topic of spirituality, but also because it points the way to a retelling of the very history of psychology: a retelling in which questions of spirituality come to assume a central place.

There are at least three concrete reasons as to why a consideration of Dostoevsky's work is salient for critical psychologists articulating a discourse on spirituality. First, the medium of Dostoevsky's critique is that of the novel, but Dostoevsky uses this medium to directly explore and present *psychological* issues. In particular, the interpersonal dynamics of shame, pride, suspicion, arrogance, humility and humiliation are a constant preoccupation in Dostoevsky's novels and short stories. Given the textual turn that has occurred, not just in critical psychology, but in the social sciences in general, the problem of narrative forms of psychological work both within and outwith literature becomes newly interesting and worthy of study. Although I will not deal with the narrative turn in psychology (Sarbin, 1986), I will, in a later section of the paper, address Dostoevsky's novelistic style in relation to his broadly psychological and spiritual problematic.

Second, in discussing novelistic style I will also show that Dostoevsky has greatly and directly influenced critical thinkers such as Bakhtin and Girard who have in turn become important figures in the theoretical background of contemporary critical psychology. Given that both Bakhtin (1997) and Girard (1997) acknowledge that many of their key concepts derive from a close reading of Dostoevsky (such as Bakhtin's contrast between monologic, dialogic and polyphonic discourse (see footnote 6)), a more direct examination of this source on the part of critical psychologists is warranted.

The third reason is that Dostoevsky was writing during a time when modern psychology was in the process of formation. Not only were writers such as Dostoevsky being acclaimed as 'psychologists', but so also were philosophers such as Nietzsche, and this at the historical juncture when Wundt set up the first experimental psychology laboratory. It is only retrospectively that we can assert that Wundt, unlike Dostoevsky or Nietzsche, was the founder of psychology 'proper'. During a time when the proper nature of psychology is itself under dispute by critical psychologists, a new importance accrues to the task of assessing psychology with this broader picture in place. In this paper I will make a partial contribution to this task by sketching some thematic continuities in the work of Nietzsche and Dostoevsky which, as I will suggest, set the scene for Freud in the wake of Darwin. This will enable me to tell the story that questions of spirituality have in fact been central to psychology since its modern inception, and this is a fact of relevance to any critical discourse on spirituality today.

I ii *The big picture: modern semantics, literature and science*
Dostoevsky articulated an account of spirituality that hinges on the tension between an acceptance of concrete, embodied and contextualised human existence as opposed to abstract and idealised forms of existence. His work can thus also be related to that of present-day political and moral philosophers who advocate a communitarian position as opposed to neo-Kantian individualism.[2] I mention this debate, which will not concern us here, only to rapidly contextualise it as a recent set of answers to the wider questions concerning spirituality and the good life provoked by the process of modernisation. It is therefore necessary to briefly reconstruct this large socio-historical theme in order to provide a big picture within which the critical psychological debate on spirituality can be seen as a continuation of themes central to the likes of Darwin, Nietzsche, Dostoevsky and Freud. Further, this will enable me to clarify some of the general issues that are at stake in any attempt to take the relationship between literature and psychology seriously.

Although there are obvious risks in any attempt to write a 'big picture' story of something as contestable as 'modernisation', courage can be taken from the fact that there is a surprisingly wide consensus amongst sociologists and social theorists today on a key theme. Namely, that certain broadly discernible structural changes in the organisation of western societies were associated, around the middle of the eighteenth century, with: 1) the development of a profound discourse of self-contained individualism; and 2) the retreat of the role and influence of organised religion. In discussing present-day religious forms, for example, Tomas Luckmann (1996) stresses that the 'private sphere' of individual consciousness was increasingly 'liberated' from social structural constraints under modernity. Like Niklas Luhmann (1995), Luckmann argues that this privatisation and individualisation (supported by novel legal provisions) is associated with a shift in the organisation of such societies from a primarily stratified form of differentiation to one based predominantly on function. In functionally differentiated societies each individual sector or sub-system (the economy, politics, education, science etc) operates with its own logic in a state of relative independence, especially from the influence of religion, which is thus relegated to an increasingly, though not exclusively, private sphere.

Otherwise widely divergent accounts converge on this theme. For the Weberians emphasis is placed on the *disenchantment* of the social world as a function of a spreading rationalism, itself made possible by the individualisation of Christianity inaugurated by Luther (Weber, 1930). For the Durkheimians, the shift to functional differentiation is grasped as a transition from mechanical to organic solidarity, the latter of which entails the erosion of previous forms of organised religion and their replacement with a new sacred cult of 'egoistic individualism' in which an image of 'man in general' comes to replace the deity of tradition (Durkheim, 1952). For the Marxists, focussing on the functions of the increasingly autonomous economic system of Capital, the abstract and general nature of this 'man in general' is targeted for historical materialist critique as bourgeois individualism and attacked as yet another ruse of ideology no different in kind to Christianity or any other 'opiate of the masses' (Marx, 1971). For the Eliasians the process of individualisation is traced to the complexification of interdependency chains that occurs during the formation of early modern states and that increases structural demands for the development of reflexive, 'civilised' (self-governing) behaviour (Elias, 1978). For the Foucauldians contemporary individualism is unmasked as the latest and most insidious form that power in its microphysical form has taken, a form often traced to modern mutations in discursive formations associated with the birth of the prison, the hospital, the asylum (Foucault, 1977). For currently dominant synthesisers of this social science tradition, such as Ulrich Beck, Scott Lash and Anthony Giddens, these social developments are associated with a (albeit non-linear) detraditionalisation which increasingly holds the individual responsible for his or her own social action and life-trajectory, leaving questions of spirituality and religion to the private sphere (Beck, Lash & Giddens, 1994).

However much one might wish to contest the details of such unidirectional developmental stories, there can be no doubt that questions of spirituality are both provoked and frustrated in this broad unfolding socio-historical context. To adopt Luhmann's terminology, the semantics of the old European tradition, adapted as they were to a hierarchically stratified social structure, falter, fail and rapidly mutate as social sub-systems such as the economy, education, the law, science, politics and art individuate and acquire relative autonomy (operative closure) in the context of increasingly functionally differentiated modern societies. As 'the individual' is effectively uprooted from a relatively fixed place in a clear social hierarchy, so the narratives – for centuries Christian in substance – that justified and perpetuated that arrangement in the old European context become inadequate and open to question. In this context new semantics are articulated, and old ones revamped, which are more adequate to the task of social communication under new and developing social-systemic conditions.

In talking of 'semantics'[3] the intention is not to propound idealism. As Foucault (e.g. 1977) is keen to point out with regard to his concept of discourse, the changes under consideration in this section were also highly material. They were economic, technological, legal and architectural as well as 'ideological'. The nineteenth century, for instance, witnessed the very material demolition and reconstruction of big cities such as London and Paris.[4] To give one potent example, the construction of the Boulevard Saint-Germain in Paris entailed the demolition of at least forty churches of equivalent scale to Notre Dame (Serres, 1995). 'Semantics' haunt real architecture, and the newly developing semantic forms were accompanied by the widespread construction of appropriate buildings: the great nineteenth century Museums, educational institutions, and scientific establishments, for example.

During this period new semantic categories emerged from numerous sources. New semantics of human rights, for instance, were emerging from political and legal sectors. Such semantics were materially situated in the very constitutions of emerging Nation States – France and the USA in particular – in the second half of the eighteenth century. Here, however, interest falls onto two distinct sources of semantics: science and literature.

Modern science, especially as it comes to differentiate itself into specialisms dealing with human and social objects throughout the nineteenth century, comes to play a new and important role as a supplier of new authorised semantic categories and techniques for making sense of and acting on human existence and its place in the natural and social worlds. However, not only science, but literature too – which under modernity can already be considered as part of a self-referential art sector (Luhmann, 2000) – must also be considered a key player in the task of supplying those texts which mediate the human sense of what it is and what it ought to be. Dostoevsky's vivid descriptions of existential crisis and of loss of vision, value and perspective, should therefore be seen not just as specific and local responses to the more general trends sketched above, but also as a weaving of new semantic categories – new texts of identity – which become widely and rapidly disseminated with the help of printing and distribution technologies[5] and this to a mass audience more and more disposed to having an interest and appetite.

Of course Dostoevsky's novels are works of art and not science, just as *The Origin of the Species*, for all its rhetorical merits, is a work of science and not art. Dostoevsky was not interested in providing scientific explanations for the personalities of his characters, and nor was he particularly well placed so to do. Nevertheless, both the semantics emerging from literature and those from science share an overriding concern with the problem of 'the individual' and in this sense are equally dealing with questions of *psychology*. Indeed this combination of a *clear functional separation* between art and science (which follows from the fact of the existence of two functionally distinct social sectors) with a nevertheless *shared concern with the predicament of the individual* is what lends critical vitality to the theme. Dostoevsky, for instance, was well aware of the claims emerging from the natural sciences of the

West, and, as will be further argued, much of the critical force of his work is owed to a profoundly felt need to show up the limitations of these for an understanding of human nature. He would have agreed with John Dewey's observation that the replacement of religious beliefs and institutions with institutions based on the conception of human destiny as strictly historical and secular is the 'conclusion of natural science' (Vivas, 1961). At the same time, he was concerned about the plausibility of the old religious narratives, which, to his mind, he subjected to an intensity of critique the like of which they had never previously suffered (particularly in the *Grand Inquisitor* passage of the *Brothers Karamazov*). In this sense, Dostoevsky's mature novelistic psychology represents a re-forging of Christian semantics in the quasi-empirical format of carefully observed and strategically staged prose-craft.

Section II: Darwin, Dostoevsky, Nietzsche, Freud

II i *Orientation*

Dostoevsky was writing during a time when modern psychology was in the process of formation. To give a flavour of this, it is instructive to imagine the year 1879 – less than a decade after the first Vatican council announced the new dogma of papal infallibility. In that year, as Dostoevsky was writing his greatest work, *The Brothers Karamazov*, Wilhelm Wundt was busy setting up the first experimental psychology laboratory in Leipzig. Meanwhile Nietzsche was retiring from his university post at Basle, writing the three parts of *Human, all too human,* and about to proclaim himself the *first genuine psychologist*. Nietzsche, it is interesting to observe, acclaimed Dostoevsky 'the only psychologist from whom he had anything to learn' (Wellek, 1962). Meanwhile, in Vienna, the young Freud was absorbing, both directly and indirectly (Ellenberger, 1994), the heady brew of Nietzschian and Dostoevskian psychology that, as will be further discussed, would influence psycho-analysis. During this birth phase, then, the form that psychology should take was, to put it colloquially, 'up for grabs'. Claims to speak the truth of psychology were ringing out from literature, philosophy, biology, medicine, theology, psychophysics and doubtless other locations as well.

That Dostoevsky was a *psychological* novelist, and perhaps the first of this category[6] is common knowledge (Encarta Encyclopaedia). As discussed by Wellek (1962), this 'dissector of sick souls' was referred to by De Vogue (1886) as the 'Shakespeare of the lunatic asylum'. Vissarion Belinsky – the critic who had acclaimed his first novel, *Poor People* (1846) – severely criticised his second novel, *The Double* on the grounds that it was too psychological: 'The business of doctors and not poets'. Dmitry Merezhkovsky (1902) went as far as to compare him to Goethe and Leonardo for his combination of science and art: 'What is called Dostoevsky's psychology is ... a huge laboratory of the most delicate and exact apparatus and contrivances for measuring, testing and weighing humanity. It is easy to imagine that to the uninitiated such a laboratory must seem something of a devil's smithy' (cited in Wellek, 1962:3).

Despite the explicitly psychological content of his writings, however, Dostoevsky was distinctly critical of the incipient specialist scientific psychology of his day.[7] Towards the end of his life he commented explicitly on his status as a psychologist as follows: 'They call me a psychologist; this is not true. I am merely a realist in the higher sense, that is, I portray all the depths of the human soul' (cited in Wellek, 1962:3).

The use of the word *soul* here is, of course, not accidental, and points to the spiritual basis upon which Dostoevsky departs from the science of his time. The use of the word *realist* is equally deliberate, and points to the *empirical* basis upon which he departs from the received religion of his time.

It was not only the emergence of Dostoevskian psychology that was characterised by a deep concern, positively or negatively inflected, with spiritual questions. So too was the philosophical work of Nietzsche and the psychoanalytical work of Freud and, as we shall see, the earlier influential work of Darwin.[8] In short, a reconstruction of the fluxional moment of psychology's birth shows that the reworking of spiritual semantics was central to its emergence. Consider the following quotation from *Demons* spoken by Shatov, but reflecting the author's own enduring concerns:

> There has never yet been a nation without a religion, that is, without an idea of evil and good. Every nation has its own idea of evil and good, and its own evil and good. When many nations start having common ideas of evil and good, then the nations die out and the very distinction between evil and good begins to fade and disappear. Reason has never

been able to define evil and good, or even to separate evil from good, if only approximately; on the contrary, it has always confused them, shamefully and pitifully; and science has offered the solution of the fist. Half-science has been especially distinguished for that – the most terrible scourge of mankind, worse than a plague, hunger, or war, unknown 'til our century. Half-science is a despot such as has never been seen before. A despot with its own priests and slaves, a despot before whom everything has bowed down with a love and superstition unthinkable till now, before whom even science itself trembles and whom it shamefully caters to.

(Demons: 251)

II ii *The priests and slaves of half-science*

Dostoevsky has Shatov present 'half science' in the most negative possible terms as a despot, new to the nineteenth century, which has usurped the place of religion. The phrase 'half science' draws attention to the partially scientific nature of the newly emerging scientific specialisms dealing with the nature and conduct of individual and collective human beings. It also draws attention to the incompleteness of the attempt to grasp the metaphysical aspects of human existence in terms of a combination of rationalism and naturalism. A tentative definition of half science would hence be: a half scientific knowledge that tells only half the human story. His rhetoric encourages us to think of this despot in terms of extreme superstition and strong human emotions such as love, fear, humility and shame. He thus leads us to think of its scientificity as a masquerade, albeit one that even science proper is powerless to expose. In inviting us to think questions of good and evil next to questions of positive knowledge he draws attention to the troubled spirituality at the core of modern psychology.

It is of course necessary in this context to address the figure of Friedrich Nietzsche. In Ellenberger's (1994: 274) words, Nietzsche was the 'Prophet of a New Era'. He cites Ludwig Klages' statement that it was Nietzsche who was the true founder of modern psychology. For present purposes it is enough to point out that both Nietzsche and Dostoevsky, in their different ways (the way of philosophy as opposed to art), were struggling against the prevalent intellectual climate emanating from Europe mid-way into the second half of the nineteenth century. That climate can best be summed up by using the terms that negatively define the typical twenty-first century critical psychologist:

positivism, scientism, evolutionism. Hence a common theme in Dostoevsky's novels, as in Nietzsche's works, is a critical attack on Enlightenment philosophy and its newer (predominantly) materialistic and mechanistic variants that include Marxism as well as social Darwinism and utilitarianism.[9]

Both Nietzsche and Dostoevsky, then, were critics of the emerging 'half-science'. Through articulating an alternative version of psychology, they both found themselves put forward as 'true' originators of a 'true' psychology whose truth lies in the fact that it does not split itself off from questions of ethics, metaphysics and aesthetics in the name of positive knowledge. This new existentialist[10] thought thus constituted a break both with the unrealism of a scientific rationality applied to human beings, and with traditional religious forms that acknowledge irrationality but spurn realism. It is therefore not so surprising to find striking communalities in the 'true' psychologies of Dostoevsky and Nietzsche. Here I will limit myself to discussing two such common themes: a concern with *unmasking* and an interest in the limitations of rationality that coheres in the concept of the *unconscious*.

Through *unmasking* half science, the true psychology can be revealed, itself a series of masks. This theme is grounded upon a dim view of human nature as devious, deceptive and power-seeking. 'With all that which a person allows to appear, one may ask: what is it meant to *hide*? What should it divert the eyes from? What prejudice should it conceive? How far goes the subtlety of this dissimulation? How far does he deceive himself in this action?' (Nietzsche, cited in Ellenberger, 1994: 273). Dostoevsky (1991), in the novel which established the existentialist theme of *the underground* (a book which Nietzsche discovered in French translation), in turn defines the human as 'a creature on two legs and ungrateful' and is scathing about the utilitarian notion of 'enlightened self-interest':

> Oh tell me, who was it who first announced, who first proclaimed that man only does vile things when he does not know where his real interests lie? and that if he were enlightened, if his eyes were opened to his real, normal interests, he would at once cease doing vile things and would immediately become good and honourable, because being enlightened and understanding where his real advantage lay, he would indeed see his own personal advantage in goodness, and because it is well known that no one can knowingly act against his own personal advantage, he

would find himself as it were obliged to do good. Oh, you child! You sweet innocent babe! (22).

For both Nietzsche and Dostoevsky, the deception of others is ubiquitous and endemic. However, added to this is the conviction that we are so adept at deception that we rapidly come to deceive even ourselves. This notion of other-deception leading to self-deception gives a pivotal role to the notion of a powerful *unconscious*. Nietzsche took this to the extreme of assuming that consciousness is little more than a fantastic commentary on an unconscious text inaccessible to reason. Likewise, Dostoevsky speaks of the unconscious determinations of action and his notion of the *underground* (a state engendered by manifold forgettings and avoidings) was a direct influence on Freud (Girard, 1997). I will limit myself to two telling quotations from the *Notes*:

> What does reason know? Reason knows only what it has managed to find out (the rest, perhaps, it will never discover; that's no comfort, but why not say it?), whereas human nature acts as a whole, by everything that is in it, consciously and unconsciously; and even if it lies, it still lives.

> In every man's memory there are things which he does not divulge to everyone, but really only to friends. And there are those things which he doesn't even divulge to friends, but really only to himself, and then as secret. And, finally, there are those which a man is afraid to divulge even to himself, and every respectable person has accumulated quite a few of these. One might even say: the more respectable the person, the more of these he has.

Returning to the quotation with which this section began, we can read Dostoevsky here, and elsewhere, as endeavouring to remove the supposedly neutral and objective mask from half science, thereby exposing its hidden despotic, superstitious half: the half that would usurp the place of religion in taking the human psyche as an object of positive knowledge. The territory of the human psyche thus becomes the battleground on which a novelistic critical psychology (a higher realism that 'portrays all the depths of the human soul') challenges the right of half science to occupy the place once held by religion. Nietzsche too unmasks the pretensions of enlightenment thought, exposing the bloody origins of its high moral position and insisting upon its continued reliance on the mundane operations of power. The stakes are laid out. If God is dead, is he to be: 1) quietly replaced by positive knowledge? 2) resurrected in (another) new form? Or 3) replaced by those strong enough to acknowledge their fate as supermen?

II iii *A hymn and a secret*

In the previous sections I have argued for: a) the psychological nature of Dostoevsky's work during the birth period of modern psychology; b) the fact that he was critical of psychology and distanced himself from that label; and c) a structural similarity between the philosophical psychology of Nietzsche and the novelistic psychology of Dostoevsky that is informed by a shared critical relationship to enlightenment philosophy and the 'half science' that emerged from it during the nineteenth century. In the following section I will briefly turn to the part played by Darwin in the story I am telling. In so doing I will give an unorthodox reading of Darwin that turns to some less formal aspects of his work. This detour is necessary because the centrality of Darwin's thought to the development of modern psychology, and especially to the fluxional moment in its history that I am considering, can not be overestimated (Richards, 1996). Along side the hymn of *natural selection*, relating to positive knowledge, was a secret – spoken in hushed tones and addressed implicitly – relating to spirituality. Already with Darwin, in other words, we can see the divided structure of 'half science' and the masked character of the side concerned with spirituality. Doubtless this masking is itself a product of the mode of operation of the scientific system, which must concern itself with the publication of data and of theoretical propositions designed to illuminate that data, rather than with metaphysical speculations (Luhmann, 1990). Nevertheless, a purely logical precondition of the work of unmasking undertaken by Dostoevsky and Nietzsche is, of course, that a form of knowledge exists that keeps half of itself a secret: 'To avoid stating how far I believe in materialism, say only that emotions, instincts, degrees of talent, which are hereditary are so because brain of child resembles parent stock' (Darwin notebooks, Gruber, 1974: 80).

Darwin, like his grandfather and his father before him, 'believed' in materialism. This comment from his notebooks refers to what should and what shouldn't be made public in the publication of his masterwork *The origin of the species*. It is further apparent from his notebooks that Darwin was deeply interested in the spiritual and 'metaphysical' implications of this belief, (although this interest remained in his private notebooks). A consistent theme is the *translation* of Christian metaphysical themes into a strictly materialist vocabulary. In this sense the *Origin* can be thought of as a Rosetta stone that provides the key for the discursive transformation of spirit into matter. Consider the following three extracts from the notebooks (Gruber, 1974):

> The above would make a man a predestinarian of a new kind, because he would tend to be an atheist. Man thus believing, would more earnestly pray 'deliver us from temptation', he would be most humble, he would strive 'to do good' / to improve his organisation / for his children's sake and for the effect of his example on others' (74).

> Origin of man now proved – Metaphysics must flourish – He who understands baboon would do more toward metaphysics than Locke (84).

> The mind of man is no more perfect than instincts of animals to all and changing contingencies, of bodies of either – Our descent, then, is the origin of our evil passions!! The Devil under form of Baboon is our grandfather! (123).

This last proposition from Darwin not only reveals a burning, yet hidden, interest in translating Christian metaphysics, with all its ethical and spiritual implications, into materialism; it also indicates a profound and personal interest in psychology, and particularly with the state of his own (doubtless material) soul. It is astonishing how preoccupied Darwin was with his own ancestry, not just in the obvious sense of his evolutionary biology, but also in the form of his relationship to his father and his grandfather. The simplest way to illustrate this is by quoting from the notebooks:

> My father says he thinks bodily complexity / and mental dispositions / oftener go with colour, than with form of body. – thus the late Colonel Leighton resembled his father in body, but his mother in bodily and mental disposition. My father has seen innumerable cases of people taking after their parents, when the latter died so long before, that it is extremely improbable that they should have imitated (1).

> My father thinks people of weak minds, below par in intellect, frequently have bad memories for things which happened in early infancy (2).

My F. says there is a perfect gradation between sound people and insane.
– that everybody is insane at some time (13).

My Grand F. thought the feeling of anger, which rises almost involuntarily when a person is tired is akin to insanity. (I know the feeling also of depression, and both of these give strength and comfort to the body) (14).

My father quite believes my Grand F. doctrine is true, that the only cure for madness is forgetfulness (18).

Pride and suspicion are qualities, which my F. says are almost constantly present in people likely to become insane. – now this is well worth considering (20).

People, my father says, do not dream of what they think of most intently … my father's test of sincerity (22).

My father thinks that selfishness, pride and kind of folly alike … is very hereditary (25).

My Father says on authority of Mr. Wynne, that bitches' offspring is affected by previous marriages with impure breed (32).

My handwriting same as Grandfather (83).

Plato / Erasmus / says in Phaedo that our 'imaginary ideas' arise from the pre-existence of the soul, are not derivable from experience – read monkeys for pre-existence (129).

Questions of positive science, of evolutionary theory and the observations which support it, are juxtaposed with deeply existential questions, with questions of madness and sanity, with questions of affects and ethics, of personal identity, and all in the context of an overriding mimetic preoccupation with the figures of father and grandfather. Although not answerable, it is interesting to pose the question of which of these two halves of Darwin's work, the manifest or the hidden, was the dominant motivation. Did the metaphysics and the psychology, so concerned with genealogy, follow from the biological theory, or was the biological theory inspired and provoked by the metaphysics and psychology, with its fascination with self in relation to ancestry? For sure, they appear like rival twins or, to allude to a theme that Dostoevsky would make his own, as *doubles* (Chizhevsky, 1962).

Consider the following highly suggestive extract from Darwin's notebooks, in which he *translates* eternal punishment by way of an unconscious doubling of father and son:

> The possibility of the brain having whole trains of thought, feeling and perception separate from the ordinary state of mind, is probably analogous to the double individuality implied by habit, when one acts unconsciously with respect to more energetic self, and likewise one forgets what one performs habitually – Agrees with insanity, as in Dr. Ash's case, when he struggled as it were with a second and unreasonable man. – If one could remember all one's father's actions, as one does those in second childhood, or when drunk, they would not be more different, and yet they would make one's father and self one person – and thus eternal punishment explained (80).

II iv *Freud the father?*

It is interesting that Darwin associated the identity of father and son with eternal punishment, and that he identified his own descent, from his father, his grandfather, and 'a baboon', as 'the origin of evil passions'. Such associations, of course, now have a distinctively Freudian ring to them, and so it is fitting that Freud's relationship to our problematic be dealt with here. To do so, however, it must first be noted that Freud had his own peculiar relationship to father figures. For example, at seven or eight years of age, Freud urinated in his parents' bedroom and recalls being reprimanded by his father: 'the boy will never amount to anything'. Of this incident, Freud wrote: 'This must have been a terrible affront to my ambition, for allusions to this scene occur again and again in my dreams, and are constantly coupled with enumerations of my accomplishments and successes, as if I wanted to say: "You see, I have amounted to something after all"' (cited in Tomkins, 1963: 513). Freud's boundless ambition to become a great intellectual figure was driven, according to his own account, by a troubled relationship to the father figure.

Was Darwin – undoubtedly a model of intellectual accomplishment – Freud's father too? Was Dostoevsky? Nietzsche? These are not aimless questions, but questions concerning influence and intellectual descent, not to mention the complexities of paternal identification. Concerning father complexes, for instance, consider that Dostoevsky's master-work *The Brothers Karamazov* is a story of patricide: the murder of a father, Fyodor Karamazov. Consider also the ringing words of Fyodor's son, Ivan, spoken at the trial: 'Who of us does not desire his father's death?' Of course the profound similarities of psychological content between Dostoevsky's work and that of Freud have long and often been pointed out, but I wish to draw attention to a far more specific relationship of resemblance: a relationship of admiration and influence that might almost be called paternal. Freud, it must be remembered, referred to this last work of Dostoevsky's as simply the 'most magnificent novel ever written' (Freud, 1962). Further, can admiration be taken further than stating that Dostoevsky's place in world literature is 'not far behind Shakespeare'? Dostoevsky is for Freud another model of a person who has *amounted to something.*

And yet, in the same article from 1928, Freud goes on to submit the novelist to a character assassination whose extreme viciousness is rivalled only by its groundlessness. The ultimate irony is that Freud chose to call the article in question *Dostoevsky and Parricide.* In brief, Freud diagnoses two personality traits – 'boundless egoism' and 'a strong destructive urge' – that together constitute the essential character of a criminal. He then draws up a list of defects including: sado-masochism; a displaced narcissism; a mania for gambling which reflects masturbatory anxiety; an instinctual character which when combined with neurosis leads to loss of ego unity; and a constitutional bisexuality which is inferred from 'his remarkable understanding of situations which are explicable only by repressed homosexuality, as many of his novels show'. In the light of all this, it is considered 'highly probable' that Dostoevsky's 'so-called epilepsy was only a symptom of his neurosis', the latter being, naturally, swiftly linked with coitus and traced ultimately to 'the shattering experience of his eighteenth year – the murder of his father'. Dostoevsky's own account that the fits began after his imprisonment in Siberia are dismissed since 'there is reason to distrust the autobiographical statements of neurotics'.[11] Finally Freud reaches his theme of parricide. In a fascinating textual technique which itself suggests the psychological proximity of this relationship for the author, Freud addresses Dostoevsky directly: 'You wanted to kill your father in order to be your father yourself. Now you *are* your father, but a dead father' – the regular mechanism of hysterical symptoms. And further: 'Now your father is killing *you*'.

Who exactly is killing whom in this bloodbath of words? Should Freud have said instead 'now your son is killing *you*'? Certainly, in this frenzy of violence disguised as neutral medical observation, we are left in no uncertainty that Dostoevsky is not a man to be trusted as a psychologist and that Freud, who understands the novelist's great strengths but also his profound weaknesses, is to be so trusted. It has since been established, incidentally, that Dostoevsky's father was not murdered, but died in 1839 of natural causes.[12]

It seems clear that Freud the son wished to take Dostoevsky's place. What place? As Freud describes it, the place of the 'teacher and liberator of humanity' that Dostoevsky was unable to fully occupy on account of his alleged neurosis. Freud goes further and begins using spiritual terminology. Without this neurosis 'the greatness of his intelligence and the strength of his love for humanity might have opened to him another, an apostolic, way of life'. Instead it was left to Freud to become this *apostle* of liberation.

And what about that other contender for the title of psychologist, Nietzsche? The philosopher is given lighter treatment. In *Beyond the pleasure principle* (Freud, 2000), after insisting that he has carefully avoided philosophy, Freud states: 'Nietzsche, another philosopher whose guesses and intuitions often agree in the most astonishing way with the painfully laborious findings of psychoanalysis, was for a long time avoided by me on that very account; I was less concerned with the question of priority than with keeping my mind unembarrassed'. So, rather than opting for violent confrontation, Freud *avoided* Nietzsche for a long time. *Avoidance* here, of course, has a strongly psychodynamic meaning. It does not mean that Freud did not know Nietzsche's work. On the contrary, the implication is that he has 'for a long time' been aware that Nietzsche's 'guesses' *pre-empted* (is this a question of priority?) his 'painfully laborious' findings. The philosopher, it seems, was merely an embarrassment to Freud, compared to the threat apparently posed by the novelist.

The three brothers Karamazov, as is commonly observed, each represent a significant aspect of the human character: Dimitri, the body with its passions; Alyosha, the spirit; and Ivan, the intellect. If we change plots briefly and consider Darwin as the father, then Nietzsche, Dostoevsky and Freud would be three brothers, and the rivalries would be fraternal rather than paternal (fraternal rivalries have an equally strong mythical heritage). Each brother uses his inheritance to invent his own version of psychology: Dostoevsky, the artist, invents a novelistic psychology; Nietzsche invents a philosophical psychology; and

Freud invents a scientific psychology. Each did so, in their different ways, and also by drawing upon numerous other sources, by unmasking the hidden side of Darwin's great idea. Freud, the youngest brother, but as a scientist the most direct heir, drew upon the work of Dostoevsky and Nietzsche. He added to the Darwinian theme of biological descent a historical and psychological dimension. The condition of we human animals being able to live together in a civilised fashion, he tells us, is that mechanisms are set up which prevent the expression of that animality. As works such as *Civilization and its discontents* (Freud, 2000) and *Totem and taboo* (Freud, 1978) insist, having the ego and superego is the price we pay for civilisation. In short, at the origin of the human collective and of human identity is a *necessary denial of Darwin's 'baboon'*. We must repress our animality if we are to live together in a workable collective, hence the functionality of the necessary delusion that we are, as creatures created in God's likeness, higher than the animals. With Freud's help, we can see why there was a 'pressure' to repress one half of the 'true psychology'. We have a vested interested in not knowing who we are. But more, we are invited to consider Darwin in a new and even more heroic light. He *dared* to speak the truth, even if only one half of it was spoken publicly. He dared to name the un-nameable. He looked into the face of god and dared to report that he made out the features of a baboon. And now, standing on the shoulders of giants, Freud can for the first time look down upon God himself. But what will be of greatest interest to the last sections of our paper, is that this can yet be presented as the *overcoming* of arrogance:

> In the course of centuries the naive self-love of men has had to submit to two major blows at the hands of science. The first was when they learnt that our earth was not at the centre of the universe but only a tiny fragment of a cosmic system of scarcely imaginable vastness ... The second blow fell when biological research destroyed man's supposedly privileged place in creation and proved his descent from the animal kingdom and his ineradicable animal nature. This revaluation has been accomplished in our own days by Darwin, Wallace and their predecessors, though not without the most violent contemporary opposition. But human megalomania will have suffered its third and most wounding blow from the psychological research of the present time which seeks to prove to the ego that it is not even master in its own house, but must

content itself with scanty information of what is going on unconsciously in its mind (Freud, 1975: 326).

Here the spiritual battle is no longer between go(o)d and (d)evil, but between science and human arrogance. We unscientific narcissists believe ourselves better than animals. What once looked like a path to redemption (the overcoming of animality) now shows up as naive self-love. God is the Devil in baboon form, and Good is evil arrogance. The values have truly been re-valued. To borrow and bastardise a psycho-analytical turn of phrase, science is here invested with holy cathexis. Freud the new Apostle now has the liberating knowledge. But, remember, in this discourse it is to this flaw, this narcissism, that we owe our community and our identity. That is why Freud was so pessimistic and jaded about the liberatory prospects of the future, and believed himself to be bringing a plague to North America when he spread the word of psychoanalysis. Thank god we vainly believe ourselves not to be animals.[13]

Section III: Spirituality and novelistic style

III i *Orientation*

I have told a story about how a return to the nineteenth century shows that the reworking of spiritual semantics was central to the emergence of modern psychology. The figure of Dostoevsky's 'half-science' was explicated with reference to Darwin.[14] The psychologies of Dostoevsky and Nietzsche were presented as a critical confrontation with the masked aspects of half science (notably its usurpation of the place of religion) and an articulation of new quasi-spiritual, existential semantics that are psychological in so far as they focus on the theme of the individual. These semantic reformulations in the wake of Darwin (but, of course, not only Darwin) set the scene for Freud who shapes them into the form of the (purportedly) positive science of psychoanalysis. Hence in this fluxional moment in psychology's history, we can distinguish the emergence of a scientific, a novelistic and a philosophical psychology. In the final sections attention will be turned to a brief account of Dostoevsky's spirituality in which Nietzsche will be used as a point of contrast. If Dostoevsky's solution to the crisis in spiritual semantics is a re-working of Christian themes of humility and concern for the other in a new existential context, then this can be contrasted with Nietzsche's solution of blasting through slave morality with a philosophically galvanised super-human individuality.

III ii *The paradox of the parasite in paradise*

Given that this is not the place to provide a detailed exegesis of the form and content of Dostoevsky's writings, I will proceed in a controversial fashion by extracting a simplified theoretical structure from these works. My main influences here are Bakhtin (1997) and Girard (1997), arguably the two Dostoevsky critics who are of greatest interest to critical psychologists. Both acknowledge that many of their key concepts derive from a close reading of Dostoevsky. Girard's concern is mainly with content. He concentrates on questions of desire and its relation to political ideals. The ideals of a utilitarian philosophy grounded in 'enlightened self-interest', for instance, hold that the human predicament can be solved by freeing individuals from religious faith and the shackles of local community belonging. Once freed, they can spontaneously follow a course of action that is simultaneously beneficial for the individual and for society as a whole. Girard's Dostoevsky offers countless refutations of this dream, and illustrates the irrationalities of desire and its rootedness in relations with others. The *underground man*, for instance, demonstrates with his own life how the paradise of enlightened self-interest turns paradoxically into an obsessive interest in others that leads to self-destruction. In this sense, Dostoevsky offers an important reflection on the *limitations* of the modern dream of self-interested individuality.

Bakhtin, on the other hand, concentrates on formal questions of style. He offers the following decisive comment: 'the orientation of one person to another person's discourse and consciousness is, in essence, the basic theme of all Dostoevsky's works' (1997: 207). It is certainly the case that a key feature in all of Dostoevsky's work, from *Poor Folk* to the *Brothers* is an acute awareness on the part of his characters and narrators of the interlocutor or addressee to whom their discourse is directed. As Bakhtin (1997) describes in his chapter on *Discourse in Dostoevsky*, words are thought or spoken always with a *sideways glance* to another person. He calls this an 'epistolary form' since the discourse of letters typically carries exactly this acute awareness of the addressee to whom it is directed, and takes into account the possible reactions and replies of the other. In Dostoevsky's writing, the response of this other person is perpetually anticipated and the discourse bears clear marks of this preoccupation. This other person is very often not physically present, but their imaginary presence transforms the consciousness, and the discourse, of the speaker or thinker. Both Girard and Bakhtin, then, draw attention to the centrality of the role of alter in the consciousness and desires of ego. Girard contends that Dostoevsky reveals the mimetic nature of desire itself, by which he means that desire originates neither with the desiring subject, nor in the desired object, but through a process whereby the desires of a model, a third party, are emulated.[15] In an attempt to combine Girard and Bakhtin's insights, we might say that in Dostoevsky, one person's discourse is always already *parasited*[16] by that of another, which takes up home in it, transforming it in the process. This transformation is seen in the fact that each utterance and each action is demonstrably permeated with the anticipated response of the other.

Girard and Bakhtin illustrate how the problem of the relationship between self and other is Dostoevsky's perpetual concern ('the manner of their embedding within a discourse – in their own or in the discourse of others', as Shotter and Gergen (1989) put it). We might say that it is from the crucible of this relationship, in all its possible permutations, that Dostoevsky draws his work. Anything that is expressed, whether a spoken word or a physical movement, potentially invites an intense *reaction* between self and other. This reaction may be harmonious, but in Dostoevsky it usually involves struggle, shame and humiliation. Whatever the outcome (joyful or shameful), we might say, as a minimal theoretical formulation, that anything expressed can be *transformed* in this crucible. Perhaps it will be parasited and used for other, negative, purposes. Perhaps it will be joined symbiotically with the word of another, creating something new but positive. Awareness of this situation brings into being a distinction between the outside (what is expressed) and the inside (namely, what we hold back from the crucible of the self-other encounter). What is kept inside is not exposed, directly at least, to the possibility of transformation. But of course this holding back of one's word or one's action does not stop the dialogue. It does not prevent the possibility of parasitism. This is the first paradox of the parasite. The dialogue simply takes up residence in the private world of the self. The crucible is internalised. The Other – threatening parasite or loving symbiote – takes up residence within. It goes *underground*.

Self, as Dostoevsky concretely illustrates through his novelistic style, is always mediated and refracted through the consciousness of another. The heroes of his novels struggle with the consciousness of the other that has taken up residence in their own. As put by Bakhtin (1997: 207):

> The hero's attitude toward himself is inseparably bound up with his atti-
> tude toward another, and with the attitude of another toward him. His
> consciousness of self is constantly perceived against the background of
> the other's consciousness of him – 'I for myself' against the background
> of 'I for another'. Thus the hero's words about himself are structured
> under the continuous influence of someone else's words about him.[17]

Paranoid suspicions and delusions of grandeur alike take place within this crucible in which one's very desires are blurred with those of another. When desires are frustrated – when the voice within punishes more than it rewards – another, redoubled attempt to chase out the parasites begins. The hero tries all the harder to break free of the influence of others. At this point the quest for psychological autonomy can begin, and with it the desire to discover one's own, true, authentic, fundamental desires: those not seeded by parasites. To escape the voice of the other the hero must fundamentally *not care* about the other, and must transcend them:

> I smiled contemptuously, and walked along the other side of the room,
> straight opposite the sofa, alongside the wall, back and forth between the
> stove and the table. I wanted, with all my might, to show them that I did
> not need them; meanwhile, I deliberately stamped my feet, coming down
> on my heels. But it was all in vain. *They* didn't pay me any attention. I
> had the patience to walk up and down like that, right in front of them,
> from eight o'clock to eleven o'clock, keeping always to the same spot ...
> 'I'm doing it because I want to, and no one can stop me'.
>
> *(Notes from the Underground*: 77)

As Dostoevsky makes clear in the above extract, the endeavour to escape by not caring is doomed to a paradoxical failure since the hero cares only too much about being seen not to care. The parasites that are chased out once again return with renewed vigour, now so amplified that the host's condition begins to border on self-delusion. In summary, I have outlined a theoretical structure involving two stages of what we might call *parasite chasing*, each of which results in a situation in which the parasite is increasingly *internalised* and *amplified* in significance. First an 'inner / outer' distinction emerges (which constitutes the first stage of internalisation of the chased parasite). Second, attempts are made to evict the internalised parasite through a programme of authentic autonomy seeking (which drives the parasite deeper within and conceals its very existence from the hero, who is thereby self-deceived).

III iii *Pride and suspicion are qualities which my F. says are almost constantly present in people likely to become insane – now this is well worth considering ...*

The above discussion enables a clearer picture of Nietzsche's solution to the nineteenth-century crisis in semantics. This in turn provides a point of contrast for understanding Dostoevsky's alternative position. Nietzsche's solution can be translated as the attempt to use philosophy to drive out the parasitical voices of others – particularly those associated with the slave morality of Christian concern for the neighbour – in a quest for radical autonomy. Christian humility is dismissed in favour of the proud affirmation of superhuman status, as reflected in Nietzsche's use of chapter titles such as 'why I am so wise', 'why I am so clever' and 'why I write such good books'. Given the quotation from Darwin with which this sub-section began, there is some justification for noting that Nietzsche found madness at the mountaintop of his delusory autonomy. His famous suspicion and pride escalated into the delusions of grandeur and persecution that would today be associated with paranoid schizophrenia. Freud too, as we are on the topic, was notoriously proud and suspicious in his private life. He was painfully jealous in his relationship with Martha,[18] and often complained of having been 'betrayed' by his friends and followers (such as Fliess, Adler, Jung and Breuer).[19] His pride, as we have seen, is likewise notorious. Freud said of himself that: 'A man who has been the indisputable favourite of his mother keeps for life the feeling of a conqueror, that confidence of success that often induces real success' (Tomkins, 1963: 511). Of course Freud's solution of turning to natural science in order to re-forge modern semantics provided him with the security of psychological distance (speaking 'in the name' of science) that Nietzsche lacked. These points about pride and suspicion are relevant: first, because the dynamics of pride, suspicion, shame and humiliation are the constant subject matter of Dostoevsky's novels; and second, because it is in relation to these affect dynamics that Dostoevsky's 'spirituality' can be understood.

For Dostoevsky, Nietzsche's position is the flawed solution of the 'Man-God'[20] depicted so starkly in the figures of Raskalnikov (*Crime and Punishment*) and Ivan Karamazov (*The Brothers Karamazov*).[21] Dostoevsky rejected this solution for the same reason that he laughed at the utilitarian dreams of a polity grounded in a rational self-interest predicated upon the notion of individual desire (as depicted by the heroes of *Notes from the Underground* and *The Idiot*). These solutions and positions are explored in the form of characters consumed by their attempt to escape the crucible of self-other relations. Their supposed autonomous desire is thoroughly caught up in the play of mimetic identifications. Following that desire and removing obstacles to its satisfaction can thus by no means represent viable solutions to social or personal problems, let alone a stable basis for rational self-interest. The same applies to Dostoevsky's critique of the radical revolutionary movement in the Russia of his lifetime (*The Demons*). Stavrogin, the spiritual leader of the movement, for all his expressed egalitarian desires, is revealed to be intelligent but shallow and preoccupied with his Man-God escape from the judgement of others. Beneath the surface of the revolutionary ideals and desires – embodied in the character of Pyotr Stepanovich Verkhovensky – lurk psychological instability, murder, madness and suicide.[22] Beware those who profess and desire to be saviours of humanity and yet who are prepared to cheat, lie and kill real flesh and blood people in order to bring about their abstract ideals. *Demons* is prophetic in relation to what later happened under Stalin.

Dostoevsky identified the positions associated with nihilism, utilitarianism and radical socialism with a general European philosophy that is spiritually atheist or agnostic, politically reformist or socialist and morally secular. It was his rejection of this philosophy that positioned him on the Slavophil side of the raging Slavophil versus Westerner controversy in Russia. Raskalnikov, Stavrogin and Ivan Karamazov are deeply influenced by European thought. Raskalnikov, for instance, wants to be a Napoleon – a self-interested, enlightened European individualist. He undertakes his double-murder in the spirit of an experiment to test his independence from the judgement of the unenlightened. Killing or suicide (in the case of Kirillov in *Demons*) or debauchery (in the case of Stavrogin) are tests of the *overman* or 'Man-

God'. If one can resist being dragged down by the judgement of others with regard to murder, these characters believe, one can resist anything. Once free of the parasites, one will discover the truth of morality.

In these ways, the hero, professing to be the liberator of humanity, becomes progressively interiorised and, with that, progressively detached from the everyday life of the ordinary people (who are typically despised as a result). The hero becomes sucked up and trapped into the life of an 'idea': a virtual and disembodied existence. The concrete and local are loathed, and the abstract and general adored. At the extreme of this process, Dostoevsky evokes one of his most powerful themes: the theme of the double. The novel by that name depicts a grey civil servant, Golyadkin, who meets his double during a phase of intense preoccupation with the inner voices of others. Borrowing one of Darwin's phrases quoted earlier: 'he struggled as it were with a second and unreasonable man'. Once these voices have been driven out to the point of self-delusion (to the point, that is, where one deceives oneself that one is free of them), then they return, in Dostoevsky's hands, in the form of powerful and tormenting hallucinations. Ivan Karamazov and Nikolai Stavrogin, likewise, meet their double in the form of the Devil. The second paradox of the parasite comes with the recognition on the part of the chaser that the chased parasite is no one but them.

Again abstracting from Dostoevsky's work, we might say that the double emerges at an extreme point of the denial of the concrete interpersonal world and the corresponding loss of existential foundation. The world of the idea splits from that of concrete existence and the double emerges from that split. The Devil, for Dostoevsky, is not associated with the red heat and flesh of concrete existence, horns and all. Rather the devil emerges when concreteness has been forsaken. The Devil emerges as a double from the split between concrete and abstract. The hero tries so hard to forsake the concrete that it comes back, in intensified and perverted form, as a double. Perhaps that is why depictions of the Devil show him red and embodied. He is a paradoxical perversion: that which the hero knows himself to be but refuses to acknowledge. We might say that the worship of the real Devil (refuge in the abstract) invokes the forsaken concrete that is mistaken as the Devil due to its horror to the hero. Frankenstein's monster is the forsaken concrete of a man obsessed with the 'idea' of life. Mr Hyde emerges as the forsaken sexual and violent concrete of a Jekyll too proud and ashamed to lose his social status.

III iv *My father quite believes my Grand F. doctrine is true, that the only cure for madness is forgetfulness*

Juxtaposed next to the Westerner heroes appear, in Dostoevsky's novels, a collection of Slavophil heroes. Alyosha Karamazov and Father Zosima, in *The Brothers Karamazov*; Sonja and the police inspector in *Crime and Punishment*; Tikhon in *The Demons*, and so on. These are humble characters who do very little but who are in close contact with the lives and feelings of others around them. About them there is comparatively little to say. They understand. They show compassion. They recognise themselves to be ridiculous, holy fools. This is well expressed in the final paragraph of a short story from 1877, *The dream of a ridiculous man*:

> I'll go further: suppose it never, ever comes true, and there is no paradise (now *that* I do understand!), well, I'll still go on preaching. And yet how simple a matter it is: in one day, *in one hour* it could all be brought about at once! The chief thing is to love others as one self, that's the main thing, and that's it – absolutely nothing more is necessary: you would immediately discover how to bring it about. And yet it's just the old truth after all – an old truth a billion times repeated and preached, though it fell on stony ground, didn't it? 'The cognition of life is superior to life, the knowledge of the laws of happiness – superior to happiness!' – that's what has to be fought against! And I shall. If only everyone desired it, it could all be brought about at once.

These holy fools are hated by the Westerner heroes who are nevertheless drawn to them, and love them. They both withdraw from and are drawn to the one thing that leads to the most emotionally intense passages in Dostoevsky's writings: *confession*. They are drawn to come down, for one moment, from the lofty heights of Man-God abstraction and to speak simply and truthfully about those things best kept hidden. They are drawn, eyes wet with tears, to cross that fraught threshold – policed by the most powerful emotions – where a Man-God becomes a God-Man.

Conclusion

I hope to have shown that the articulation of a critical psychological discourse on spirituality involves more than the opening up of a new and relatively unexplored subject matter for contemporary study. Attention to the broad theme of spirituality also provokes and necessitates a re-visioning of the history of psychology. Focussing on Dostoevsky in relation to Darwin, Nietzsche and Freud, I have contributed to this task by showing the extent to which the emergence of modern psychology was about the reworking of spiritual semantics. This has in turn required a broadening of the definition of psychology to include, at the very least, a novelistic, a philosophical and a medico-scientific variant (usually serious historical attention is focussed only onto the experimental scientific variant). I have presented each variant as a re-fashioning of spiritual discourse in an historical context where the old European Christian religious narratives were rapidly losing plausibility amongst a modernised intellectual elite. For Nietzsche the transcendence of these old narratives in the figure of the *overman* is at the heart of psychology. For Freud, spirituality is to be subsumed by positive knowledge. For Dostoevsky, Christian virtues of honesty and neighbourly love are recast in novelistic form as a solution to problems of arrogance, transcendence and abstraction associated with modern individualism. A reconsideration of these excluded forms of psychology is necessary if we are to avoid their return as distorted doubles.

Notes

1. I would like to thank Monica Greco, Lisa Blackman, Neil Washbourne and Corinne Burns for their comments on the ideas presented here.
2. Influential authors such as MacIntyre (1985), Taylor (1989) and Sandel (1982) proposed community based solutions to problems they identified with the rights-based individualism of, for example, Rawls (1971). The argument was that a rights-based emphasis on justice pits the individual against society, and overlooks the role of the latter in constituting the individual in the first place. These debates mirror those in moral psychology between Gilligan and Kohlberg (see Gilligan, 1982).
3. My use of the term *semantics* is motivated by the over-use of the concept of *discourse* in critical psychology to the point of evacuating the word of any meaning. Whilst the latter is drawn largely from a French post-structural tradition, the former derives from a German tradition that demonstrates a radical shift in the meaning of basic semantic terms used to describe society and time that occurred during the late eighteenth century (Koselleck, 1978; Krauth, 1984). Luhmann developed this tradition in a

direction that to a large extent parallels Foucault's (e.g. 1969) use of discourse. The key difference is that Luhmann attempts to read the influence of social structure into the historical semantics of discourse (Luhmann, 1998).

4. It is crucial that Dostoevsky's prime geographical reference points were not Paris or London but Moscow and St Petersburg. Nineteenth-century Russia was barely industrialised and, in spite of reforms such as the emancipation of the serfs in 1861, the social system remained predominantly differentiated by hierarchically organised strata. Nevertheless, Russian intellectuals were deeply influenced by European thought and practice, and this engendered an historically important Russian debate known as the Slavophil/Westerner controversy. Dostoevsky's evolving philosophy of *pochvennichesvo* (concerning the Russian soil) could be characterised as an attempt to reconcile these two warring (especially in the 1860s) positions (Jones, 1991: viii). It is important to acknowledge in this context the anti-semitic aspects of Dostoevsky's work. See section 1, chapter 2 of the March 1877 edition of the *Writer's Diary* (Dostoevsky, 2000) for example. Without doubt, the problematic of nationalism, a key theme in the nineteenth century and a corollary to the theme of individualisation, is of central importance to an understanding of Dostoevsky's work, although I will not discuss it further here (see Frank, 1986).

5. Much of Dostoevsky's work was published in a series of journals founded by Dostoevsky himself. For instance, with the help of his brother Mikhayl he founded *Vremya* (Time) in 1861, in part to publish *House of the Dead*. This was followed in 1864 by the review publication *The Epoch*, in which the first part of *Notes from the Underground* was published.

6. The best source here is Bakhtin (1997), who credits Dostoevsky with the invention of the polyphonic novel. In contrast with monologic, in which the authorial voice rises above that of the characters, in a polyphonic novel the world is viewed from the perspective of each of the characters, thus enabling a more developed portrayal of psychological preoccupations.

7. This *critical psychological* aspect emerges at various junctures, such as the section 'Malicious Psychologists', which appears in chapter 1 of the December 1877 edition of the *Writer's Diary* (op cit), the various discussions of psychology in *Crime and Punishment*, and 'Psychology let loose', which appears as section 9 of book 12 in *The Brothers Karamazov*.

8. Although not the theme of the current paper, it is also well documented that several of the immediate precursors to the 'new' American psychology that emerged at the end of the nineteenth century were employed in US universities with a clearly religious agenda and had strong spiritual based beliefs in the potential of psychology as a discipline (see Richards, 1996, on Porter and McCosh). William James himself famously gave up psychology for philosophy, the better to settle his own raging spiritual preoccupations. The emergence of German experimental psychology was also permeated with spiritual concerns. The heated debate between the Würzburgers and the Wundtians was in large part structured by the 'conflict of the confes-

sions' (*Konfessionenstreit*) endemic to the modern German cultural landscape (Kusch, 1999). The former were either Catholic (as with Buhler, Marbe and Messer) or Protestants with strong Catholic leanings (as with Külpe). Wundt, Protestant in spirit, objected to the Catholicism of the Würzburgers.

9. The counterpart of these scientific influences in literature was the naturalistic realism that had been typified in the work of Balzac and developed in Europe by the likes of Flaubert and Zola. Dostoevsky's first novel, *Poor Folk* was celebrated by the influential critic Belinsky precisely because the latter saw in it an exemplary form of naturalism that expressed the favoured intellectual and ideological sentiments (inspired by the European revolutionaries). As Dostoevsky's spiritual views developed (and a key event here was his period of Siberian exile) he broke with the revolutionary groups of his youth and likewise with realism in the sense described above. His criticism of 'half science' reflects this break with realism indicated in the previously quoted self-designation as a realist only in the 'higher sense'. But it should also be noted that this break with realism, and Belinsky in particular, was also provoked by the extreme development of the psychological dimension in Dostoevsky's writing – the very development for which Belinsky criticised *The Double*. Dostoevsky is very clear about this link: 'I am merely a realist in the higher sense, *that is, I portray all the depths of the human soul*' (emphasis mine).

10. Kierkergaard must also be mentioned here. As put by Vivas (1962): 'With Kierkergaard... [Dostoevsky] was one of a small number of men who helped us to forge weapons with which to fend off the onrush of a naturalism bent on stripping us of our essentially human, our metaphysical, reality'.

11. And this despite Dostoevsky's own lucid discussion of the psychosomatic origins of Smerdyakov's epilepsy in *The Brothers Karamazov*.

12. It had been widely rumoured that Dostoevsky's father was murdered in 1839 by a group of serfs while Fyodor was away at the Petersburg Academy of Military Engineering. Good recent archive research, however, looked to the reports of the local authorities and found that two doctors had certified the cause of death as a bout of apoplexy from which Dr Dostoevsky had long suffered. Apparently the rumour of murder was spread by a neighbour in the hope of purchasing their property on the cheap (Frank, 1990).

13. As Sophocles puts it in *Oedipus Rex*: 'How dreadful knowledge of the truth can be when there's no help in truth!'

14. I am not claiming that Dostoevsky was referring directly to Darwin. Darwin's influence on Dostoevsky was indirect (see Wellek, 1962, Girard, 1997).

15. A simple example would be the rivalry between two small children, wherein both come to desire a toy (object) because the other appears to desire it. Another humorous example is provided by Cervantes' *Don Quixote* who copies the desires of the chivalrous knights of the middle ages that he reads about.

16. I am using parasite here in the very literal sense discussed by Serres (1982): para and site – on the side. Eating next to and feeding on, we might say.
17. The connections here to Sartre, himself heavily influenced by Dostoevsky, are evident, although Sartre's solution is somewhat different.
18. Tomkins (1963: 524) discusses Freud's mental state. Regarding jealousy, Freud demanded that his wife Martha abandon her family as a token of her love for him, and wrote of one rival: 'When the memory of your letter to Fritz … comes back to me I lose all control of myself, and had I the power to destroy the whole world, ourselves included … – I would do so without hesitation'.
19. For instance, Freud wrote to Abraham: 'I have always sought for friends who would not first exploit and then betray me' (Tomkins, 1963: 525).
20. Given my historical concerns, I will continue to use Dostoevsky's sexist formulation, even though it correctly invites consideration of the masculinist bias of his work.
21. Needless to say, followers of Nietzsche condemn Dostoevsky for this view. Georg Brandes (1889), for instance, proposed that Dostoevsky preaches: 'the morality of the pariah, the morality of the slave' (Cited in Wellek, 1962).
22. Needless to say, Marxist critics condemn Dostoevsky for this view. Maxim Gorky (1905) condemned him as 'Russia's evil genius' and he was effectively forbidden during Stalin's reign. There has also been a tendency for Marxist critics to divide Dostoevsky in two. For instance, Lukacs (1943) celebrates his 'instinctive sympathies' whilst condemning his 'overt ideology'. Bakhtin's (1998) emphasis on polyphonic form as opposed to content can also be seen as a means of effectively obscuring Dostoevsky's evident spiritual intent (for more on which, see Vivas, 1962).

References

Bakhtin, M. (1997) *Problems of Dostoevsky's poetics*. Minneapolis, MN: The University of Minnesota Press.

Beck, U., Lash, S. & Giddens, A. (1994) *Reflexive modernization – politics, tradition and aesthetics in the modern social order*. Cambridge: Polity Press.

Chizhevsky, D. (1962) 'The theme of the double in Dostoevsky'. In R. Wellek (Ed), *Dostoevsky: a collection of critical essays*. Englewood Cliffs, N.J: Prentice-Hall.

Dostoevsky, F. (1846/1997) *The Double*. Translated by C. Garnett. London: Dover Publications.

Dostoevsky, F. (1864/1991) *Notes from the Underground*. Translated by J. Kentish. Oxford: Oxford World Classics.

Dostoevsky, F. (1868/1983) *The Idiot*. Translated by D. Magarshack. Harmondsworth: Penguin.

Dostoevsky, F. (1871/1994) *Demons*. Translated by R. Pevear & L. Volokhonsky. London: Vintage Classics.

Dostoevsky, F. (1877/1999) *A Gentle Creature, White Nights and Dream of a Ridiculous Man*. Oxford: Oxford World Classics.

Dostoevsky, F. (1880/1994) *The Brothers Karamazov*. Translated by I. Avsey. Oxford: Oxford World's Classics.

Dostoevsky, F. (1997) *A writer's diary*, Volume 2: 1877-1881. Translated by K. Lantz. Evanston, Illinois: Northwestern University Press.

Durkheim, E. (1952) *Suicide*. London: Routledge & Kegan Paul.

Elias, N. (1978) *The civilizing process, Vol.1: The history of manners*. Oxford: Basil Blackwell.

Ellenberger, H. F. (1994) *The discovery of the unconscious*. London: Fontana Press.

Foucault, M. (1977) *Discipline and punish: the birth of the prison*. London: Allen Lane.

Frank, J. (1986) *Dostoevsky: the stir of liberation, 1860-1865*. London: Robson Books.

Freud, S. (1962) 'Dostoevsky and parricide'. In R. Wellek (Ed), *Dostoevsky: a collection of critical essays*. Englewood Cliffs, N.J: Prentice-Hall.

Freud, S. (1975) *Introductory Lectures on Psychoanalysis*. Harmondsworth: Penguin.

Freud, S. (1978) *Totem and taboo*. Harmondsworth: Penguin.

Freud, S. (2000) *Civilization and its discontents*. London: Norton & Co.

Freud, S. (2000) *Beyond the pleasure principle*. London: Norton & Co.

Gilligan, C. (1982) *In a different voice: psychological theory and women's development*. Cambridge MA: Harvard University Press.

Girard, R. (1997) *Resurrection from the underground: Feodor Dostoevsky*. New York: The Crossroads Publishing Company.

Gruber, H.E. (1974) *Darwin on man: A psychological study of scientific creativity*. Wildwood house: London.

Jones, M. (1991) Introduction, *Notes from the Underground*. Oxford: Oxford World Classics.

Koselleck, R. (1978) (Ed) *Historische semantik und begriffsgeschichte*. Stuttgart.

Krauth, W. (1984) *Wirtschaftsstruktur und Semantic: Wissenschaftssoziologische Studien zum wirtschaftlichen Denken in Deutschland zwischen dem 13. und 17. Jahrhundert*. Berlin.

Kusch, M. (1999) *Psychological knowledge*. London: Routledge.

Lucacs, G. (1962) 'Dostoevsky'. In R. Wellek (Ed), *Dostoevsky: a collection of critical essays*. Englewood Cliffs, N.J: Prentice-Hall.

Luckmann, T. (1996) 'The privatisation of religion and morality'. In P. Heelas, S. Lash & P. Morris (Eds), *Detraditionalization*. Oxford: Blackwell.

Luhmann, N. (1990) *Die wissenschaft der gesselschaft*. Frankfurt.

Luhmann, N. (1995) *Social systems*. Stanford, Cal: Stanford University Press.

Luhmann, N. (1998) *Love as passion: the codification of intimacy*. Stanford, Cal.: Stanford University Press.

Luhmann, N. (2000) *Art as a social system*. Stanford, Cal: Stanford University Press.

MacIntyre, A. (1985) *After virtue: a study in moral theory*. London: Duckworth.

Marx, K. (1971) 'The Jewish question'. In D. McLellan (Ed), *Early texts*. Oxford: Blackwell.

Pevear, R. (1994) Introduction, *Demons*. London: Vintage Classics.

Rawls, J. (1971) *A theory of justice*. Cambridge, Mass.: Harvard University Press.

Richards, G. (1996) *Putting psychology in its place*. London: Routledge.

Sandel, M. (1982) *Liberalism and the limits of justice*. Cambridge: Cambridge University Press.

Sarbin, T. (Ed) (1986) *Narrative psychology: the storied nature of human conduct*. New York: Praeger.

Serres, M. (1982) *The parasite*. London: The John Hopkins University Press.

Serres, M. (1995) 'Paris 1800'. In M. Serres (Ed), *A history of scientific thought*. Oxford: Blackwell.

Shotter, J. & Gergen, K. (Eds) (1989) *Texts of identity*. London: Sage.

Taylor, C. (1989) 'Cross-purposes: the liberal-communitarian debate'. In N. Rosenblum (Ed), *Liberalism and moral life*. Cambridge, Mass.: Harvard University Press.

Tomkins, S. (1963) *Affect, imagery, consciousness. Volume 11: The negative affects*. London: Tavistock.

Vivas, E. (1962) 'The two dimensions of reality in The Brothers Karamazov'. In R. Wellek (Ed), *Dostoevsky: a collection of critical essays*. Englewood Cliffs, N.J: Prentice-Hall.

Weber, M. (1930) *The protestant ethic and the spirit of capitalism*. London: Unwin University Books.

Wellek, R. (1962) (Ed) *Dostoevsky: a collection of critical essays*. Englewood Cliffs, N.J: Prentice-Hall.

The subjectivity of money
Critical psychology and the economies of post-structuralism

Nick Mansfield

His formative problem was doubtless money, not sex.

Barthes, 1977, p45

Abstract

Recent theory in critical psychology and elsewhere has looked to post-structuralism to provide more useful models of subjectivity and its relationship to power, identity and culture. Post-structuralist theory is often understood as a radical critique of contemporary power relations, and thus society in general. Foucault, Lyotard, Irigaray and Derrida often envisage the inter-relationship of subjects in contemporary power regimes as 'economic'. This is a significant development in an era whose only universal language of social meaning is economics. The aim of this paper is to show how post-structuralist theory both describes and enacts what it means to be a subject in such an economy, where identities circulate only in so far as they can be queered, and where structures operate only by way of their deconstruction. Post-structuralism does not merely replicate the logic of an economised world, but helps us to understand the cultural and historical forms that have made such a world possible. By outlining what post-structuralist theory means by the economy of subjectivity, this paper helps to clarify its value for contemporary psychological and cultural theory.

I

I want to situate what follows in relation to the project of critical psychology by commenting on a recent article by Margaret Wetherell (1999) in *Theory and Psychology* on the comparative value of Marxism and Foucauldian discourse analysis in approaching the issue(s) of contemporary subjectivity. I don't want to adjudicate this debate, nor even enter into it, but I do want to comment on the way Foucault is introduced here. According to Wetherell's article, Foucault's critical genealogy measures out our imagined interiority in an account that makes possible its maximum articulation – the opening of its obscurities, and the tracing of its linkages. Our subjectivity thus appears as dynamic and plural, fluid and complex, and our discourse is unregulated by conventional binary oppositions. She writes:

> What post-structuralist writers such as Foucault offer... is a way out of [the] constraining logic of the individual vs. the social. Again we can find in this work a new and often much more productive way of studying subjectivity which moves us past wearisome debates of nature vs. nurture and the individual vs. social relations. Rather than look at the individual and the social as separate but related entities, investigation is focused instead on modes or practices of subjectification, the rituals and routines which produce human natures in the plural and our very sense of 'individuality'. Indeed Foucault's work suggests that it is a case not of choosing to articulate or choosing to hide a conception of human nature but of asking a different kind of question altogether (Wetherell, 1999: 402).

We are familiar with this sort of representation of post-structuralism from the last thirty years of radical cultural theory: it 'offer[s]... a way out', is 'more productive'; it 'moves us past' and is 'far-reaching', 'asking a different kind of question altogether.' There are a number of unaddressed problems in this article, however, and they spring from the implication that Foucault's work can be harmonised with an albeit circumspect understanding of progress, that it is in fact a form of moral and political engagement (404). The first set of problems cluster around the un-named theorist of genealogy, and I mean Nietzsche, whose work remains not so much the ghost in the machine of post-structuralism, but the enduring source of its provocation, a provocation that is neither reduced nor domesticated by our ability to turn post-structuralist insights into water-tight methodologies. In short, behind Foucauldian evocations of the political, which are rare, and often subsumed into more idiosyncratic usages like 'governmentality', and 'power/knowledge', lies not a sense of a hypothetically shared, open and potentially rationalisable human community, nor a public sphere that can eventually be attuned or even improved according to any standard of measurement, but a permanent state of antagonism between quantums of force that are only known fleetingly as modalities of power and strategies of resistance. In other words, it is not possible to integrate Foucault's Nietzschean inheritance into a model of human improvement without sacrificing the complexity and irresolution of its image of intersubjective relations, which is in fact what Wetherell finds useful in the first place. In fact, Foucault's understanding of human subjectivity leads us away from the image of 'society' towards something else altogether (which, as I will argue, he calls 'economy').

The second set of problems critical genealogy proposes to us is linked to the first, by the way our work itself must also partake of this same volatility, that the subjectivity we live and the account of it we produce can never stand opposite one another in the way that, for realism, word stands in relation to thing, or representation to world. Or in short, a Foucauldian subjectivity can never be simply an object for an investigating subject, and putting it this way makes obvious the entanglement here of one type of subjectivity with another and one type of discourse with another, to the point where the flows and conjunctions that allow us momentarily to signify our subjectivity to one another never really stabilise or make sense in the way we once thought they would, when we believed with Freud, that analysis could make appear in the light what arose in the dark, or allow what defied speech to speak.

Foucault's recurrent solution to these two problems was to use metaphors that could both summarise his image of the subject, and poeticise his writing. In the first case, a society of endless and reversible, yet patterned antagonisms could be described in an accessible way without caricaturing it as a predictive and predictable structure. Secondly, the metaphor itself signalled the extravagantly literary dimension to his theorising, substituting for scholarly pedantry a kind of intimidating rhetorical charisma. The clearest examples here are the use of the panopticon in *Discipline and Punish*, and the conception of the 'modern' mission of subjectivity as a kind of (aesthetic) avant-gardism of the soul in the late paper 'What is Enlightenment?' These metaphors capture both the slipperiness of the state of subjectivity in which we subsist, and the self-consciousness of the writing as which theory appears. The achievement of these metaphors is to occlude the path to demonstrability – how could we prove either empirically or metaphysically that our modern subjectivity is panoptical, or that the broadest future for subjectivity is radically aesthetic? Instead, they offer a kind of maximum resonance, a felt access to endless theoretical improvisation and correspondence. Defensible truth is replaced by a discursive opportunity that clarifies an image or dimension of what we are, while encouraging a practice of signification that might make everything move. These metaphors, thus, operate before and, in the end, without the rigour and finality of any other than an intuitive, or at most, a literary verification. They do not hierarchise the many possible discursive practices which could be used to articulate the subject: metaphysics, theory, fiction, history, diary or just plain bitching. Indeed, they encourage any of these genres to recognise itself in the others.

The aim of this paper is to investigate another example of a metaphor which performs this same complex function for post-structuralism: the metaphor of economy. What is to be achieved by this is quite simple. For post-structuralism, 'economy' seems to be the easiest way of imaging the interpenetration, circulation and exchange of concepts, signifiers, identities, bodies, affects and subjects. In this way, it gives us access to post-structuralism as a kind of representation of social, subjective and discursive processes as analogous to one another. Yet its obvious metaphoricity also clarifies the status of post-structuralism as itself a cultural artefact. The metaphor of economy is the point where contemporary theory simultaneously defines itself and its world. In short, it helps us see what critical psychology, for example, is taking on board when it adopts a Foucauldian methodology.

II

We live in an age whose last remaining grand narrative is economics. Given the revulsion with which humanist and post-humanist culture alike greet the economic, it is curious to say the least, that radical cultural theory embraces this term as an image of its means and meaning. Indeed, in post-structuralism, the word 'economy' is greeted in an enthusiastic, yet quietly neutral way, as a term that is both facilitating and dry, explanatory and impersonal, the thing that both entraps us and allows our escapes. In short, an unaddressed ambivalence has settled on the notion of economy in our theory. What satisfies us, what is satisfied when Foucault calls our libidinal set-up an *economy* of bodies and pleasures' (Foucault, 1980: 159)? Or when psychoanalysis talks of the 'economic' model of the subject? Or Lyotard's 'libidinal economy' (Lyotard, 1993), Irigaray's 'economy of fluids' (Irigaray, 1985), Baudrillard's political economy of the sign (Baudrillard, 1981), Barthes's notion of a semiological value that is economic (Barthes, 1968: 54), and so on and so forth? To post-structuralism, we are not living in a garden, a kingdom, a hierarchy, a family, a race, a structure, a super-structure, a regime, a system, a world, an ontology, or an age. We are living in an economy, and the post-structuralism that makes this witness is not the post-structuralism that commands our will to subversion, our duty of dissent. It is the post-structuralism that reveals itself as the language of the times, whose lexicon of circulation, investments, flows, limits, returns, of possibility and excess will remain as not the cultural logic, but the rhetorical endowment of an age whose only image (dream, language, fantasy, confession) of universality is economics.

But we must be careful not to identify this economy too readily with the models of economics that we have inherited. We are not encountering here the mere displacement into culture and subjectivity of an economics already fixed and knowable in its own natural material domain, that either determines the shape of culture and subjectivity, or lends them its logic. The economy we meet in post-structuralist theory does not merely replicate the more literal economies of commodities, labour and capital. Nor does it simply show that radical cultural theory is in fact a capitulation to or collaboration with the logic of neo-liberalism and the market. The conception of economics in theory can do as much to de-legitimise as to legitimise rogue consumer capitalism. On the other hand, this is not at all to say that Foucault's economics, and the economics of Smith, Ricardo, Bentham, Marx, Jevons, Keynes, Becker, Sen, Friedman, of the invisible hand, surplus value, marginal utility, the general theory, monetarism, micro-economic reform, games theory, and so on and so forth are unrelated. As Marian Hobson reminds us, the classic strategy of post-structuralism is to move 'upstream' (Hobson, 1998) from a structural opposition, in order to reveal the inchoate form out of which that opposition is generated. The economics of theory and the economics of the real instantiate a logically anterior potentiality, one that makes them both possible, while also making it possible to identify and interrogate them. This broader economics is the one that I hope to begin to reveal in this paper, and the larger project of which it forms a part.[1] My hunch is that post-structuralist theory does not provide us with superior, transcendent or

ultimate models of subjectivity, textuality and power, but is a significant cultural artefact in its own right, one that enacts this broader
economics at the same time as it tries to describe it (this paper being no
exception). In the end, my aim is to discover the logic through which
our many economies – our economies of labour, commodities and
capital as well as our economies of subjectivity and intersubjecivity –
reach the point where they can be articulated.

What then are the attributes of this broader economics? Amongst
post-structuralist thinkers, it is Jacques Derrida who has been most
enthralled by the metaphoric potential of economics. As Derrida
painstakingly reminds us, the etymology of 'economics' leads us to the
Greek word *oikos*, and thus to the management of the household as the
core of all transactions (Derrida, 1988: 184). Thus, every use of the
word economics is always already metaphorical, whether it is in our
parlance or our parliaments, government policy or business theory, my
anxious calculations on the back of a payslip or the writings of a
Friedman, Sen or Becker. Indeed, Derrida implies that money may
prove the key to metaphoricity itself (Derrida, 1982). But it is in
Derrida's response to Lacan's seminar on Poe's 'The Purloined Letter',
that we can start to elucidate the definition of economy that we are
seeking. Here the economy is put in apposition with 'the determination
of the proper, the law of the proper' (Derrida, 1988: 184). Economy is
thus produced as a caused event, one to be identified with ownership,
order and the most intense source of meaning in Lacan – in fact, the
very principle of meaning-making – the law. Yet, the law, even in its
most absolute Lacanian sense, remains endlessly divisible. Derrida
argues that the unity on which identity depends is vulnerable to an
endless and automatic dissemination. No singularity, whether semantic, conceptual or political, can resist being dispersed into an endlessly
redistributing field of possibilities.

If we are talking about a signifier, this dissemination defies the logic
of meaning to the point where meaning itself can only be hypothetical.
Yet, the material gravity of the concept of economy reminds us that
however fleeting, illogical or theoretically unverifiable the law of the
proper – and all the entities which depend on it – may be, they remain
the law, property remains the law, and identity is a *fact*, even in its
dispersal. Economics then is determined as a law that is endlessly divisible. The exempla of this law are thus established in their most
rigorous, stable sense as identity, value, product or management. Yet, at

the same time, economy requires them to appear only as the freak residue, the momentary crystallisation of unstoppable flows, into which they must always automatically disappear, and out of which again they must prepare to be suddenly, unexpectedly yet inevitably reproduced as something completely different altogether. Identities – whether financial values, modes of political self-recognition, or incandescent instantiations of desire – are all at once ruthlessly fixed and endlessly unstable, redolent with purpose, but open to possibility. This mode of *différance* – or, given its coincidence of historical immobility and irrepressible flow, it may be better to call it *indifférance* – is the meaning of economy in post-structuralism.

From this point, the easiest option would be to follow a path conventionally identified as postmodern and say that dissemination mocks or ruins the law, and that deconstruction produces a phantasmagoria of ever-dispersing and discontinuous disjunctions, that knows no stabilities. Yet it is absolutely crucial for us to remember that the law *persists*, even in its discredited state, marshalling real effects, continuing vicious histories, operating violent systems, bullying the other, and ourselves when other, with theoretical totalities; and these totalities endure even though no-one might believe in them, even though the identities on which they depend are recognised to be mere signifiers and are transmitted in the world mainly in a disseminated formlessness. Our impulse has continually been to try to re-invent the imagined disjunction between, say, knowable identity and the internal instability that subverts it as a kind of politics that will re-install some sense of priorities in us. The face-off between identity politics and queer theory is a version of this will-to-politics. Wetherell's reading of Foucault is, of course, another. But the important thing to recognise here is that these putative alternatives are inter-dependent – indeed inseparable – because of their location in a larger frame of exchange and possibility, in short, in an economy that does not need to choose, and thus does not own up to a politics. The choice between identity and its deconstruction is not enough, therefore. It does not capture either the quality or the quantity of economic activity to which we are subject. Identity fixes a place in the world and a moment in time, yet it also activates the pluralities into which it can shatter, and beyond that the inexhaustible field of meanings, unmeanings and non-meanings that it automatically evokes simply because of its position in the stream of signification. In sum then, we co-ordinate our identities, but only as still-frames in the endless multiplication and division that inevitably queers them, because behind these momentary fixities is an irresistible flux which threatens and thrills us with enlivening substitutions and decompositions, in which we both recognise and refuse our new truth. In other words, we are the law and its dissemination, living out these contradictions in a flow of exchange that still defines value, of bargaining that still respects fixed price, of absurdity that still reproduces meaning.

III

But can we really describe this contradictory set of incommensurable and ineluctable relationships between law and its deconstruction, identity and its dissemination, as subjectivity? Perhaps the best way to answer this question is by a return to the thinker who first problematised the subject in the very way Foucault was to develop, and that's Nietzsche, or the Nietzsche in Lyotard, who writes towards the very end of *Libidinal Economy*:

> So you see how we have a *theatrics of masks without faces*: every effect is a mask, and just as there is no cause, there is no face. These masks mask no lost origin... they become conductors of one another, without it being possible to assign them an order of appearance, without a law of concatenation, and therefore according to anonymous singularities (Lyotard, 1993:259).

Subjectivity here has no ontology as selfhood, as face. Being is not as self, but as mask. 'Being *is* mask,' as Jean Granier puts it (Granier, 1977: 191). This implies that whatever we mean by 'we' live(s) in a world of masks without faces, of effects without causes and so on. These masks circulate amongst and between themselves, without hierarchy, without meaningful relationship. Yet ironically, they join, they become mutual in irreducible and unsystematisable, in Lyotard's usage, 'anonymous' events, events which inevitably arise, at least phenomenologically, as an unignorable reality in a given moment.

Thus, in a single 'event', the mask both asserts and deconstructs identity. Even though they connect the play of masks with fixed moments and episodes, such events still disseminate us into an unde-limited range of intensities that can only be known by their linkage to one another and another and another *ad infinitum*. Yet how can we call this infinity that is often seen as 'possibility', but that does not even respect the binary between possibility and impossibility, how can we call it subjectivity? What is our relationship to this economy, these events?

They both include and limit us. They may be made up of our experience, but they may be larger than it, incorporating what we must take to be either the experience of the other, or hypothetical experience, or both. They include, therefore, an experience that is not or at least might not be experienced, an experience for which we must find a new term, a subjectivity without experience if you like. Models or images of the subject as an economic conjunction cannot reduce a necessary dimension of subjectivity that is purely hypothetical, that only relates to experience because it is not experienced. It is the subjectivity that we *might* connect to, the one that we *might* have, which means that in the greater part or at least a little in every part, our experience of subjectivity will always be defined by what we will not experience.

To find an example of such an event that connects both the hard material reality of the historical moment, and the opening onto the infinite possibilities of intersubjective substitution and enlargement, we need look no further than the commodity, that most modern trope of economics which not only appealed to Marx, because it seemed to allow him to quantify the process of exchange in human terms, but that has also fascinated recent theorists of the culture of postmodernism because it seems the key to the signification of subjective desire in the act of consumption. If the value of the commodity is in the amount of labour time invested in it, then everything we eat, wear, touch, the walls that enclose us, the machines for which we labour and that carry us from one work-station to another, that fill the world with noise and movement and production and exchange, then each of these *things* is only the objectification of work. And as the turning of work into material resistance, they are the substantiation not only of time, but of somebody's time, not only of will, but of some momentary embodiment of will, not only of production, but of intention, and these (and there could be more), this person in time, this localisation of will and purpose, what else is this but a type of subjectivity, not a definition of the subject, but dimensions of it at least, enough of it for us to say that what classical economics and its antagonists offer us in the labour theory of value is the commodity not made calculable in the moment of exchange, but the world made animate, made *animist* by the subjectivity invested in every one of its hardnesses, in every product, and everything is a product, till what we inhabit in this room, or as we touch this page, what happens is not a calculable translation of economic materials of meaning, but the subjectivity of the other trapped within it, walled into the surfaces of the world like a victim or a villain in a story of Poe's, so that when I touch the commodity with my skin, how close do I come not to the mathesis of the economic but its cruel and charismatic flesh, how easily, how lightly do I brush up against the sweat of the labouring face, and the blood that coils within?

But from Marx onwards, the commodity has never been simply an embodiment of the act of production or exchange. It is also a focus of desire and consumption. As we purchase, touch, imagine, represent, taste, exhaust and repudiate each of these things, and we too are things, are we not linked to the subjects who might or might not at any moment perform the same act of purchase, touch, imagination, representation, taste, exhaustion or repudiation? Do not infinite possibilities of subjectivity multiply inward to the heart of the commodity and outward from the imagined privatisation of the moment we call interest? In this most definite economic event, therefore, in which we make contact most desperately with the law of the proper, we connect with the subjectivities that have gone before us, and those who might stand in our place. In a little part, by way of the predictable shape of this definite experience, our sense of our own possibility must touch all the experience we may or may never have.

Traditionally, our deconstruction of the subject has not cared for the distinction between the mask that we wear, and the mask that could be, but has never been, worn. In a sense, the term we have become accustomed to calling both these masks and all masks together is *culture*, our reading of which has become a perpetual phenomenology of the conductivity that links all those masks with and without a face. But culture is only an historical term, used to analyse or describe the masks that we have already contrived. The future is not so knowable. Our future is not vested in possibility, but in the impossibility of impossibility, that nothing might not happen.

IV

What I want to say is quite straightforward: that what we know as culture or as the genealogy of power/knowledge, or simply as this conductivity of masks without faces is economics, and that when we see the triumph of economics as a society's or an epoch's last remaining authoritative language of meaning what we are seeing is not the triumph of instrumental rationalism, nor philistine materialism, nor liberal humanism. What we see is the ascendancy of what post-structuralism both knows and embodies – knows because it embodies – this subjectivity of the economic, that subjectivity both with and without experience, both with and without identity – and that when we 'touch', either literally or figuratively the commodity, or the thing, or the law in its hard material instant, we touch it backwards towards the labouring subjectivity embedded in it, and outwards towards the other possible subjectivities we stand in for. This is what economics means, the interpellation of our subjectivity by a subjectivity we have not experienced, a subjectivity that always requires the impossibility of impossibility. And, what is most important of all, in doing this, we do not distinguish our 'real' experience from that subjectivity without experience that is the possibility in which we invest our interest. Instead, our impulse is to conflate our subjectivity with this subjectivity without experience, to dream of ourselves endlessly out there in the flow, seeking returns, fucking others, being fucked, yet being unfucked by them as well, active but somehow weightless, real but only in so far as virtual. So what Foucault's phrase teaches us is that bodies and pleasures and subjectivity too are all in this economy, that even when it is most real, what subjectivity is subject to is an hypothesis of circulation and transfer, in which experience only makes sense, only attains its reality as a lapse of non-experience, and that subjectivity will always be an enthusiasm and a disavowal, an incredible intensity and a weightlessness, a material fact and an endless imagination.

Foucault's work is consistently read to say that it is practices of subjectification co-ordinated with the disciplinary apparatuses of power/knowledge that we need to subvert, that a fluid self-reinvention can promise us some image of freedom. Yet the economy shows us that such a separation is not available. The subjectification we have inherited, and the possibility Foucault proposes, are entangled in an infinite process of interchange where fixity and fluidity only make meaning with one another, not as alternatives. Thus 'possibility' does not free us from system. System is a mere version of possibility, and thus bears it in and as itself. Embracing possibility is not then a denial of system, but an immersion in system's concealed, even disingenuously disguised reality. This is not to say that possibility merely returns us to the entrapments of the system, which cannot simply be seen to govern the unstable field in which possibility can be imagined. Rather, both system and the possibility we are supposed to prefer to it, are part of a larger phenomenon, a subjectivity that can appear as both a representative of the system and a denial of it, as an embodiment and denial of identity, as a celebration of the truth of experience and an endless advance beyond the limitations of experience.

Thus, what the post-structuralist use of the metaphor of the economic confronts us with is the insight that the subjectivity we must contest is not the subjectivity of the disciplinary apparatus, nor power/knowledge, nor structure conceived in any way, but a subjectivity that can lend itself to all these things while still remaining a subjectivity of endless self-disavowal in which we slip from one economy to another, from the economy of money to the economy of the sign to the economy of bodies and pleasures, finding, in a sort of incessantly available double-click, transitions and translations which consistently re-assert and subvert what we have thought of as manageable social identities, ourselves, our typologies, or our places. And the problem for us is that this subjectivity simply does not turn self-consciousness into self-improvement. The self that is recognised enters a currency of possible identities that have equal weight whether they are experienced or not. In fact, this distinction becomes unimportant.

Our hope would be that we could provide a *model* of this subjectivity, or an explanation of where it comes from. To propose such knowledge is to re-enact habitual strategies of evasion by imagining an alternative level of discourse that would claim that it itself and its subjectivity can stabilise. But this subjectivity knows only metaphor, and thus can only produce a discourse that is as unstable as itself, that will always decompose in the face of theory, philosophy, metaphysics or ontology, a decomposition and recomposition that become its life. The economy meets the theoretical strategy of evasion, with its own petty, even cheeky, hyper-evasion. The subjectivity of the economic intensifies our belief in experience as simultaneously real and hypothetical, just as we learn to kill on behalf of the identities that no longer remain stable and self-identical, and it is only from this point, without the guiding lights of culture, science and philosophy, all of which it mocks, without the guiding light of theory, that we must begin to theorise it. But most importantly, to revert momentarily to the issue of agency and the public, this subjectivity is not that of a society or a system, that we can then objectify and analyse. Economic subjectivity is the subjectivity that we are living, and in which our pleasure and our pain is both enwrapped and dispersed. And although we must maintain a rigorous critique in the face of the oppressions of race, gender and sexuality that we see all around us, we should not be consoled by the thought that this is enough, or that such politics deals at all with our pleasure and pain or the radical convergence that will not let us keep them apart.

V

But, of course, in an economy, there is always a trade-off between opportunity and cost, which are not always to be located in the same people. Let me refer to a case study:

A miller promises the king that his daughter can spin straw into gold. The greedy king locks her away, threatening to kill her if she does not fulfil the promise. Her sorrow is relieved by a strange little man who performs her task for the return of her first-born child. Yet even when she is queen and has given birth to a child and he comes to fulfil the bargain, he offers her another possibility: if she guesses his name she will be absolved of her debt. The name is overheard for her by a servant, and the little man explodes with rage, stamps his foot through the floor and dies.

The queen is a victim of a promise she has not made about a skill no-one can have, which she hires for a child she is not expecting at a price she can afford to pay only by chance. Yet from these experiences she does not have – the promise, the weaving, the child, the eavesdropping – she is remade a queen, and lives happily ever after, conjoined with the highest metaphor of the social law, the king. The bargain always contains the faith that somehow the connection we do not yet have to something we do not know about will make us. And this necessity will not only make us, it will make us real. This is the bargain we have no choice but to engage in if we are to live economically.

Yet what the story tells us is that the little man will die. He cannot even be protected by his absurd name. Both Lyotard and Deleuze argue that the proper name, because it is a uniqueness, is somehow protected from the iron-cage of discipline and systematicity to which all other signification remains prey. Deleuze writes of the proper names in Nietzsche, that they are 'neither signifiers nor signified... There is a kind of... a perpetual displacement in the intensities designated by proper names, intensities that interpenetrate one another at the same time that they are lived, experienced, by a single body' (Deleuze, 1977:

146). Proper names then do not belong to the system and structure of language. In all their authority and charisma, proper names turn the contingent linking of any phonemes we might have inherited into an institution, that then specifies them in and as the 'single body.' The old burdensome weight of system and structure is sloughed off in the dream of the uniquely individual, the un-natural, the impossible or bizarre.

Derrida, however, has gone much further to argue in *Glas* (Derrida, 1986) and elsewhere, that in fact proper names help us to imagine language without the reductive resort to an unliveable logic of system and structure altogether. Proper names do not provide an autonomous individual space separate from the crushing dominance of system and structure. They show that the latter only emerge as images in the unstable flow of the trace and différance. In the economy, there is no freedom from freedom. We are told repeatedly that the little man's name could not be more unique, more idiosyncratic, less trapped by systemics. Yet Rumplestiltskin is not a victim of system, structure, ideology or even power, but of the economy that produces and locates the subjectivity of the queen in a network of possibilities and non-experiences. It is not system that kills the little man, who, certainly in every logic but the fantastic, has earned his wage. It is the economy of possibility and impossibility that the queen could call on, even when she was a peasant girl, about whose head, and without whose knowledge, men were making ridiculous deals: the possibility that there was someone who could weave straw into gold, and someone who might overhear an absurd name. It is these weaknesses in the texture of fate – talents and experiences that we do not have, but that the bargains we make every day make ours without our ever needing to know or experience them – that we now believe in, and that all too quickly come true for and as us. In sum, the story of Rumplestiltskin undoes the post-structuralist platitude that what inhibits us is system and structure, and that an 'undefined' freedom (Foucault, 1984:46) is found in pursuing the proper name's evasion of this entrapment out into the flow and indeterminacy – the impossibility of impossibility – that theoretical rhetoric has romanticised as economy. It is the proper name, and its link to the inconceivably possible, in other words, the economy, that kills the little man.

Yet we don't care! The princess is released from her bond, and this is all that matters to us. In this way, the little man's death gives us pleasure, or at least the ecstatic relief from tension that Freud understood as pleasure. We live out these sorts of entanglements every day, and shrug our shoulders at the unknowable complications and consequences – lived, but perhaps not by us – they must bring. We know that when we have sex, our DNA, our stress, our fury, our passion links and twines with multiple flows, both physical and abstract, of the living and the dead, the sick and the well, who have been where we are, or will be there later, or who simply might be there, the others who we know and do not know, who we teach and from whom we learn, how to twist our bodies, how to ask, how to call out. And when we eat, our bodies are forever arching over duties, sufferings, cheatings, ideas and inspirations, the dreams and prosperities sacrificed for work and fulfilled by work. And in this economy we burn with our love and our fury, with our longing and our satisfaction, because our dreams are endless and our bodies are hot. We simply cannot have the pleasure without the death, we have always known that, but it is equally true that we always end up taking the side of the princess, and thus we can't have the death without the pleasure.

VI

So given this intense ambivalence, what could possibly be our way out of the economy? It is after all, a 'way out' that Wetherell sees Foucault as offering. Foucault imagined that a renewal of subjectivity would be possible by way of a quasi-voluntarist self-reinvention analogous to art. Art, intoxication, religion, desire and suicide traditionally function as our arsenal of escape. Yet each is only one romantic enthusiasm, or one day, ahead of the economy, which is itself replete with images of ways out, offered as putatively original contrivances that are available either to affectively transcendent 'individuals' – the entrepreneur, the star, the success story – or to those courageous enough to imagine the abandonment of unified subjectivity altogether.

The challenge is to think the chiasmus of death and pleasure simultaneously, that we will never have the one without the other. Yet, that even as we can think this double-thought, we will never be reconciled to the economy, nor will it finally accommodate us. We lack the right sort of agency, and it will never make its ephemeral stabilities truly comforting. We must live simultaneously the economy's pleasure and its terror, its beauty and its inconvenience: exhilarating shopping and degrading anxiety, global deprivation and titillating novelty. The economy kills us every day and kills others for us, though never in our name; but it also gives to us and we take, charges and excites us, bores us and relieves our boredom. It almost has a love for us, and we spasmodically, selfishly, love it. We detect our advantage in it, repeatedly, serially offered to us, and we seize that advantage in moments of flamboyant privacy, of an abandonment of ourselves before ourselves, of excess and secrecy. And this combination of murders we do and do not commit, and loves that do and do not exalt and exult us, this is the subjectivity with and without experience of the economy. We do not choose it, and we equally choose not to evade it. Our indulgence and impulsiveness sit side by side with our seamless critical theory. We will never be at home in it, nor will we ever stop letting it find us, and all this despite the savagery that a materialist analysis consistently, almost irrevocably recalls to us in a language we cannot deny, but seem unable not to ignore.

The whole logic of a 'way out' towards which our critical intelligence prompts us falters before the deconstruction of the binary opposition between inside and outside, which is the absolutely fundamental philosopheme of post-structuralism, and that is echoed in the title of Wetherell's article 'Beyond Binaries.' The economy does not know its outside. The subjectivity we seek to know and the discourse we seek to produce can never stand outside of and opposite one another in a way that can propose a radical alternative, or even convince us that something as dependent on the subject/object dichotomy as 'analysis' is possible, whether we mean psychoanalysis, social analysis or discourse analysis.

So what path then is available to critical psychology? It is impossible to disentangle our subjectivity from the economy, and we must recognise that the same is true of our discourse. Critical psychology must not refuse to pursue a Foucauldian methodology, but must recognise its metaphorical logic, a logic that suspends both the injunction to truth, and the usual teleology of critical thought. What is required therefore is a broader, more eclectic discourse, one that can match the fluidity of the economy with processes that are as fictional as they are analytical, as destructive as they are enlightening, as disorienting as they are progressive. Our discourse of subjectivity should not offer truth, or meaning (the (a)trophies of system) or difference and possibility (the naïve hopes of those who saw the image of economy as radically deregulatory of culture and politics). Instead it should charge up what in the economy is most typical: its unresolvable disjunctions between experience and insight, knowledge and praxis, its obscure indifferences between exposition and strategy, interpretation and invention; in short, to plunder its incommensurabilities. This sort of improvisation does not easily lend itself to clinical practice, though the discourses of practice must be part of its work. Theory has a duty to support practice, but it is also obliged to cross the horizons to which difficulty and provocation lead us. In an economy, a psychology seeking to understand the situation of the subject must also be a psychology that endlessly recounts without reducing to truth the pain and pleasure of subjectivity all along its dim and tortuous line – a line that includes statistics and theory, but also poetry and graffiti – exposing and expounding it, squeezing the bruise of subjectivity till it aches and we laugh, till we scream and come alive.

Notes

1. This essay is part of a book-length project entitled *Other Economies: Subjectivity After Derrida*, which analyses the economic as a way of understanding the significance of post-structuralist thinking on subjectivity, in Foucault, Lyotard, Irigaray and especially Derrida's analyses of Marx, Bataille, Levinas, psychoanalysis and the gift.

References

Allison, D. (1977) *The new Nietzsche: contemporary styles of interpretation*. New York: Dell.

Barthes, R. (1968) *Elements of semiology*. Annette Lavers and Colin Smith (Trans). New York: Hill and Wang.

Barthes, R. (1977) *Roland Barthes by Roland Barthes*. Richard Howard (Trans). London: Macmillan.

Baudrillard, J. (1981) *For a critique of the political economy of the sign*. Charles Levin (Trans). St Louis: Telos Press.

Deleuze, G. (1977) 'Nomad thought'. In D. Allison (Ed), *The new Nietzsche: contemporary styles of interpretation*. New York: Dell, 142–149.

Derrida, J. (1982) 'White mythology'. In A. Bass (Trans.), *Margins of philosophy*. Brighton: Harvester Press, 207–71.

Derrida, J. (1986) *Glas*. J.P. Leavey and R. Rand (Trans). Lincoln NE: University of Nebraska Press.

Derrida, J. (1988) 'The Purveyor of Truth'. In J. P. Muller and W. J. Richardson (Eds), *The purloined Poe: Lacan, Derrida and psychoanalytic reading*. Baltimore: Johns Hopkins University Press, 173–212.

Foucault, M. (1977) *Discipline and punish: the birth of the prison*. Alan Sheridan (Trans). London: Allen Lane.

Foucault, M. (1980) *The history of sexuality, volume 1: an introduction*. Robert Hurley (Trans). New York: Vintage Books.

Foucault, M. (1984) 'What is enlightenment?' In P. Rabinow (Ed), *The Foucault reader*. Harmondsworth: Penguin Books3. 2–50.

Granier, J. (1977) 'Perspectivism and Interpretation'. In D. Allison (Ed), *The new Nietzsche: contemporary styles of interpretation*. New York: Dell, 190-200.

Hobson, M. (1998) *Jacques Derrida: opening lines*. London and New York: Routledge.

Irigaray, L. (1985) *This sex which is not one*. C. Porter and G. Gill (Trans). Ithaca, NY: Cornell University Press.

Lyotard, J. F. (1993) *Libidinal Economy*. I. Hamilton Grant (Trans). London: The Athlone Press.

Wetherell, M. (1999) 'Beyond binaries'. *Theory and psychology* 9(3): 399–406.

Entranced
Embodied spirituality on the post-industrial dance floor

Hillegonda C. Rietveld

Abstract

In this article, spirituality will be explored within a post-human context through a case study of the contemporary post-industrial dancing body[1] at post-rave dance clubs and parties characterised by DJ produced techno-house music. The mental state of this body is driven outside of daily perceived psychological boundaries by an amplified pulsating electronic rhythm, whereby such altered states of consciousness can be chemically enhanced by the use of dance drugs. As the dance floor 'peaks', in the words of its technician, the DJ, the dancing crowd can reach a transcendental moment perceived as a timeless forever now. For example, Sylvan notes in Traces of Spirit *that: 'The first theme that stands out as nearly universal in the dance floor experience of the rave subculture is that of trance' (2002: 127).[2] Such a state of trance, or peak-experience, produces a subjective perception of spirituality that seems to exist outside of the boundaries of material reality. However, the discussion will show that experiences of spirituality are, in fact, produced within the embodied lived experience of specific material and cultural contexts. In this case, these contexts are provided by the gendered discursive field of global post-rave cultures and their dominant musical genre, techno-house.*

Analytical matrix

The argument in this article was initially inspired by Bataille's almost casual definition of the spirit as 'subject-object' (1989: 15), the merging of self with the other-as-thing. This, Bataille explains, involves the reduction of the other to an objectified thing, followed by destruction of the object, to release its spirit in death. In the case of post-industrial marathon electronic dance events, I will suggest, the opposite occurs of what Bataille proposed; instead of destroying the other in order to achieve spiritual merging, a sense of the self disappears. Hereby the self is experienced as a merging with the surroundings in a spiritual manner, a merging with what in the clear hegemonic day light would be conceived of as the other. This other could be the object as presented in the technological metaphors of techno, whereby the self is defaced ('off your face' is a popular phrase amongst dance drugs users), producing a peak-experience subjectivity playfully identified here as a 'sacrificial cyborg'. Yet, with reference to ideas developed by Irigaray (2002), the other could also be the realm of the other subject, the social surroundings, producing a 'subject-subject' relationship and a (sometimes real, sometimes simulated) sense of 'communal soul'. In this article, one can also find glimpses of the idea that spirituality is closely tied in with the embodied subjectivity of gendered sexuality. In short, a contemporary sense of spirituality is achieved on the dance-floor in a variety of ways. In intense cases, the contemporary dance club could be regarded as a secular type of night-time church and the free open-air party as a post-historic tribal rite.

Historian Michel Foucault has demonstrated, for example in the context of sexuality (Foucault, 1984), that the subject never exists in a vacuum – it is embodied.[3] The subject's relationship with the other is never the same, it changes through time, discursively. As such, despite the experience of the spiritual as universal, disembodied and transcendental, this is an illusion; the notion of spirit is unstable, depending on historical and material contexts. The methods of observation and analysis in this article are therefore inter-disciplinary in the style of critical cultural studies.[4] Hereby, the intersection between a material embodied world and the formation of a subjective understanding of spirituality is partially based on ethnographic data as well as on historical work.

As a white North-West European female, I have spent several decades at several hundreds of post-rave and post-disco dance events in the UK and elsewhere, on other continents,[5] as a 'punter' on dance floors and as an academic researcher. I have also spent some time in the UK and Benelux as a dance DJ and composer in a male-defined dance club industry. My (rarefied) version of a 'peaking' dance floor is, then, an amalgamation from my lived experiences of a wide range of dance events:

> The amplified dance music carries me into another plane of experience, its regular beat comforting me while a world of musical textures, rhythms and visual impressions whirls around me. I forget about how I arrived here, about my usual daily life, myself. My body seems to have shed its burdens of human existence, its limitations reduced: free at last, free at last. Time is now and always, fragments of seconds, breaking to a blur of party weekends, then smoothening out into a transcendental sense of forever. Bodies of fellow dancers brushing, strangers have gone, we are all friends, in it together, we are as one. Thinking in terms of differentiation eliminated – being, immersed. Stepping out of this sense of immersion, walking now around the periphery of the event, I notice the repetitive 4/4 beats of a house music related dance music that is pumped out of a rather oversized set of speakers, flanking a person wearing headphones, the DJ, playing recordings, mixing them seamlessly, taking control over the mood of the party. Meanwhile, lights and smoke are interfering with the visual field, making clear observations cumbersome. The dancing crowd of people looks like a mass, some people more individuated than others, swayed by musical manipulations, by visual fragmentation and enhanced by dance drugs.

Post-industrial dance-floor

Although showing similarities in terms of the intense experience of freedom (see also: Pini, 2001; Rietveld, 1993), the peak-experience on the post-rave dance floors is experienced by dancers in a variety of manners depending on what embodied self they feel they are liberated from (Fikentscher, 2000; Rietveld, 1998). Here discussion will focus on the historical context of rave-inspired (in other words: post-rave) events that feature techno-house hybrid musical genres, the (global) post-industrial dance floor of the late 20th to early 21st centuries. Such events are not necessarily exactly identical to specific English raves of the early 1990s (Rietveld, 1993; Pini, 2001), but are partially inspired by them, mixing their formal elements with other sensibilities, normalising and localising their cultural potential.

Initially given shape by the well-documented explosion of UK rave and club culture (Collin, 1997; Garratt, 1998; Reynolds, 1998), a noticeable intensification of such DJ-led dance gatherings took place in the 1990s, coinciding in terms of global territory with societies in the process of post-industrial change. In the UK, the energy of Thatcherite post-industrial upheaval, combined with dance drugs and house music (especially Ecstasy and acid house), propelled 'raves' in 1989 into mass mediated shock events (Rietveld, 1993; Thornton, 1995), resulting in both global 'super club' brands and nomadic counter cultural sound systems. Although post-rave dance culture is seemingly calming and maturing in the UK, post-rave dance events have erupted elsewhere. Related dance gatherings take place in USA, Europe, Israel, South Africa, India, South East Asia, Australia, New Zealand, China, Japan, South America. Such geographical locations are all, arguably, in one way or another characterised by global capitalist urbanisation and by degrees of (post)-industrial development.

Admittedly, the notion of the post-industrial is problematic. It is based on the acceptance of an 'information revolution' which Robins and Webster aptly describe as a 'cocktail of scientific aspiration and commercial hype' (1999: 89), that obscures historical and material power relations in a neo-conservative fashion (Kumar, 1995). Ignoring complex social and historical analysis, technology acquires immanent agency. Information communication technology (ICT), especially in its digital form, seems occult in its mystery, perfect for inspiring techno-paganism (David, 1998: 183). In such a discourse, the arrival of ICT appears as a divine deliverance from outer space, changing industri-alised societies accordingly from their base in manufacturing industry to information-led economies. Yet, the idea of the post-industrial era has inspired artists and policy makers alike, since it is attractive in its apparent simplicity, making the hype a reality or, indeed, 'hyperreality' (Baudrillard, 1987: 16). As a hegemonic myth, the post-industrial and its 'information revolution' identifies a symbolic relationship between human and technology, especially between man and machine, which in turn is worked out in the cultural and subjective domain, such as in its dance rituals.

Spirit-matter
Addressing spirituality in 'the information age' in *TechGnosis*, Davis suggests that the spirit could be subjectively regarded as 'a blast of the absolute' (Davis, 1998: 6), pure information, subjectively comparable to digital data, which seems to exist magically independent of matter.

By contrast, Davis suggests, the soul is analogue, a source of creativity, tied to the emotions and desires of the body as well as to mythologies; in other words, tied to cultural production. This separation, of seemingly non-physical entities, offers an attractive construct in a time when analogue communication media are replaced by digital media. For example, in electronic music, as digital technologies were introduced into the production process, analogue technologies gained by contrast an aura of authenticity (Goodwin, 1990), feeling 'warmer', fuller, more organic, and a more 'soulful' texture and sound. Davis' distinction between spirit and soul as digital and analogue respectively, shows a particular reworking of the mind/body split of the European enlightenment, removing the body one more step towards a post-human subjectivity; the digitised ghost, it seems, now operates in an analogue machine. This construct shows a shift of the spiritual into a domain of what Yurick calls 'electromagic' voodoo (1985: 24). The organic human brain is capable of operating in a complex ever-changing environment, yet the domain of the digital is invisible to the human eye, while its speed of processing of information makes it impossible for the human mind to keep up with certain calculations. Only an interface can humanise such alienating digital processes.

Yet, the idea that 'spirit is excluded from matter' is an 'illusion', as Susan Griffin bluntly puts it (in Springer, 1996: 25). Such a duality disregards the fact that digital data nevertheless have a human and social source. Neither would a spirit/matter duality explain how the embodied act of dancing to a musical aesthetic could indeed produce a spiritual experience. As literary theorist Eagleton put it so succinctly: '(a)esthetics is born as a discourse of the body' (1990: 13), part of a material and discursive context. Within Bakhtin's dialogics, furthermore, the aesthetic can be regarded as a type of empathy or melting between self and other (Todorov, 1984: 98). This is comparable to orgasm, as well as to the experience of a peak-experience when dancing to a repetitive beat for a length of time at techno and house related dance parties, or to taking empathy inducing drugs, such as Ecstasy. Pini points out that 'raving' is 'commonly experienced as involving a dissolution of the division between self and other and between inner and outer' (2001: 160). The result of this melting of self and other (community), of human and thing (cyborg), of subject and object, produces a sense of encompassing intimacy with what, according to Bataille, could be perceived as the spirit of the other, the thing, the object. In the case of the spirit being 'subject-object' (Bataille, 1989: 56), I suggest that the interface between complex technology and humans could be regarded as a spiritual tool.

Techno: interface

Techno works both as an interface and as a musical aesthetic discourse to make sense of the relationship between humans and ICT:

> (Techno) seems to mirror the feeling of non-specific dread that many people now feel when they think about life, the world, the future; yet it also expresses a feeling of bliss (Toop, 1995: 89).

As a musical genre, techno can be understood as both futuristic electronica and industrial nostalgia. It is abstract and foregrounds seemingly other worldly machine noises rather than producing a simulated version of acoustic musical instruments. Its speeds, rhythms and structures can vary widely, from break and broken beat to chillout music. Most commonly, though, and of importance to the dance events discussed here, is when its syntagmatic structure is supplied by house music. As a post-disco party music, house features a repetitive 4/4 beat and a speed of 120 or more beats per minute and is mostly produced with electronic instruments. House provides a ritual musical structure to a broad and inclusive 'church' and can feature a range of textures, from electronic to organic, and may support a range of attitudes, from abstract to humanist, including techno's machine aesthetic (Rietveld, 1998a). Important to the current discussion is that, when fused with house, techno becomes a powerful physical and spiritual means of confirming a subjective relationship with technology.

The term 'techno' was initially inspired by Toffler, who in 1980 popularised the idea of an information-based post-industrial society in *The Third Wave*. Toffler suggested that the 'agents' of this new era, this new wave, were the 'Techno Rebels' (in Savage, 1996: 315), people who would be able to take control over technology for their own purposes. As a genre, techno utilises relatively accessible electronic music technologies, widening the use of ICT to a rebellious DIY underground resistance; music by the people for the people, in effect a type of electronic folk music (Rietveld, 1998b: 261). The term 'techno' and its vaguely futuristic implications struck a chord with producer Juan

Atkins and his DJ-producer friends in early 1980s Detroit, as well as with the British music industry and press who marketed Detroit techno and the ideas around it to a wider world audience.

In 1980s Detroit, the car industry had vanished and businesses moved out to the suburbs, leaving this city to rethink its post-industrial future in terms of information technologies (Sicko, 1999). Similar shifts in industrial and urban structures have occurred elsewhere. In New York, hip hop spawned the electro genre (with the robot dance, globally popularised by Michael Jackson) during the early 1980s, which left its mark on early forms of techno. Also in the early 1980s, in one of Chicago's areas of deserted warehouse spaces, a black Latino gay club called The Warehouse lent its name to the musical selections of its resident DJ, Frankie Knuckles; this was music from 'the 'house', in other words, house music. In the UK, sound system parties utilised disused industrial storage and factory spaces. At the very end of the 1980s, similar events, much larger in scale, gained the tag of 'rave' in the UK, increasingly organised in the countryside, signifying an urban disappearance from intensifying surveillance by police and press, fuelled by moral panic, whilst enabled by ICT (Collin, 1997). Elsewhere, especially during the 1990s, one can find similar uses of empty warehouses (San Francisco, Melbourne, Sydney, Bangkok, Lisbon, Berlin) and, increasingly during the 1990s, of non-urban spaces (Australian bush, Israeli desert or Japanese mountains for its urban 'refugees', and Thai islands, Peruvian mountains or Goan beaches for global urban tourists). At the same time, the UK's super clubs developed in the 1990s as a result of the overwhelming success of this type of dance gathering. Since the middle of the decade such clubs, like Ministry of Sound based in London, have attempted to gain a share of a potential global market.

Detroit techno was a combination of European and African-American futurisms; as Derrick May famously put it: 'It's like George Clinton and Kraftwerk are stuck in an elevator with only a sequencer to keep them company' (Barr, 2000: vii). In Germany, during the 1970s, Kraftwerk's 'Man-Machine' music brought the electronic avant-garde, including its machine aesthetic heritage, into the popular domain, with tracks like *Trans Europe Express* (1978). Meanwhile, in 1970s USA, funk music articulated changes in industry and in black civil rights politics; funk made sense of the identity crisis experienced by black male 'blue collar' workers as they lost jobs in the failing manufacturing industry in the 1970s economic downturn (Ward, 1998). An intense sense of rootlessness found expression in 'the discontinuum of AfroDiasporic Futurism' (Eshun, 1998: – 003). In the case of George Clinton's Detroit-based spaced-out funk, Afro-centric imagery of Egypt's pyramid gods was combined with the idea that the black man came from outer space (Toop, 1995). Hereby the Afro hair-do signified black pride, in a counter-cultural let-your-hair-grow manner, as well as the psychedelic antennae that reached out into the universe.

Global trance

More convulsive psychedelic sentiments were tried out in an excessively raw form in the early to mid 1980s in Chicago. Ron Hardy's legendary drug fuelled marathon DJ sessions, a mixture of raw edgy electronic weirdness, including industrial punk funk from the USA and Europe, enabled the birth of acid house in 1997. This African-American deconstructed post-human form of house music, exemplified by Phuture's seminal *Acid Trax* (1987), inspired a generation of producers, including the techno creators of Detroit, the rave generation in the UK and a range of trance tribes around the globe.

As a genre, trance can be described as an, initially German, abstracted marriage between techno and house music. Trance is favoured in the early 21st century at rave-styled events (often 'psychedelic'), as well as by super club DJs (the 'epic' version). It exists in parallel fashion in a wide variety of geographical locations, Goa, Bangkok, Australia, Japan, Germany, the UK, South Africa, Israel, Greece, and in a diversity of spaces, from legislated clubs to squat and countryside parties. Alongside other forms of techno, during the late 1990s trance became a dominant genre at the Love Parade in Berlin. This is a yearly techno driven political demonstration celebrating the re-unification of Germany, attracting over a million young people in one day by the end of the 1990s. Another example can be found in the new age realm; Earthdance is a yearly trance event, inspired by Tibetan Buddhist pacifism, that takes place in 45 countries, from London to San Francisco to Melbourne, all venues linked by internet, promoting world peace. Meanwhile, UK based dominant dance music magazine 'DJ' showed in its yearly poll of October 2002 that a significant number of non-English DJs were applauded for their trance sets. Since it is extremely difficult for non-Anglo-American artists to break into the British music world, this shows the overwhelming effectiveness of trance across national borders. It could be seen as a global dominant for raves and post-rave events, and is also stylistically incorporated into the corporate pop aesthetic.

Trance is extremely functional; it only makes sense within the specific ritual of DJ-led, rave-styled dance gatherings. In addition to a relentless industrial machine aesthetic (whether psychedelic or epic), the pulsating house beat and seamless disco mixing, it features a hypnotising tonality. House's melodic content and groin moving funk bass lines have been stripped and replaced by repetitive half-note shifts that leave the listener in a perpetual state of body-denying suspense, while, occasionally, a randomised sequence weaves its psychedelic squelches through the mass of electronic sound. Skilfully manipulated by the DJ at a dance event, the tracks glide into each other, deleting individual differences between them. Typically for the structure of trance, breaks from the bass drum pulse are programmed, as a rest from the physical exhaustion; here dancers can ritually predict a build-up of suspense, as a succession of chords elevates the spirit and the arms. A euphoric catharsis is produced (every time!) when the pulse of the 4/4 bass kick drum (its mechanical heart beat) returns, literally producing a 'kick', an adrenaline rush. The effect is comparable to a roller coaster ride, where the car is pulled to its highest point, people bursting with suspense, higher, higher... and then let loose to the forces of gravity with thundering abandon. From there, the beat carries on, and on, seemingly endless (until the next euphoric break), producing a temporal sense of a forever present. This experience, artificial and machine-like as it may be, is perceived as transparently natural and tribal, somehow acutely pre-historic. For example, in the context of an Australian setting for trance, Cole and Hannan's interviewee remarked in 1995:

> (l)ike the aborigines, aeons ago, that contemplated the planetsphere, whilst hitting their sticks, blowing thru a hollowed out pipe (ie a didjeridu). These open-air, wilderness, tribelic, pagan-like parties (rituals) are along the line of primordial communion (*original spelling*, 1997: 5).

Sacrificial cyborg

The very dancing to house music at dedicated dance gatherings is ritualistic, in open-air events as well as in urban settings. I would like to propose that this ritual context revolves, in the case of techno, around the merging, psychedelic, sexual, spiritual relationship with technology, especially ICT, in a post-industrial society. Bataille (1994) argues in *Theory of Religion* that humanity defines itself in separation from the non-human, from objects or things. He then proposes, inspired by the Aztec death cult of human sacrifice, that in death or in destruction of the object, the thing/animal/body releases its spirit. Therefore, through sacrifice, the object-as-thing becomes intimate to the subject, the self, in a spiritual sense. Adapting this idea may help understand interface spirituality as provided by techno on the dance floor. When being conscious of the self, this is an imagined object of our observation. By suspending that particular object, the subject ceases to be. As the dancer 'gives up', as it is said, their 'body and soul' to the rhythmical music, there is a temporary destruction of the imaginary self.

As self-consciousness disappears, the dancer enters into a spiritual world, filled with impressions produced through the music. For example, techno can, at times, feel like a forceful technological cyclone wrapping our beings. In the excesses of gabba ('gabber house', an originally Dutch form of extremely fast 'industrial' techno), a masochistic serenity is produced when the pain of industrial pounding noise leads to comforting numbness. Meanwhile, deep house, with its analogue sounding textures and more human pace, melts us subjectively into the dancing crowd. Roused by sensory over-stimulation, a dancer may be overcome by a state of trance, ranging from emotional/orgasmic ecstasy to indeed a type of spirit possession (Rouget, 1985). Trance especially seems to be made for this purpose.

At the peak of the night

This peak-experience is a trip into the void: time, space and sensory input fragmenting and collapsing, yet held together by the repetitive beat; suspended, the spiritual hedonist is rendered speechless and unable to articulate; being everything and nothing; part of the all; complete, yet empty. 'Zero is immense', notes Land, in the context of Bataille: '(t)he nihil of annihilation is the nothing from which creation brings forth the being' (Land, 1992: 101). The techno DJ can function as a type of shaman, taking the congregation on a journey of speed, in some cases with peaks and lulls, but mostly faster and faster into the void and to the other side of the night. It is only before and after the nothingness of the peak-experience, that this unbearably ungraspable gap is filled by normalising discourse, like domesticating a divine monster. In this case I would like to suggest that techno and its subgenres, such as trance, acts out, or metaphorically articulates, the very ICT that affects and, for some, threatens to undermine everyday social identities. We act out our becoming cyborg in our convulsive dance into the void, filling that void in turn with ways to connect and make sense of this experience. This can be a techno-pagan post-historic or a more refined spiritual feeling, abstract and indefinable, zen-like.

In techno mutations like trance (German origin) and gabba, the 4/4 beat of house and disco takes on a Teutonic 'motorik' (Reynolds, 2000: 31), a metronome piston noise of industrial machines, seemingly reinstating a nostalgic masculinity of industrial modernity. This rigid machine beat was developed, according to Reynolds, by German bands like Neu! in the 1970s:

> Krautrock brought into focus an idea that had been latent in rock (...) that the rhythmic essence of rock – what made it different from jazz – was a kind of machine like compulsion ... There was a spiritual aspect to all this, sort of *Zen and the Art of Motorik Maintenance*: the idea that true joy isn't liberation from work, but exertion and fixation, a trance-like state of immersion in the process, regardless of outcome (33).

It is through combination with this industrial rock aesthetic that techno has gained its global popularity. The 'protestant' North European work ethic, arguably underlying the first industrial revolution, is here translated into music and leisure. At dance events featuring trance, techno-house and rave inspired dance gatherings, one sees this work taken to an extreme, in order to reach a peak experience: the complex demanding logistics of a night out, the pushing of the body beyond endurance in physical exercise, sleep deprivation and drug use.

The experience of 'freedom' from the self is thereby a complex production of a particular embodied self through the engagement of a range of practices of self-production, which are enabled by the historical assemblage of post-disco and post-rave dance music and their specific structural contexts. Fikentscher (2000), for example, has produced an ethno-musicological account of how black gay dancers on New York City's underground dance-floors work hard to reach their peak-experience through a physical engagement with underground disco and deep house. Dance drugs may enhance such complex production of the (free) self; in the contexts of raves and rave inspired clubs in London, Pini (2001) and Malbon (1999) provide detailed descriptions of how their interviewees work hard to reach a drug induced peak-experience and to maintain that experience.

Various dance cultural scenes seem to display a 'macho' atmosphere around drug use, where it can be important to show off how much battering the (imagined 'once warrior') body can endure. Dance drugs aid a dancing cyborg identity, as the chemicals enhance the nervous system to mesh with the technological sensibilities that techno offers. Like legal drugs in our post-industrial society, dance drugs work to abolish an awareness of the body, or rather, to unmake an awareness of its limitations. Dance drugs are body technologies, with a profound effect on the mind, on subjectivity. Yet, the body itself is subjectively disregarded in this process, just as '(t)he denial of the body ... is but symptomatic of the lack of mind body integration within society at large' (McNiff in Barrett, 2002: 119). Mind-altering drugs temporarily enhance required mental faculties, at the cost of the organism that supports it. Not only is the self tampered with subjectively, in some social environments (such as the post-industrial north of the UK); one also sees a tendency towards (an almost) physical self-annihilation.

As body technologies, drugs help the user to plug in, jack into, or merge with, a matrix of aural, tactile and visual sensations. The experience of the matrix is kind of 'pre-historic' on an individual level, a vaguely remembered feeling that came before the conscious formation of the subject. Especially in enclosed environments, such as clubs, the warm, moist bodies of the crowd within a dark space or distorted visual field produce an environment akin to the womb. As the amplified pulse of bass drum inescapably enters and embraces the body in a tactile manner, it seems to acts like a mother's heart beat. In the context of popular music, Middleton calls this pulse the 'primal metaphor' (Middleton, 1990: 288). This regularity, embracing heartbeat and 'motorik' at once, provides an androgynous 'pre-Oedipal' framework (Rietveld, 1993), into which the dancer loses a sense of self, however temporarily, whilst feeling safe.

Such a repetitive musical structure synchronises the crowd, affecting the body's own pulses, which can produce a profound experience of transcendental universality, where time seems suspended, a forever here and now (Bradley, 2001). The continuous exercise, sometimes for hours on end, may stop an awareness of the limited body and self. This is combined with the ritualistic predictability of the DJ-led dance event. In the context of techno paganism, Davis observes that 'ritual passes the intellect and stimulates (...) on a more subliminal level' (1998: 183). This is a powerful cocktail, slotting together perfectly in its affect on a subjectivity similar to the one found in Baudrillard's exploration of the disappearing dialectic of 'alternative strategy' in postmodernity: 'The sublime has passed into the subliminal' (Baudrillard, 1987: 54).

As the crowd moves in unison, the individual, at times, gains a subjective experience of being absorbed and becoming part of a larger timeless organism, of bodies, music, machine aesthetic, clearly tactile and acoustic but blurry in the visual field. As techno music and post-rave dance gatherings foreground their technological imagery as an abstraction, this metaphorical 'womb' has a machine-like quality, a matrix in terms of both womb and grid system, making the experience of self-annihilation and rebirth in the context of a machine aesthetic a deeply spiritual cyborgian suture. It is at the same time a sacrifice of the body-as-organic as well as of the self-as-thing. Hooked chemically and sensorily into the machine pulse of techno (Plant, 1993), the post-industrial alienated individual sacrifices her or him-self ritually to achieve a spiritual transition into a cyborg-like subjectivity. This is the peak-experience, one that does not always materialise, but one that is nevertheless profound and unspeakable when it occurs.

Man–machine

Although thousands of girls and women attend rave-related events (Pini, 2001; Rajandran, 2000), the 'man' in the techno-based man-machine relationship is quite male. A post-industrial crisis in masculinity seems to have been produced due to a dread of the obsolete male body, no longer needed in heavy industries. For example, in a study of heterosexuality in the UK, it was found that: 'In the social construction of heterosexuality it is the male who is embodied – in his body – and the female who is disembodied' (Holland et al: 117-118). Yet, the physical assertion of the male body seems to be denied in increasingly ICT enhanced work environments. At the same time, arguably, a feminisation of the labour force occurs (Morley, 1996; Springer, 1996), whereby it is more attractive to hire (lower paid) women under casual work contracts. Meanwhile, feminism has had a head start in assessing gender roles compared to debates on changed masculinity, leaving men discursiveless prepared for their changing work function and the subjectivity this produces. Almost nostalgic for a futurist past, techno music seems to channel this gendered identity crisis.

Men – black, white, Asian, straight, gay, teenage, middle-aged – ener-
getically dance to a range of post-human techno versions on a mutated
disco dance floor. This may seem a strange way to reconfirm one's
masculinity. Unlike couple dancing, disco group dancing is historically
associated with the feminine, with women and gays. House music,
providing the dominant structure for techno, developed in the 1980s
from the underground disco that structured highly sexualised gay
scenes (Fikentscher, 1999; Thomas, 1995). However, drug use has physically 'loosened up' the heterosexual masculine body. Especially the
entactogenic (dance) drug Ecstasy (MDMA) seems to have had an
androgynising,[6] even infantilising (Rietveld, 1993), psychological effect
on its users (Henderson, 1997). Nevertheless, such androgenising effects
are not complete, while the popularity and availability of Ecstasy has
been uneven since the days of UK raves around 1990. During the 1990s,
phallocentric heterosexuality has clearly re-emerged within a party
structure that initially undermined it. As a result, at heterosexual male
dominated techno-house and trance events, the homosocial gaze is
deflected from fellow dancers towards the DJ. The profoundness of this
situation becomes clear when one realises that the DJ is not particularly
exciting to watch (someone wearing headphones, usually too absorbed
with the equipment and music selection to look up). In fact, the DJ is
sometimes even invisible (because of smoke and visual effects, or
because the DJ is too far away). At techno events, dancing can be
regarded as a male bonding, (Rajandran, 2000) comparable to football
matches (Verhagen, 2001).[7] Here one finds an environment that favours
a subject-object relationship, where the object is found in the technological metaphors of the dance music. Such events provide spaces for
men to experience a sense of wholeness undisturbed by gendered difference. Instead, a technophile fetishisation of potentially threatening
technology takes place (Springer, 1996; Rietveld, 1998a). The man-
machine is a subject-object relationship in which 'the machine' plays a
role in the game of (spiritual) seduction. Not only do dancers give themselves up to the machine metaphors of the music, there is also a
self-absorbed masculine pleasure in taking control over this cyborg relationship, as DJs, producers and programmers (Rietveld, 1998a). If
'subject-object' is spirit, it is also the experience of fetishised orgasm;
this is what makes techno sexy to some.

Social and industrial relations are changing for women as well; they
too attempt to negotiate their relationship to the emerging 'paradigm' of

ICT. Despite a male majority in the organisation of techno events, there is an increasing involvement by women, as DJs and, sometimes, as producers. Between 1997 and 2002, up to 10% of Top 100 DJs in the yearly UK based 'DJ' (magazine) poll have been female and the most successful ones play techno. Reactions from crowds are mixed, from male hecklers as well as supporters to friendly female admiration. However, there is a twist in the sexual politics of techno, exactly because the visual focus has moved from the people on the dance floor to the DJ. There have been reports of women on the dance floor who have displayed confusion when being led by a female DJ. Men, on the other hand, especially the dancers rather than the promoters, increasingly seem to welcome female DJs in the domain of techno. Huyssen (1986) has suggested in context of the feminised robot in Fritz Lang's 1926 film *Metropolis*, that 'the vamp in the machine' normalises the male experience of new technology. The potentially spiritual experience of cyborgian merging is thereby positioned in terms of a male-defined heterosexual sexuality. In the case of female techno DJs, the focus of male heterosexual energy on the female DJ powerfully deflects the idea of homo-eroticism in a homo-social environment, enabling both male bonding as well as a sexualised, yet spiritual, man-machine bonding in a time of social transition.

The techno/trance interface offers a precarious liberation to women, it seems, either in the form of androgeny or of a sexual metaphor for technology. A cyborg subject position is a 'body without organs' to borrow Deleuze and Guattari's concept in Potts, who summarises Irigaray's critique of this idea, in that it 'amounts to the annihilation of female embodiment before a female-defined corporeality even exists' (2001: 158). Although female techno fans undeniably exist, they are outnumbered by male fans. Many women seem to be more into the social scene than into techno's technological metaphors, as subjects relating with other subjects: the people; the sharing of dance drug experiences; the possible subcultural attitudes; the mutual engagement with music through dancing (especially the intricate techno footwork called 'Melbourne Shuffle' in Australia, a speeded up mix of Irish and jazz dance steps); the socially produced fashions. In short, women seem to engage in a range of experiences other than a masculine ritual of self-annihilation.

Communal soul

Irigaray (2002) has suggested on the basis of comparative European socio-linguistic research with boys and girls that the definition of human self in relationship between subject and object, as Bataille proposed, is quite masculine. Instead, she found that girls define themselves more in relationship with other subjects, rather than with objects or things; rather than a masculine subject-object relationship, a 'feminine' subject-subject relationship was noted. Similarly, in contemporary dance culture it is striking, for example, that specialist record shop owners and promoters alike have noticed that most women prefer more melodious and embodied forms of dance music. Such music sets up a relationship with the human world, rather than with the post-human world of things. This includes soulful vocal club music and deep house music, which the techno fraternity often dismisses as 'handbag' music, referring to an accessory associated with the feminised realm.

Like soul music itself, the musical skills and attitudes of many African-American house music singers and producers, male and female, are rooted culturally in gospel music. For the current discussion of gendered engagement with dance culture, it is telling that women represent a matriarchal majority in gospel based church communities, in the USA as well as in the UK. In gospel, harmonies between the voices articulate an embracing community, and chord progressions 'lift up the spirit'. It is as if energy is channelled from the rhythmically moving lower part of the body into the cerebral. Pratt (1990) has suggested that as an overwhelming soundscape, acting as a spiritual re-energiser, Gospel music can be part of 'a larger strategy of survival' (49). For those who feel they have been dislocated in a political sense, made homeless in more ways than one, intense dance parties that engage in a subject-subject relationship can provide a strong sense of community.

In the case of old-school 1980s African-American and Latino house music, instead of directing one's devotion to Jesus, the gospel inspired focus was to physical love and on a sense of hope for the (repressed) community (Fikentscher, 2000). Phrases like 'someday', 'we'll make it to the Promised Land', 'holding on' which can be found in African-American deep house are all directly related to the hopeful musings of gospel. Orgasm was sometimes bluntly celebrated in house lyrics from Chicago (Rietveld, 1998) making the profane sacred in the process. Here one finds a celebration of freedom from repression, from limitations imposed by discourses of racism, homophobia and/or sexism: '(t)he sacred is (...) a privileged moment of communal unity, a moment of the convulsive communication of what is ordinarily stifled' (Bataille,

1985: 242). Again, such experience of unshackling can produce a peak-experience, of losing a sense of material boundaries, lifting oneself into the spiritual realm.

Although aimed at a gay crowd, the Chicago house scene also attracted male and female heterosexuals, whereby it was 'hip to be gay' in order to gain access to the intense fun of the party (Rietveld, 1998a: 21). Kevin Saunderson, part of the seminal (heterosexual) brotherhood of Detroit techno innovators, observed the following about DJ Knuckles' early 1980s sessions at Chicago's The Warehouse, where the sound system was allegedly fantastic:

> I'm sixteen years old, don't know anything about gay people, so I'm sitting on the wall the whole night, you know, guarding my butt and everything, right. And anyway, after a while … you start to see the people having fun and getting into the music and these people (are) just so free. I mean, just animated, arms all over the place, jumping on top of speakers, dancing with this person, prancing over this side, on the wall, climbing the walls on top, above 'em (Bidder, 2001: 18-19).

This statement illustrates the uneasy, yet curious, relationship between gay club culture and heterosexual masculinity. The dance style described was called 'jacking', a dance floor variant of copulating movements. The term itself, though, is a mechanistic subject-object metaphor, creeping into the early house imagination, preparing for a discursive development towards techno. People jacked with each other to the music, with walls and with the speakers (Bidder, 2001; Rietveld, 1998a).

Deep house is tantalisingly tactile in its deep penetration and full embrace of the body through its loudly amplified low-frequency bass lines. The 4/4 'foot' of the bass drum, mostly an analogue sound, has a warm 'feel', while its African-American and Latino syncopations move the body in a variety of directions, in contrast to the uni-directional macho 'motorik' of its European counterpart, trance. In the dark space of the dance floor, the dancer gives in to the musical spirit of communal intimacy, a 'subject-subject' spirituality, perhaps even to something comparable, Davis' idea of analogue soul (1999). There are some forms of techno which manage to achieve this as well, mostly African-American and mostly a crossover with deep house's bass lines and soulful analogue feel. In current deep house, deep in its emotional response, the sexual is often less explicit. While the 'motorik' accompanies a possession trance with the machine as its imagined 'animal' (Rouget, 1985), deep house's orgasmic ecstasy articulates a relationship with a community. In both cases, however, such rituals strengthen vulnerable identities in times of change. Gay club cultures and African-American forms of dance music have pioneered in this, as subjectivities which have been under siege for so long that powerful forms of dance music and partying have been produced to heal this sense of unease, this continuous need for a rite of passage.

Outro: embodied spirituality

Although the above discussion, addressing techno's post-industrial gender politics and its production of a spiritual peak-experience, may suffer from generalisations for the benefit of argument, a common theme emerges in the experience of the relationship between human and machine in post-industrial societies in globalised parts of the world. This experience is worked out through a range of interfaces. Techno, as an interface, works powerfully when combined with the ritual music of house music in a post-rave setting. A subjective state of a peak-experience is produced by the discursive realm of social-economic shifts, gendered sexuality, racial identity, musical structure, the DJ's programming of the night and the swaying mass of bodies, at times enhanced by dance drugs. The aimed-for peak-experience may not always be reached and may vary widely in terms of intensity. In addition, as the relationship to the machine in post-industrial societies varies, a techno-house post-rave ritual will take on a variety of additional local meanings.

Importantly, what the above discussion shows is that as the relationship with the other shifts, the spirit, the experience of an unrestrained relationship between self and other, does so as well. Despite its transcendental and universal appearance, the spirit is produced in and by the material and historical context of the subject. Therefore, in contrast to a traditional conceptualisation that splits spirit and matter, the spirit is always embodied. Subjectivity is hereby not a rarefied and an individual matter, but is socially and culturally produced in specific complex material and historical contexts, of which the above may be regarded as a small case study.

Notes

1. The body is subjected to discourse and thereby becomes a subject, gaining a sense of subjectivity in the process.

2. 'Rave subculture' is a crude shorthand, used by Sylvan in a wide sense of the word, going historically back to the seminal 1980s Chicago house scene (Rietveld, 1988a). There are some problems with this phrase. Firstly, 'the' implies a homogeneous subculture, while in reality it covers a wide range of related localised scenes, musical histories, technologies and similar post-industrial angst in need of repeated rite-of-passage (as this article will argue). Secondly, the term 'subculture' can be problematic, in that it presupposes a stable social identity; instead it seems more useful to conceive of an engagement with a dance scene as an unstable process.

3. Subjectivity is not an individual rarefied essence but, rather, produced through a set of cultural and communicative structures collectively known as the discursive field, which itself changes historically within specific material contexts.

4. Critical cultural studies is an inter-disciplinary field within humanities and social science, researching and analysing culture in terms of its hegemonic structures. Employing ethnographic methods as well as analysis of the discursive construction of identity, this study field provides a critical anthropology of one's own culture and its subjective experience. Yearly book reviews can be found in *The Year's Work in Critical and Cultural Theory* (McGowan, 1994-2002), while a solid historical introduction can be found in Turner (1996).

5. USA, Belgium, the Netherlands, Germany, Norway, Spain, Portugal, Goa, Bali, Thailand, Tokyo, Singapore, Melbourne, Sydney.

6. The term 'enactogenic' indicates an increase in tactility and empathy. This enables the user of MDMA to immerse, for example, into the audio-tactile environment of the dance floor (Rietveld, 1993; 1998a). A subjective state emerges that finds sensuality in every fibre of its being. With so much gained, there is nothing to lose; androgyny is thereby not the same as emasculation, but rather a moment where fear of lack evaporates.

7. Before football matches were 'feminised' (in the UK), creating a family-friendly environment with seating and additional entertainment, such events, with their standing terraces and swaying crowds, were very much geared towards male fans.

References

Barr, T. (2000) *Techno. The Rough Guide*. London: Penguin.

Barrett, E. (2002) 'Knowing and feeling: new subjectivities and aesthetic experience'. *International Journal of Critical Psychology* 5: 113-123.

Bataille, G. (1985) 'The Sacred', in A. Stoekl (Ed.), *Visions of Excess: Selected Writings, 1927-1939*, A. Stoekl with C. R. Lovitt and D. M. Leslie Jr (trans.) Manchester: Manchester University Press.

Bataille, G. (1989) *Theory of Religion*. R. Hurley (trans) New York: Zone Books.

Baudrillard, J. (1987) *The Ecstasy of Communication*, New York: Semiotext(e).

Bidder, S. (2001) *Pump Up The Volume*. London: Channel 4 Books.

Bradley, B. S. (2001) 'An approach to synchronicity: from synchrony to synchronisation'. *International Journal of Critical Psychology* 2: 119-141.

Cole, F. and Hannan, M. (1997) 'Goa Trance'. *Perfect Beat*, Issue 3, Vol .3: 1-14.

Collin, M. with Godfrey, J. (1997) *Altered State: The Story of Ecstasy Culture and Acid House*. London: Serpent's Tail.

Davis, E (1998) *TechGnosis: Myth, Magic and Mysticism in the Age of Information*. London: Serpent's Tail.

Eagleton, T. (1990) *The Ideology of the Aesthetic*. Oxford: Basil Blackwell.

Eshun, K. (1998) *More Brilliant Than The Sun: Adventures In Sonic Fiction*. London: Quartet.

Fikentscher, K. (2000) *'You Better Work!' Underground Dance Music in New York City*. Hanover and London: Wesleyen University Press.

Foucault, M. (1984) *The History of Sexuality: An Introduction*. London: Peregrine.

Garrat, S. (1998) *Adventures in Wonderland: A Decade of Club Culture*. London: Headline.

Goodwin, A. (1990) 'Sample and Hold; pop music in the digital age of reproduction'. In S. Frith and A. Goodwin (Eds.), *On Record; Rock, Pop and the Written Word*. London: Routledge.

Henderson, S. (1997) *Ecstasy: Case Unsolved*. London: Pandora.

Holland, J, Ramazanoglu, C., Sharpe, S., Thomson, R. (1998) *The Male in the Head: Young People, Heterosexuality and Power*. London: The Tufnell Press.

Huyssen, A. (1986) 'The vamp and the machine'. In: *After The Great Divide: Modernism, Mass Culture and Postmodernism*. Basingstoke and London: The Macmillan Press.

Kumar, K. (1995) *From Post-Industrial to Post-Modern Society: New Theories of the Contemporary World*. London: Blackwell.

Land, N. (1992) *The Thirst for Annihilation: George Bataille and Virulent Nihilism*. London: Routledge.

Malbon, B. (1999) *Clubbing: Dancing, Ecstasy and Vitality*. London: Routledge.

McGowan, K. (1998-2001) *The Year's Work in Critical and Cultural Theory*. The English Association: Blackwell and Oxford UP.

Middleton, R. (1990) *Studying Popular Music*. Milton Keynes: Open University Press.

Morley, D. (1996) 'Postmodernism: A Rough Guide'. In J. Curran, D. Morley and V. Walkerdine (Eds.), *Cultural Studies and Communication*. London: Edward Arnold.

Pini, M. (2001) *Club Cultures and Female Subjectivity: The Move from Home to House*. Basingstoke: Palgrave.

Plant, S. (1993) 'Building The Hacienda'. *Hybrid* 1: 3-11.

Pott, A. (2001) 'The Body without Orgasm: becoming erotic with Deleuze and Guattari'. *International Journal of Critical Psychology* 3: 140-164.

Pratt, R. (1990) *Rhythm and Resistance: explorations in the political uses of popular music*. London: Praeger.

Rajandran, S. (2000) 'The Female in Rave Culture: The Adventures of Galactic Canary in Buenos Aires', a Richter Fellowship proposal, supervised by J. Tobin, University of California, Los Angeles.

Reynolds, S. (1998) *Energy Flash: A Journey Through Rave Music and Dance Culture*, London: Macmillan.

Reynolds, S. (2000) 'Kosmik dance: krautrock and its legacy'. In Shapiro, P. (ed.) *Modulations: A History of Electronic Music, Throbbing Words on Sound.* New York: D.A.P./Distributed Art Publishers.

Rietveld, H. (1993), 'Living the Dream'. In Steve Redhead (ed.) *Rave Off, Politics and Deviance in Contemporary Youth Culture.* Aldershot: Avebury/Ashgate.

Rietveld, H. (1998a), *This Is Our House: House Music, Cultural Spaces and Technologies,* Aldershot: Ashgate.

Rietveld, H. (1998b) 'Repetitive Beats: free parties and the politics of contemporary DiY dance culture in Britain'. In G. McKay (ed.), *DiY Culture: Party and Protest in Nineties Britain,* London: Verso.

Robins, K. and Webster, F. (1999) *Time of the Technoculture: From the Information Society to the Virtual Life,* London: Routledge.

Rouget, G. (1985) *Music and Trance: A Theory of the Relations between Music and Possession,* Chicago: The University of Chicago Press.

Savage, J. (1996) 'Machine Soul: A History of Techno'. In *Time Travel. From The Sex Pistols to Nirvana: Pop, Media and Sexuality, 1977-96* (first published in Village Voice, Rock & Roll Quarterly, summer 1993). J. Savage (ed.) London: Chatto & Windus.

Sicko, D. (1999) *Techno Rebels: The Renegades of Electronic Funk,* New York: Billboard.

Springer, C. (1996) *Electronic Eros: Bodies and Desire in the Postindustrial Age,* London: The Athlone Press.

Sylvan, R. (2002), *Traces of Spirit: The Religious Dimensions of Popular Music,* New York and London: New York University Press.

Thomas, A. (1995) 'The house the kids built: the gay black imprint on American dance music'. In C. K. Creekmur and A. Doty, *Out in Culture: Gay, Lesbian and Queer Essays on Popular Culture* (first published in Out/Look, summer 1989), London: Cassell.

Thornton, S. (1996) *Club Cultures: Music, Media and Subcultural Capital,* Cambridge: Polity.

Todorov, T. (1984) *Mikhail Bakhtin: The Dialogical Principle,* Manchester: Manchester University Press.

Toop, D. (1995) *Ocean of Sound: Aether Talk, Ambient Sound and Imaginary Worlds,* London: Serpent's Tail.

Turner, G. (1996), *British Cultural Studies: An Introduction,* London: Routledge.

Verhagen, S. (2001) 'To Be or To Wannabe: Over Gabbers, Jeugdculturen en de Media', Sociology Master's dissertation, Supervisor F. van Wel, University Utrecht.

Ward, B. (1998) *Just My Soul Responding: Rhythm and Blues, Black Consciousness and Race Relations,* London: UCL Press.

Yurick, S. (1985) *Behold Metatron, the Recording Angel,* New York: Semiotext(e).

Creative knowledge

Ann Game and Andrew Metcalfe

Abstract

This piece sets out some of the central ideas involved in a relational logic, the basis of creative knowledge. These include: dialogue, presence, flesh of the world, participation, the whole, infinitude, mystery, love and implication. Whereas post-structuralists deconstruct binary oppositions through a third term, relationality involves an infinitude that cannot be counted. It is an experience of presence.

Introduction

In 1996 we published a book, *Passionate Sociology*, which offered a post-structuralist and deconstructive account of sociological knowledge, drawing heavily on writers like Barthes, Cixous, Derrida, Foucault and Irigaray. In this piece we want to outline the key conceptual concerns of a more recent book *The Mystery of Everyday Life*, in particular drawing out the significance of relationality for understandings of knowledge. Between *Passionate Sociology* and the new book there has been a conceptual shift from an understanding of knowledge based on desire to one based on love, together with a developing appreciation of the spirit in knowledge and learning. The central idea in *The Mystery of Everyday Life* is that the site of life is in the *interbeing* of relations, and that, consequently, a living creative knowledge emerges in and through relationships, through dialogue.

The exercise we are offering here is constrained: it is, loosely speaking, an exercise in self-criticism, a reflection on the issues which *Passionate Sociology* was unable to recognise, enunciate or think through. But we hope this initial constraint has a benefit for readers, for, by articulating the heart- and gut-felt desires, defences and connections that underlay the poststructuralism of *Passionate Sociology*, we hope to help readers recognise the deeper workings of other examples of poststructuralism. We stress, though, that this task of extending from the poststructuralism of *Passionate Sociology* to the work of other poststructuralists is one that readers will have to make for themselves. It is an intellectual exercise that requires a heart-felt sense of the reader's own implication. We stress too that the change we are discussing here is not apostatic: rather than reporting on a shift from error to a correct line, we are continuing a process of dialogue. Far from being abandoned, *Passionate Sociology* continues to teach us about the implications of *The Mystery of Everyday Life*.

Dialogue

The physicist David Bohm provides a clear account of the dia-logic of dialogue. Bohm found that his interests in a folded universe could be pursued through and within everyday dialogue, which he saw as the unfolding of meaning. Here is an example of his understanding of dialogue:

> The weekend began with the expectation that there would be a series of lectures and informative discussions with emphasis on content. It gradually emerged that something more important was actually involved – the awakening of the process of dialogue itself as a free flow of meaning among all the participants. In the beginning, people were expressing fixed positions, which they were tending to defend, but later it became clear that to maintain the feeling of friendship in the group was much more important than to hold any position. Such friendship has an impersonal quality in the sense that its establishment does not depend on a close personal relationship between participants. A new kind of mind thus begins to come into being which is based on the development of a common meaning that is constantly transforming in the process of dialogue. People are no longer primarily in opposition, nor can they said to be interacting, rather they are participating in this pool of common meaning which is capable of constant development and change. In this development the group has no pre-established purpose, though at each moment a purpose that is free to change may reveal itself. The group thus begins to engage in a new dynamic relationship in which no speaker is excluded, and in which no particular content is excluded ... [G]oing further along these lines would open up the possibility of transforming

not only the relationship between people, but even more, the very nature of consciousness in which these relationships arise (Bohm, 1985: 175).

Dialogue, then, is not based on interaction, exchange or the reconciliation of different positions, for all these conventional logics imply the persistence of individual selves and distinct positions. Instead, dialogue implies a 'new kind of mind', a form of consciousness that isn't located in any or even in all of the individual participants, even though it operates through them.

Within a dialogue no *one* possesses knowledge. Indeed, a mutual unknowing is the basis of dialogue's inherent creativity. Only when the positional laws of identity are suspended can life become inspired, allowing us to enunciate ideas that are ours but which we couldn't have said or even remembered by ourselves, allowing us to carry the dialogue at the same time as it carries us, and allowing the play of differences and similarities out of which the new emerges.

Desire

In *Passionate Sociology*, following French feminist and post-structuralist thought, we took the undoing of the Hegelian scenario of desire as our starting point. But despite all our attempts to refigure desire, the primacy of separate terms remained: self, identity and linearity are unavoidable where there is desire.

The Hegelian scenario goes like this: knowledge is always ultimately about the self; it involves a desire for self-knowledge, to know oneself finitely, as an independent identity. But since we live in a world of others who are different from ourselves, our search for self-certainty compels us to know these others, to master their otherness. Hence desire: a yearning towards that other that we would master.

Desiring self-certainty means that we don't simply want to know something for its difference, but to make it the same as ourself, a mirror. Our desire is to negate the other's difference from us, for as long as there is difference, we can't be certain of our self-sameness or our masterful independence. And so, in our desire to stand alone, we deny our dependence on others, our relations with others.

As Hegel points out, this negating brings to light the very dependencies we would deny. This has been the crucial point for contemporary theorists, who see in this undoing the possibility of an alternative, positive structure of desire, one in which the relation and difference could be acknowledged. Cixous, for example, speaks of a desire which 'would keep the *other* alive and different' (1986: 79), and of a movement towards the other in a proximity that avoids merger or appropriation.

However, we are still presuming the primacy of separate terms and a linear, Euclidean logic when we talk this way of a 'self moving towards', of being in a state of 'becoming', of 'never arriving', of an end endlessly deferred. The basic formulation of desire – self and other – refers to two terms that interact with each other, rather than a relational logic. It is the intersubjective possibilities of these *two* terms presumed by desire, that is often mistaken for relation.

Love: I-Thou

'Love is *between I* and *Thou* ... Love is responsibility of an *I* for a *Thou*.'
Buber, 1958: 14-15

In contrast with notions of intersubjectivity, Martin Buber's 'I-Thou' relation refers to a primary relationality: '*I-Thou* establishes the world of relation' (1958: 6). 'I become through my relation to the *Thou*; as I become *I*, I say *Thou*' (1958: 11). I and Thou have no bounds; they are not limited by identity; they are neither subject nor object. 'When Thou is spoken, there is no thing': in each Thou we address the eternal and infinite Thou (1958: 4-6).

I-Thou is a meeting, a direct, spontaneous encounter, not filtered through the preconceptions, categorisations or comparisons that characterise the subject-object relation of 'I-It'. This meeting is recognition of our ethical implication: I am necessarily connected with the other, to whom I am bound to respond. Response, for Buber, is the foundation of responsibility. And in order to be able to listen and respond we need to be empty of our self. We need to live our relationality, our interbeing.

This listening is the basis of knowledge. Through dialogue 'it is possible to meet and know the other in his concrete uniqueness and not just as a content of one's experience' (Friedman, 2002: xiii). In order to experience difference, we must let go of self and identity. In other words, this way of knowing is founded on a compassionate, ego-less love.

The unknowable

Deconstructions of Hegel focus on the impossibility of a complete mastery, knowing the total: there is always an excess that is the unknown. Logically, this unknown is elsewhere, eluding us in an endless deferral that produces a restless 'never settling' movement (Cixous 1986). Thus, despite the undoing of mastery, a desiring knowledge is still governed by an end.

In contrast, knowledge based on an I-Thou relationship is a *meeting* with the unknowable. It is an experience of presence, occurring, as T.S. Eliot puts it:

> At the still point of the turning world. Neither flesh nor fleshless;
> Neither from nor towards; at the still point, there the dance is,
> But neither arrest nor movement. And do not call it fixity, where past
> and future are gathered. Neither movement from nor towards (*Burnt
> Norton*).

And, in contrast with post-structuralists' 'elsewhere', in an I-Thou relation we experience mystery in the here and now of the everyday:

> I possess nothing but the everyday out of which I am never taken. The
> mystery ... has made its dwelling here where everything happens as it
> happens (Buber, 1966: 18).

Just as the unknowable is not the opposite of the known, something that can switch from unknown to known, the unsayable is not the opposite of the sayable. It is its precondition, the basis of its significance. Thus, Merleau-Ponty (and Castoriadis) say that the impulse to speak comes from

> a void which swells in the already said; a void which is determined in the
> sense that the one who is about to speak knows that there is something
> other and more to be said than what has already been said, but nothing
> positive beyond that fact, beyond the fact that it is not said by what has
> already been said (Castoriadis, 1984: 132).

The things we can say 'lean' on this tangible (swelling) sense of void, which can only be discussed in words but which can never be exhausted or expressed through words. The unutterable and unknowable cannot be represented because they are not thing-like. They are in-finite or no-thing-like. They can, however, be known, through participation.

Flesh of the world

Merleau-Ponty uses the term 'flesh of the world' to describe this experience of participation. We are made of the same stuff as the world, and this, for phenomenologists, is how we know. Since 'we are in the world', part of the 'closely woven fabric' of 'reality', knowing happens within this weave (Merleau-Ponty, 1962: x-xii). 'Immersed in the visible by his body ... the see-er does not appropriate what he sees ... he opens himself to the world ... my body is caught in the fabric of the world' (Merleau-Ponty, 1964: 162-3). We know the world with and through our bodies: 'Things arouse in me a carnal formula of their presence' (Merleau-Ponty, 1964: 164). We are in the world, and the world is in us: relational logic reversibly entwines inside and outside:

> Since things and my body are made of the same stuff, vision must somehow take place in them ... 'Nature is on the inside', says Cezanne. Quality, light, colour, depth, which are there before us, are there only because they awaken an echo in our body and because the body welcomes them (Merleau-Ponty, 1964: 164).

Implication

The ethical implication of this entwining may become clearer through a more specific example. The Buddhist monk Thich Nhat Hanh tells a story of a leaf that illustrates the logic of interbeing:

> One autumn day, I was in a park, absorbed in the contemplation of a very small but beautiful leaf, in the shape of a heart. Its colour was almost red, and it was barely hanging on the branch, nearly ready to fall down. I spent a long time with it, and I asked the leaf a lot of questions. I found out the leaf had been a mother to the tree. Usually we think that the tree is the mother and the leaves are just children, but as I looked at the leaf I saw that the leaf is also a mother to the tree. The sap that the roots take up is only water and minerals, not good enough to nourish the tree, so the tree distributes the sap to the leaves. And the leaves take the responsibility of transforming that rough sap into elaborated sap and, with the help of the sun and gas, sending it back in order to nourish the tree. Therefore, the leaves are also the mother to the tree. And since the leaf is linked to the tree by a stem, the communication between them is easy to see ...
>
> There are hundreds of thousands of stems linking us to everything in the cosmos, and therefore we can be (1988: 24-25).

Thich Nhat Hahn says that the form of 'leaf' is only a part of the leaf; the leaf is also the whole tree; the leaf is in the tree, and the tree is in the leaf. Another way of saying this is 'the leaf and the tree are implicated in each other', as parents and children are. We could also say, following this logic, that in this leaf there are other trees of the past and the future, and other beings too, living now. Furthermore, through this falling leaf we can get a sense of the way in which spring is in autumn, and autumn in spring, life in death, and death in life. Most importantly, if we respond to the leaf we are acknowledging that *our* life and that of the leaf are implicated. We are allowing the leaf to remind us that we are linked to everything in the cosmos.

Interest

When we take an interest in the world, in this leaf, say, we find the world both interesting and interested. *Inter* means between and *esse* means to be. Interest is life between, a sense that is also evoked when we define an interest as a concern. The mutuality and care involved in interest suggest then a very different basis to knowledge than desire's motivation: a humble curiosity and gratitude rather than mastery.

The interest that allows creative knowledge and learning emerges from the infinitude of interbeing. No longer able to distinguish inside and outside, self and other, we find that in attending to the topic of interest we move closer to our own heart. By participating in what we study, independent it-ness is transformed to a Thou-ness. And *we* are necessarily changed in the process.

Inclusion

Whereas the I-It relation is exclusionary, the I-Thou relation is inclusive, as Buber shows:

I CONSIDER A TREE.

I can look on it as a picture: stiff column in a shock of light ...

I can perceive it as movement: flowing veins on clinging, pressing pith, suck of the roots, breathing of the leaves ...

I can classify it in a species and study it as a type ...

I can subdue its actual presence and form so sternly that I recognise it only as an expression of law ...

I can dissipate it and perpetuate it in number ...

In all this the tree remains my object, occupies space and time ...

It can, however, also come about ... that in considering the tree I become bound up in relation to it. The tree is now no longer *It* ...

To effect this it is not necessary for me to give up any of the ways in which I consider the tree. There is nothing from which I would have to turn my eyes away in order to see, and no knowledge that I would have to forget. Rather is everything, picture and movement, species and type, law and number, indivisibly united in this event.

Everything belonging to the tree is in this: its form and structure, its colours and chemical composition, its intercourse with the elements and with the stars, are all present in a single whole (1958:7-8).

In contrast with an *It* or an object, this whole is an infinitude, without bounds or limits, an infinitude that cannot be exhausted by any branch or sum of knowledge. It is important to note, however, that an inclusive logic implies the inclusion of oppositional, exclusive forms of knowledge: 'there is nothing from which I would have to turn my eyes'.

This understanding clearly has implications for the reading practices that are brought to this very article. Academic work relies on Hegelian positional and identificatory exercises, and so we have, for example, set up this article in terms of the poststructuralism of *Passionate Sociology*. Statements made at this level can be assessed for their adequacy in the usual academic ways. But to stay at that level, acting as if our identifications were definitive, is to lose the *life* of the texts we read, to ensure that we never truly *meet* them, that we never truly respond through our implication in them. Whereas some academics are fearful of putting together inappropriate texts, because they come from different nameable traditions, or speak to 'different realities', it seems to us that the identity of a text – or a person – is always emerging, endlessly re-created through open-hearted meetings between I and Thou.

Whole
Whereas a total is the sum of the parts, a whole is greater than the sum of the parts. This difference has enormous implications for understandings of knowledge.

When knowledge is concerned with the total, it studies the parts as separate identities, taking the total to be a big, bounded entity, and assumes the possibility of a complete knowledge. Knowledge concerned with wholes focuses on relations and connections, assuming that specific forms emerge through relations, and that any specific form holds within it the connections of a whole that is infinite: 'a World in a Grain of Sand'. Whereas a total is based on an exclusive logic, a whole is based on an inclusive logic that never presumes to be exhaustive. Knowledge is not an accounting of the world but a celebratory unfolding of the world's possibilities.

Whole and hole are related etymologically. From a totalising view, hole is regarded as vacant emptiness, a gap in knowledge that needs to be filled. From a wholistic view, hole refers to the no-thing that holds all things: nothing *and* everything, empty *and* full. Note also that whole and hole are related to holy. This alerts us to the sacred and spiritual associations of whole: the eternal and the infinite that we know through the part we play.

Infinitude

Post-structuralists deconstruct binary oppositions by adding a third term, but the infinitude of which we speak is not a term that can be counted. Infinity is not just endless counting but an inability to even begin counting. Not an immeasurably long way away, infinitude is right here, right now, the condition of our belonging to the universe and each other. Infinitude is the fundamental quality of all relations.

Within a relation, the other is at once different to me and the same as me, and there is a mysterious incapacity to say where the boundaries of this sameness and difference fall. The other fills me with wonder, yet this wonder teaches me about the strangeness I find in myself. From a post-structuralist perspective, this may seem to involve a restless movement between strange and familiar (Cixous, 1992: 70-71), but the experience of infinitude is one of stillness: strange *and* familiar. The medieval German priest Meister Eckhart had this logic in mind when he insisted that 'The eye with which I see God is the very eye with which God sees me.'

The ability to appreciate Eckhart's insight comes and goes according to the sorts of relations we have, the sorts of boundaries that we perceive. Ordinary life could almost be defined as the times when we live without a conscious sense of infinitude, meaning that we treat life in terms of finite entities and knowable forces acting between them. The challenge, then, is to live with the recognition that our knowledge of finite things must always be implicitly accompanied by a knowledge of the infinite. The in-finite is another word for the no-thing, and nothing, as the famous Taoist phrase has it, is the mother of the five thousand things of the world. The infinite is the often invisible ground that holds the things of the world both together and apart, holding them in relation as parts of creation.

Fluency, inspiration, enthusiasm and effervescence are manifestations of infinitude. The infinite is the source of the aura that gives special depth and wonder to the ordinary knowledge we have of the things of the world.

Presence

Another term for this aura is presence, a term with many associations: being in the presence of; experiencing Steiner's sense of real presences (1989), the tangible no-thingness of mystery; being present, in the present. Presence, rather than representation, is the hallmark of living, creative knowledge.

The present is where life is lived; it is the here and now of non-linear time where 'past and future are gathered':

> The present, and by that is meant not the point which indicates from time to time in our thought merely the conclusion of 'finished time' ... but the real, filled present, exists only in so far as actual presentness, meeting and relation exist. The present arises only in virtue of the fact that the *Thou* becomes present (Buber, 1958:12).

Whereas the I-It of representational knowledge is lived in the past, I-Thou is a relationship of presence.

Experiences such as inspiration and wonder indicate the eternal quality of presence. Think of the sense of 'newness' that we have in experiences of wonder. In those very moments of newness, we have a sense of *I know this already*; *I've always known this*. There is a repetition, but it is a repetition of an event that is *now* rather than in a chronological past: the past we are experiencing, if we can even call it that, is a living present past. In other words, newness is an experience in the eternal now of a new *and* old, now *and* then.

Wonder

It is only when we are present and open, in-relation, that we can experience the mystery of difference, experience a sense of wonder in the face of the world. A great deal of our lives is spent in a narrative mode, living in either the past or the future, striving for progress and knowledge, but the condition of presence is simply 'being present':

> Each of us is encased in an armour which we soon, out of familiarity, no longer notice. There are only moments which penetrate it and stir the soul to sensibility. And when such a moment has imposed itself on us and we then take notice and ask ourselves, 'Has anything particular taken place? Was it not of the kind I meet everyday?' then we may reply to ourselves, 'Nothing particular, indeed, it is like this everyday, only we are not there everyday ...'
>
> The signs of address are not something extraordinary ... they are just what goes on time and again. The waves of the aether roar on always, but for most of the time we have turned off our receivers (Buber, 2002: 12-13).

References

Bohm, D. (1985) *Unfolding Meaning*. London: Routledge.

Buber, M. (1958) *I and Thou*. New York: Scribner's.

Buber, M. (1966) *The Way of Response*. New York: Schocken Books.

Buber, M. (2002) *Between Man and Man*. London: Routledge.

Castoriadis, C. (1984) *Crossroads in the Labyrinth*, trans. K. Soper and M.H. Ryle. Cambridge, Mass.: MIT Press.

Cixous, H. (1986) 'Sorties: Out and Out: Attacks/Ways Out/Forays', in H. Cixous and C. Clément, *The Newly Born Woman*, trans. B. Wing. Manchester: Manchester University Press.

Cixous, H. (1992) *Readings: The Poetics of Blanchot, Joyce, Kafka, Kleist, Lispector and Tsvetayeva*, trans. V. Conley. New York: Harvester Wheatsheaf.

Friedman, M. (2002) 'Introduction'. *M. Buber, Between Man and Man*. London: Routledge.

Game, A. and Metcalfe, A. (1996) *Passionate Sociology*. London: Sage.

Merleau-Ponty, M. (1962) *Phenomenology of Perception*, trans. C. Smith. London: Routledge.

Merleau-Ponty, M. (1964) *The Primacy of Perception*. Evanston: Northwestern University Press.

Metcalfe, A. and Game, A. (2002) *The Mystery of Everyday Life*. Sydney: Federation Press.

Nhat Hanh, Thich (1988) *The Heart of Understanding*. Berkeley: Parallax Press.

Steiner, G. (1989) *Real Presences*. London: Faber.

Reviews

A. Game, and A. Metcalfe, *The Mystery of Everyday Life*
The Federation Press, Sydney 2002

Louise Chambers

he Mystery of Everyday Life begins by inviting us to consider the idea that our individualistic, purposeful, goal-directed behaviours prevent us from stumbling across other routes, other modes of being, that are focused on a de-centred self, and a form of being that exists *in relation to* the people, plants, animals, etc., with whom we interact. As we wander through the book, the reader encounters an eclectic mix of stories, myths, parables and textual channels that enable us to consider how a form of being-in-relation might be lived in our everyday lives. The story of Parzival's quest for the Holy Grail; the spontaneity of a relaxed conversation; experiences of fishing and horse-riding; comforting a child waking from a nightmare – all of these tales produce a space marked by a fork in the road: the one route signposts our desire to control, to be purposeful, to impose our fragile sense of autonomy upon the situation, whilst the other invites us to adopt a 'non-Euclidean' view of space: a space connected-to, a space of letting-go, a space of being-in-relation.

My first response to the book was to recall other meeting-points, other tensions, between Zen Buddhism and Western Culture. Robert Pirsig's classic *Zen and the Art of Motorcycle Maintenance* was necessary reading for anyone who had counter-cultural pretensions in the early 1970s; Benjamin Hoff popularised Taoism through the characters of Pooh and Piglet; the figure of the Samurai has influenced filmmakers as diverse as John Sturges, Sergio Leone, Walter Hill and Jim Jarmusch. However, whilst Zen and Taoist ideas are certainly filtered through the book (p9), other references draw from a breathtaking panoply of Western teachings: the conversion of St Paul (pp71-78); the Annunciation of the birth of Christ (pp32-33); the psychoanalytic musings of D.W. Winnicott and Oliver Sacks (pp23, 58-9); Barthian post-structuralism (p40); the post-enlightenment writings of Blanchot, Serres, and Levinas (pp45, 66, 85), and so on. This is, of course, *enlightenment*, but not as we in the West generally know it. The book seems to suggest that many of the mainstays of Zen philosophy are long-established in Western culture – albeit (with the exception of Christian teaching) at the margins: the notion of 'being-in-relation'; Flow; the 'middle-way'; music being the 'space between the notes' and writing 'the space between the words'. In fact, these concepts are so well known that they are often subjected to satire and cynicism: as I read about Bruce Springsteen's take on the creative process (p34), I was reminded of Woody Allen's injunction to 'be the ball' in the animated movie *Antz*; as I wandered through the rest of the book, I could recall Bridget Jones's feeble efforts at achieving self-fulfilment through the concept of Flow in Helen Fielding's (1996) *Bridget Jones's Diary*; and Bill Bailey's hilarious transformation, after swallowing *The Little Book of Calm*, in Channel 4's cult sitcom *Black Books*. And the notion of the 'middle way' has been completely appropriated and re-branded by the Blairite rhetoric of New Labour as an injunction to reject radical politics in favour of the bland, utilitarian philosophy of Victorian Methodism.

Consequently, I wondered, as I was reading, whether this book offers us anything that has not already been proffered (and satirised) elsewhere?

Certainly, many of the passages resonate with some of my own experiences. I enjoy wandering purposelessly around libraries and bookshops, and I love trawling aimlessly through the internet. I pick up books for no better reason than the cover looks aesthetically pleasing. I click on hypertexts at random. In both instances I have 'discovered' writings that I would never have come across had I been engaging in 'purposeful action'. Furthermore, as an avid proponent of the writings of Michel Foucault, and as a feminist, I want to embrace a position that invites us to discard the patriarchal fantasy of autonomous, controlling, omniscient selfhood, and to engage with others through a relational, collective sense of being-in-the-world.

Does this book have a function, a purpose? The paradox of *The Mystery of Everyday Life* is, of course, that to ask this question is to miss the point. If the book has a purpose, then it becomes purpose*ful* and the theme of the book is – if I have understood it correctly – to encourage us to engage with our selves and our everyday lives as though we are purposeless: to stop living through the fiction of self-autonomy and to take up a position that acknowledges our relationships with/to our fragile selves and the world in which we live. For those of us who embrace the tenets of 'critical theory' – particularly if our writing is produced in and through the labours of Saussure, Barthes, Foucault, Deleuze, Probyn and Butler, we have a difficult question to address: if we reject the phenomenological-humanist fantasy of *self-actualisation* through goal-oriented, self-motivated, conscious action, then with what do we replace this fantasy? If we reject the politics of a stable, consistent, self-centred identity, how do we ground a politics of resistance, and how do we establish our sense of being-in-the-world? The difficulty that I have with *The Mystery of Everyday Life* is both its strength and its weakness. Its strength lies in bringing together a broad array of portraits, writings, teachings, philosophies and entreatments that seem to share similar themes: the need to conceptualise time and space from a relational perspective; the importance of spontaneity; the advantages of allowing our selves moments where we are enabled to *do* nothing and to *be* nothing. Its weakness, however, is that this *bricolage* of writings offers little in the way of a concerted response to the space left by 'the death of the subject', because many of the writings – particularly those from Christian teachings – which comprise this book are implicated in the system of thinking that it is supposedly problematising.

I would guess that the authors did not intend this book to be the 'answer' to the *meaning* of (everyday) life, but instead, perhaps, to offer some spiritual guidance in relation to our encounters with our selves, our friends, our children and our undertakings. In that sense, and as a companion to *The Little Book of Calm*, I found the book most engaging but, as an introduction to the path towards a different kind of enlightenment, I would recommend Benjamin Hoff's *The Tao of Pooh*.

T.J. Csordas, *Body/Meaning/Healing*

Palgrave/Macmillan, New York 2002

Nigel J. Danby SJ

This book attends to the body in three distinct but related registers. Operating within the school of cultural phenomenology in medical anthropology, Csordas gives an ethnographic account of the ways healers within the Catholic Charismatic Renewal movement tend and attend the bodies of their 'supplicants'. Second, the concept of somatic modes of attention, which are 'culturally elaborated ways of attending to and with one's body' (p244) is developed. Third, the author presents the body as the existential ground of culture and self. These three moments are woven together throughout this book, attempting not only to theorise the body, but also to theorise with the body. In what follows, I address each of these themes in the light of my own experience of elements of Charismatic practice. I draw attention also to Csordas's ongoing and not always cordial dialogue with post-structuralist theory and bring to bear on his work some of the methods and insights of Judith Butler.

In the Catholic Charismatic Renewal movement, healing takes three forms – physical healing, inner healing of emotional illness and distress, and deliverance from evil spirits. The distinctions are not rigid, however. In the Christian tradition, physical healing is more than a restoration of health but is a mode and indicator of a deeper transformation. Likewise, a particularly recalcitrant emotional illness may be the sign of demonic activity.

Focusing on inner healing and deliverance, Csordas provides an account of the techniques advocated by Charismatic healers – healing of memories for emotional illness and the prayer for deliverance from evil spirits. These practices are complementary in 'redirecting the supplicant's attention to his action and experience in order to achieve the construction of a self that is healthy, whole and holy' (p34). In healing of memories, the supplicant is invited to relive her or his past life with an explicit awareness of the presence of Jesus, imagining him as present in the often-traumatic scenes recalled.

While the process of healing of memories is one of integration, of recognising the presence of God in episodes where God seemed absent, and of forgiving those responsible for past emotional hurt, deliverance is a process of externalisation. Healer and supplicant are involved in a process of identifying the bad spirits that oppress and harass the supplicant. According to Charismatics, once this is done, the process of deliverance is remarkably straightforward, since the demons are unable to withstand the power of God to expel them.

In providing a faithful ethnography of Charismatic healing from the point of view of both supplicant and healer, however, Csordas downplays the operations of the regime of power/knowledge at work. While it may be the case that both parties are active in the process of deliverance, there is an imbalance of power located in the healer's ownership of the gift of 'discernment of spirits', which gives him or her privileged insight into the forces at work in the supplicant, often given in the form of a divinely-inspired 'word of knowledge'.

According to Csordas's book-length treatment of Charismatic healing, *The Sacred Self* (1997), healing practice is structured by shared psychocultural themes of spontaneity, control and intimacy. This generates a contemporary demonology of bad spirits who bear the names of such traditional Catholic sins as Lust, Adultery and Gluttony as well as more 'modern' spirits of Low Self-Esteem, Anxiety and Depression. While there is no unanimity among the mostly ageing and middle-class healers as to the precise cast of this demonology, their ethical systems are predominantly profoundly traditional and conservative. Thus, they are liable to discern evil spirits of Homosexuality and Masturbation.

Place yourself for a moment in the position of a young man approaching or – just as likely within the context of a Charismatic meeting – approached by a healer. You are suffering from the emotional fallout from the ending of a gay relationship, only to 'discover' yourself oppressed by a spirit of Homosexuality revealed to the healer by the direct inspiration of God. Imagine also that any resistance you put up to this 'diagnosis' is figured as either resistance to God's healing power or as the voice of the evil spirit.

In elaborating his concept of somatic modes of attention, Csordas draws attention to the cultural rhetoric at work in the discourse of healing, which 'redirects the supplicant's attention to new aspects of his actions and experiences' (p25). However, the supplicant is not rendered as a passive recipient of a discourse which is, to use one of Csordas's least-favourite metaphors, inscribed upon her body. Csordas advocates a non-empiricist concept of meaning, whereby 'meaning is not *attached* to experience, but is constituted by the way in which a subject *attends* to experience' (p57). His cultural phenomenological approach holds that meaning is 'already inherent in basic sensory experience' (p101). Thus, the experience of supplicants is not data to be interpreted and tamed by healers or medical professionals. Neither is it constructed in and through their interpretations. Instead, 'expert' accounts are cultural objectifications of an embodied experience that is always already meaningful, and can be taken up or rejected as such.

Drawing on the philosophy of Merleau-Ponty, for whom attention is 'the active constitution of a new object', and the phenomenological sociology of reflexivity developed by Schutz, Csordas theorises attention as a 'turning towards' which is 'more bodily and multisensory ... than we usually allow for in psychological definitions' (p244). His account runs into difficulties, however, when faced with precisely the question of reflexivity addressed by Schutz and profoundly interrogated by Judith Butler (1997) in *The psychic life of power*.

Csordas's theory of somatic modes of attention works well in providing an account of particular experiences as embodied. However, when attention is turned towards oneself in the hyper-vigilance associated with hypochondria or the tolerance for self-mortification associated with eating disorders (p. 246), the somatic modes at work are more than attending to and with oneself. They turn *on* one. One becomes what Nietzche describes as 'an animal soul turned against itself', for whom reflexivity is initiated not in the phenomenological register as a form of neutral attentiveness to self and others, but is 'a consequence of conscience; self-knowing follows from self-punishment' (Butler, 1997: 22). For Csordas, as in much contemporary social theory, the body is the new mind, implying a new object and method of cultural analysis that corrects a previous over-emphasis on the cognitive. However, this can lead to a blindness to or disregard of the psychic processes at work in self-examination theorised as somatic modes of attention or Foucault's notion of problematisation.

This said, Csordas's account of the body as the existential ground of culture and self is useful in enabling us to think past the dichotomies and aporia that characterise social scientific and philosophical discourses of individual and society, subject and object, essentialism and constructivism. Csordas's paradigm of embodiment generates fruitful 'fieldwork in philosophy' (p220, citing Bourdieu), using the case of a thirty year old Navajo man suffering from a brain tumour. In placing the body at the centre of his account, Csordas is able to disrupt and interrogate the 'battle of causal arrows flying in both directions from neurology and culture'. Taking the feminist deconstruction of the dichotomy of nature and culture into a phenomenological register, Csordas presents both as 'forms of objectification or representation' (p219). In so doing, his account provides an alternative to the debate of essentialism *versus* constructivism, positing the body as 'the phenomenological ground of both biology and culture' (p237).

To adopt a phrase from Judith Butler, the body is the 'groundless ground' of culture and self. It is so neither as mute biological substrate or a blank slate upon which meaning is inscribed. To turn to, with or on the body is to actively constitute a new object in somatic modes of attention which are 'neither arbitrary nor biologically determined, but are culturally constituted' (p246). That these modes of attention, and even the possibility of attention, are structured and constrained by psychic processes indicates the need for and possibility of a post-Foucauldian social theory.

J.R. Carrette, *Foucault and Religion: Spiritual Corporality and Political Spirituality*

Routledge, London and New York 2000

Linda MacKay

At the very outset I must confess that this review will reflect more of a summary of Jeremy Carrette's thesis than a critique, given my own very incomplete, yet thankfully, evolving understanding of much of Michel Foucault's fascinating and brilliant work. Whilst complex, Carrette's work allows a student of Foucault to gain some expansive insights into the constructions of arguably the twentieth century's greatest thinker, drawing out the notion of a political spirituality of the self, and emphasising the *evolving* and *changing* nature of Foucault's thinking in relation to religion in his later work.

Chapter 1 (pp7-24) provides an examination of the production of Foucault's archaeological thinking between 1954 and 1969, and Foucault's genealogical work between 1970 and 1975. Chapter 2 (pp25-43) expands the theoretical division between 'silence' or 'spiritual corporality' – relating to the silencing powers of religion – and 'speech', or 'political spirituality', and religious authority in the demand for confession. These ideas first emerged in Foucault's 1976 work *The History of Sexuality: An Introduction,* hence Carrette uses the year 1976 to delineate ideas of early and late Foucauldian thought, whilst adding the critique that Foucault fails to locate the interconnection between the concept of silence and his work on the confessional and the interpretation of Christianity as a 'confessional religion' (p27). It is this relationship that Carrette extrapolates in his writing. Further, Carrette states that he avoids the somewhat 'murky' sphere inhabited by Foucault when he blurred the concepts of silence and discourse by referring to silence and *speech* as '*mutual dynamics in the field of discourse*' [my emphasis]. Similarly, Foucault's writings regarding speaking and silence described Christianity, prior to 1976, as an oppressive apparatus that silenced, whilst after 1976 they described it as an oppressive apparatus which demanded an utterance (pp35-36). However Carrette perceives Foucault to have seriously erred by not connecting the dynamics of speech and silence in the form of speaking that confession demands.

Chapter 3 (pp44-62) engages with the question of a 'religious problem', demonstrating to what extent Foucault examines yet holds off notions of 'religious' ideas, with Carrette giving particular emphasis to the broad role French surrealism plays in the development of Foucault's anti-humanist criticisms of philosophical epistemologies. Chapter 4 (pp63-84) continues something of this discussion when it looks at the notion of the death of God, and discusses how Foucault transports the 'spiritual', relocating it within the 'corporal' via the work of the Marquis de Sade. This chapter also points specifically to Foucault's prevailing gender blindness in failing to perceive the gendering of sexual politics.

Chapter 5 (pp85-108) examines Foucault's *The Archaeology of Knowledge* (1969, 1991) to punctuate how this work stands in opposition to notions of traditional religious ontology with its focus on religious transcendence, leading the way to notions of religious immanence. With a focus on emphasising the degree of terrain which separates Foucault from Pseudo-Dionysius epistemologically, Carrette clearly challenges any uncritical association Foucault is perceived to have had with Christian mysticism.

Chapter 6 (pp109-128) is an argument of how in *Discipline and Punish* (1975), there is a core ambivalence caused by the binary opposition between belief and practice. Foucault's 'modern soul' is constructed through the play of power and knowledge and likewise is positioned as 'a network of power-knowledge relations', a surface of disciplinary practices that shape the body (p109). Carrette argues that whilst Foucault positioned 'belief' within the (sexual) body, aware as he was of the interrelationship between belief and practice, he

> ... fails to realise that when theology is located in the body a description of social practice directly becomes a statement of embodied belief ... By rethinking religion through the body, a whole series of binary oppositions collapse. However, by maintaining the binary opposition between

body and belief in his later social and historical analysis of religion, the poverty of Foucault's underdeveloped 'religious question' is revealed (pp112-4).

What is most salient in this chapter however, is Carrette's emphasis on locating Foucault's spiritual corporality in the context of gender; however this analysis is made only too briefly. No doubt saying more about my own subjective interests, I wanted to be invited to understand more of these assertions, in particular Carrette's argument that the religious question is 'no longer the "matter" of "sexed-bodies" but also of "sexed-souls" and "sexed-doctrine"' (p127). Carrette does not examine the implications of this but instead points to the expansive work in this regard of feminist writers such as Grace Jantzen.

Chapter 7 (pp129-141) allows Carrette to discuss Foucault in relation to a de-emphasis of a 'spiritual corporality' developing a new emphasis in the form of 'political spirituality' in his examination of religion. Carrette's goal here not only is to demonstrate how Foucault's analysis of religion can be more appropriately perceived as a 'problematisation', he also endeavours to show how there are two inter-related dimensions with a single critique of Christianity – just as Foucault perceives silence and speech as inseparable, so too does he perceive notions of spiritual corporality and political spirituality. Carrette perceives Foucault as collapsing notions of the 'spiritual', the 'ethical' and 'political' into a singular focus of 'truth', 'subjectivity' and 'power', which therefore positions this work within his 1978 framework regarding 'governmentality' (p138, c.f. Foucault, 1982: 212).

In conclusion, Carrette leaves us with what he sees as the challenges Foucault offers us in regards to religious and theological thinking (pp. 142-152). He brings together the strands of Foucault's work on religion to include notions of the body and sexuality as they are constituted through religious practice and explores a political spirituality of the self. Carrette summarises:

Foucault's work on religion [operates] on the basis of five interrelated factors from his wider work: an analysis of the cultural facts (the integration of religion and culture); the historical and social location of discourse (religious immanence not transcendence [i.e. not outside the historical context and conditions of self hood]); the prioritisation of the body and sexuality (the embodiment of belief); an analysis of the mechanisms of power (the micro-politics of religious utterances and silence), and the development of a technology of the self (the religious government of the self) (pp143-4).

Carrette concludes that religion needs to be relocated 'outside the superstitions, misconceptions and illusions through which "secular" academics have so far dismissed the subject', and makes perhaps his most important assertion when he expands this to say that we need to locate religion, and indeed Foucault's religious question, 'in the very fabric of the "secular" – in the absence' (p152).

Notes on contributors

Lisa Blackman is a Senior Lecturer in the Department of Media and Communications, Goldsmiths College, London, UK. She has written at the intersection of critical psychology and cultural theory, and is currently working on a genealogy of the suffering body, exploring the connections between the emergence of self-help, spiritual healing and biomedicine.

Jeremy Carrette is Senior Lecturer in Religious Studies at the University of Stirling, Scotland, UK. He has written numerous articles on critical psychology and religion, and is author of *Foucault and Religion: Spiritual Corporality and Political Spirituality* (Routledge, 2000); and editor of *Religion and Culture by Michel Foucault* (Manchester/Routledge, 1999).

Louise Chambers is a visiting lecturer and doctoral student in the Department of Media & Communications at Goldsmiths College, London. Her present research is concerned with the relationship between psychology and the media and, more particularly, the constitution of new femininities in contemporary romantic fiction and their relationship with/to technologies of the self.

Kirsti Cheals has recently completed masterate research from which this paper is taken, and is currently working towards registration as a psychologist with an emphasis on narrative re-weavings to make sense of our life stories. Her research interests generally focus on power relationships and the re-inclusion of spirituality talk.

Leigh Coombes has recently completed doctoral research using feminist and poststructuralist theory to critically read criminal trial evidence involving expert psychological testimony. Her research interests generally focus on the interface of feminism, critical psychology, and critical legal studies.

Nigel J. Danby SJ is currently an MPhil/PhD student at Goldsmiths College, London. He is a member of the British Province of the Society of Jesus.

Ann Game is an Associate Professor in the School of Sociology, University of New South Wales. She is the author of *Undoing the Social* (Open University

Press, Toronto University Press, 1991); and co-author with Andrew Metcalfe of *Passionate Sociology* (Sage, 1996) and *The Mystery of Everyday Life* (Federation Press, Sydney, 2002).

Ian Hodges is Senior Lecturer in Psychology at the University of Westminster, UK. He teaches critical psychology, social psychology and qualitative methods. His research interests include psychology and social regulation, sexual prejudice, sexual identity and social psychological aspects of living with HIV.

Helen Lee is a lecturer in Critical Psychology at Staffordshire University, UK. Her research interests centre on the role of psychology in producing and maintaining the status quo, knowledge construction, socio-cultural and psychological construction of spirituality, and embodiment.

Linda MacKay is a family therapist in private practice as well as a lecturer at the Centre for Critical Psychology at the University of Western Sydney, Australia. She is presently completing her PhD.

Harriette Marshall is Professor in Feminist and Critical Psychology at Staffordshire University, UK. Her research interests centre around issues of identity, especially in relation to gender, ethnicity and sexuality, and the relationship between Psychology and the construction and reproduction of social inequalities.

Nick Mansfield is Associate Professor in Critical and Cultural Studies at Macquarie University in Sydney. Amongst his books are *Masochism: The Art of Power* (Westport, Connecticut: Praeger, 1997) and *Subjectivity: Theories of the Self From Freud to Haraway* (New York: New York UP, 2000). The present article is part of a forthcoming book entitled *Other Economies: Subjectivity After Derrida*.

Andrew Metcalfe is an Associate Professor in the School of Sociology, University of New South Wales. He is the author of *For Freedom and Dignity* (Allen and Unwin, 1986) and has co-authored *Passionate Sociology* (Sage, 1996) and *The Mystery of Everyday Life* (Federation Press, Sydney, 2002) with Ann Game.

Mandy Morgan is a senior lecturer in critical psychology at Massey University in Aotearoa/New Zealand. Her research interests generally focus on the relationship between feminism, poststructuralism and psychology.

Hillegonda C. Rietveld is Senior Lecturer in Arts and Media at the Faculty of Humanities and Social Science at South Bank University, London. Her publications in the field of dance cultural studies include *This Is Our House: House Music, Cultural Spaces and Technologies* (Ashgate, 1998). As member of Quando

Quango, she released several electronic dance music recordings for Factory Records in the 80s and currently appears occasionally as a club DJ.

Paul Stenner lectures in psychology at University College London. He has written numerous scholarly articles bringing the work of philosophers such as Wittgenstein, Spinoza, Heidegger, Serres and Foucault into contact with psychology, and has published empirical work on a range of substantive topics including the psychology of health, values, emotions, identity and sexuality.